DEMOCRACY, DELIBERATION, AND EDUCATION

RDD

RHETORICANDDEMOCRATICDELIBERATION
VOLUME 13

EDITED BY CHERYL GLENN AND J. MICHAEL HOGAN
THE PENNSYLVANIA STATE UNIVERSITY

Rhetoric and Democratic Deliberation is a series of
groundbreaking monographs and edited volumes focusing
on the character and quality of public discourse in politics
and culture. It is sponsored by the Center for Democratic
Deliberation, an interdisciplinary center for research,
teaching, and outreach on issues of rhetoric, civic engagement,
and public deliberation.

A complete list of books in this series is located
at the back of this volume.

DEMOCRACY, DELIBERATION, AND EDUCATION

ROBERT ASEN

The Pennsylvania State University Press | University Park, Pennsylvania

Library of Congress Cataloging-in-Publication Data

Asen, Robert, 1968– , author.
   Democracy, deliberation, and education /
   Robert Asen.
        pages   cm — (Rhetoric and democratic
        deliberation)
Summary: "Explores the ways that school board
members engage each other to make decisions
for their local communities in the United States.
Illustrates the perils and promise of local
policymaking as people seek to chart a future
course for their communities, addressing issues of
ideology, scarcity, expertise, and trust"—Provided
by publisher.
Includes bibliographical references and index.
ISBN 978-0-271-06709-4 (pbk. : alk. paper)
1. School boards—Wisconsin.
2. Deliberative democracy—Wisconsin.
3. Democracy and education—Wisconsin.
4. Education and state—Wisconsin.
I. Title. II. Series: Rhetoric and democratic
deliberation.

LB2831.A8 2015
379.1'53109775—dc23
2015003614

The Pennsylvania State University Press is a member
of the Association of American University Presses.

It is the policy of The Pennsylvania State University
Press to use acid-free paper. Publications on uncoated
stock satisfy the minimum requirements of American
National Standard for Information Sciences—
Permanence of Paper for Printed Library Material,
ANSI Z39.48–1992.

To Sue:

You are a wonderful interlocutor and an even better partner.

CONTENTS

ACKNOWLEDGMENTS

Democracy, deliberation, and education all underscore the importance of human relationships for personal growth and development as well as community well-being. In writing this book, I have experienced this dynamic as I have benefited from a community of colleagues, friends, and family who have supported my efforts and engaged with me on this project.

This book simply would not have been possible without the support of the William T. Grant Foundation. From the beginning of our discussions about a research project for the Foundation, Bob Granger and Vivian Tseng recognized the importance of a communication approach to studying issues of policymaking and evidence use. Their vision has drawn scholarly attention to these important topics, and they have been crucial to fostering interactions among an interdisciplinary community of scholars.

The fieldwork conducted in Beloit, Elmbrook, and West Bend was originally undertaken to support the efforts of the Research on Education, Deliberation, and Decision-Making (REDD) Project. Consisting of myself, co–principal investigator Deb Gurke, Pam Conners, Ryan Solomon, Elsa Gumm, and Michelle Murray Yang, the REDD team spent two years in the field attending board meetings, interviewing board members and administrators, and building relationships. While all the analysis and writing of this book is my own, I collaborated with REDD team members on some projects regarding the use of research evidence. I am a better scholar for having worked with the REDD team.

At Penn State Press, Kendra Boileau has been a valued and wise editor. I have appreciated Kendra's enthusiasm for this project and our discussions of its revisions and publication. Robert Turchick was a helpful and friendly voice at the Press during the review process. Nicholas Taylor provided careful copyediting. Series editors Mike Hogan and Cheryl Glenn have been strong supporters of this project. As an admirer of their scholarship, I am honored by their support. Dave Tell and Karen Tracy read the entire manuscript for the Press, offering insightful and detailed comments. Their efforts have made this project better.

I am extremely fortunate to have wonderful colleagues who have sustained a vibrant and supportive intellectual community that facilitates good research. Karma Chávez, Jonathan Gray, Rob Howard, Jenell Johnson, Steve Lucas, Louise Mares, Sara McKinnon, Christa Olson, Zhongdang Pan, Mike Xenos, and Sue Zaeske all have discussed various aspects of this project with me. I have benefited enormously from these discussions. I am also grateful to KC Councilor, Whitney Gent, Ken Lythgoe, Kevin Musgrave, and Brandi Rogers, who, in addition to discussing this project, helped me organize my materials, review relevant scholarly literatures, and proofread the manuscript.

I presented earlier drafts of portions of this manuscript at various colleges and universities, including Arizona State University, Carnegie Mellon University (jointly with Duquesne University, Indiana University of Pennsylvania, and the University of Pittsburgh), Georgia State University, Syracuse University, the University of Illinois at Urbana–Champaign, the University of Kansas, the University of Texas at Austin, and Wabash College. At the University of Wisconsin–Madison, I gave talks about this project in the Communication Arts Department, the Educational Policy Studies Department, the English Department, and the Interdisciplinary Training Program in Educational Sciences. I also spent a semester as a resident fellow at the UW–Madison Institute for Research in the Humanities, where I worked on the manuscript and delivered a talk. I am indebted to all the people who attended my talks at these various institutions for their astute questions and comments.

Innumerable conversations with colleagues and friends have bolstered this project. In particular, I thank the following people for their feedback and support: Elise Barho, Rachel Bloom, Geoffrey Borman, Dominique Bradley, Dan Brouwer, Rubén Casas, Kathy Chaput, David Cheshier, Jay Childers, Alan Daly, Anne Demo, Jeff Mehltretter Drury, Sara Mehltretter Drury, Chris Earle, Cara Finnegan, Kara Finnigan, Susan Friedman, Sara Goldrick-Rab, Robert Hariman, Debbie Hawhee, Aaron Hess, Mark Hlavacik, John Lucaites, Paul McKean, Kristen Moore, Chuck Morris, John Murphy, Adam Nelson, Kimberlee Pérez, Phaedra Pezzullo, Kendall Phillips, Lou Roberts, Robin Rowland, Ellen Samuels, Pete Simonson, Rohini Singh, Michael Steudeman, Mary Stuckey, Dave Tell, Karen Tracy, Brad Vivian, Mike Wagner, Stephen Weatherford, Scott Wible, Rachelle Winkle-Wagner, and James Wynn.

My family has been a tremendous support during the writing of this book. My mom, Fela Asen, has been a terrific teacher. Throughout my life, she has modeled practices of democracy and education—and deliberation, too! My children, Simone and Zac, have reminded me of the importance of orienting education toward the democratic advancement of individual and community potential. And they have reminded me that scholarship should happen within the context of a balanced life. My wife, Sue Robinson, to whom this book is dedicated, has been an incredible partner. She has engaged me intellectually, emotionally, and lovingly. Sue's multiple contributions to this project have been irreplaceable.

Portions of this book have been published previously elsewhere. A section of chapter 1, which has been condensed and revised from its original version, was published as "Lyndon Baines Johnson and George W. Bush on Education Reform: Ascribing Agency and Responsibility through Key Policy Terms," *Rhetoric and Public Affairs* 15, no. 2 (2012): 289–318. An earlier version of chapter 5, which has been significantly expanded and revised, appeared as "Deliberation and Trust," *Argumentation and Advocacy* 50, no. 1 (2013): 2–17.

Democracy and education make each other better. Over the course of his long and illustrious career, John Dewey wrote about a wide range of topics, but he never lost sight of this productive and mutually informative relationship. He recognized that democratic practices can encourage an inquisitive social spirit, while educational practices can foster skills for self-governance. Both democracy and education generate their power from people's purposeful participation, as individual energy enlivens social practice. In his trenchant essay on creative democracy, Dewey famously defines democracy as "a *personal* way of individual life; . . . it signifies the possession and continual use of certain attitudes, forming personal character and determining desire and purpose in all the relations of life." Similarly, in *Democracy and Education*, he defines education as the "reconstruction or reorganization of experience which adds to the meaning of experience, and which increases ability to direct the course of subsequent experience."[1] In both definitions, as he highlights processes, Dewey conspicuously does not locate democracy or education in institutions, procedures, or subject matters. Neither operates in only one aspect of society, nor submits itself to one technique of production, nor arises apart from people who practice it. Both cultivate a similar set of competencies and commitments, especially a practice of perspective-taking that enables individuals to discover and account for values, needs, interests, and identities different from their own. Both cultivate an appreciation of the interaction of individual and community, whereby individuals sustain the cooperative relations of community, and communities provide the resources for individuals to achieve their goals. Each prepares citizens and students to participate efficaciously in the other.

To bolster democracy and education, we may consider not only relations between democracy and education, but how democracy may operate within education as well as how education may occur in democracy. Fostering democracy in education means engaging the interest and involvement of students and stakeholders (i.e., parents, teachers, community residents) in the values, materials, processes, and aims of education. A lack of attention to interest and involvement constitutes the basis of Dewey's critique of traditional methods of education. He insists that "we never educate directly, but indirectly by means of the environment."[2] Students do not sit as empty vessels that teachers fill with knowledge. Direct instruction may instill memorization and recitation, but without their identification with the process of education, students will not learn. Democracy in education, then, arises as students, teachers, and others participate in a mutually valued process.

Education in democracy constitutes the latter as a process of learning —not an aloof, abstract process pursued apart from other concerns, but a bridging of theory and practice. Democratic publics emerge, Dewey suggests, because the consequences of human interaction extend beyond the individuals immediately involved in an exchange.[3] Publics organize to direct human action purposefully rather than responding haphazardly to the inevitable issues and concerns that arise in human society. Organized action arises because democratic practices may transform people's perceptions. In contrast to other modes of governance, democracy may prompt "a recognition that there are common interests, even though the recognition of *what* they are is confused." In *The Public and Its Problems*, Dewey maintains that this lack of recognition has held the public in eclipse, yet he discerns a solution in "discussion and publicity," which may engender "some clarification of what they [common interests] are."[4] Local communities, which may provide their members with stable footing in a complex and changing world, appear as promising forums for such discourse. A community also may offer its members the benefits of sustained interactions over time. Dewey insists that "there is no substitute for the vitality and depth of close and direct intercourse and attachment."[5] A person's confidence and skill in public engagement may increase with repeated efforts. Regular communication may permit interlocutors to judge their decisions in light of consequences, enabling them to revisit decisions when expected outcomes do not occur.

Democratic decision-making in education and educational work in democracy historically have proceeded in the United States at the local level in the thousands of school districts across the nation. The decentered character of the U.S. educational system has reflected the belief held by policymakers and citizens alike that each community presumably knows best how to educate its children, underscoring formal education's role in reaching beyond the walls of the classroom to reproduce culture and community.[6]

Appreciating this wide reach, Dewey recognizes education, "in its broadest sense," as "the means of this social continuity of life." Society does not reproduce itself automatically, nor do its members possess an innate social knowledge. Education enables youth to engage and reinterpret the values and experiences of their elders. In this process, communication plays an irreplaceable role: "Society not only continues to exist *by* transmission, *by* communication, but it may fairly be said to exist *in* transmission, *in* communication." By circulating shared meanings, communication builds community: "Communication is the way in which they come to possess things in common."[7] Yet, even at the local level, people may express different visions of community—they may have different ideas about what they hold in common. In these moments, deliberation, as a particular mode of communication, may facilitate people's articulation and negotiation of different senses of community, permitting interlocutors to chart different visions of a shared future.

At the local level, school boards historically have stood as the deliberative, decision-making bodies for education policy. Populated by community members, school boards affirm the relationship between democracy and education, representing the belief that education does not constitute a technical policy area open only to specialists. School-board members may not possess training in pedagogy, but they do hold valuable perspectives on the role of education in a community's sustenance and success. School boards often do not serve as stepping-stones for people with aspirations for state or national offices.[8] Members generally have some interest in education, although, especially recently, they may not confine this interest to public education. Both in their place in the larger structure of U.S. education policy as well as their daily operation, school boards serve as sites of local democratic engagement and policymaking. School boards present opportunities for ordinary folks to engage with policymaking. They enable laypeople not only to develop opinions about governance, as in an advisory public sphere, but also to govern themselves. Calling local public meetings "democracy's litmus test," Karen Tracy holds that how "citizens and officials go about their talking is a powerful emblem of democracy."[9] Although they offer no guarantees, school boards present the potential for ordinary people to realize democracy in education and education in democracy.

School boards play an important role in contemporary U.S. education policy, even as, in the view of contemporary observers, they have come increasingly under siege. The editor of one collection assessing the "besieged" state of school boards writes that "whereas school board members governed virtually all aspects of public education during the nineteenth century, today members must compete with political actors scattered throughout the federal, state, and local governments as well as organized interests in the private sphere."[10] At the federal level, passage of the 2001 No Child Left Behind (NCLB) Act represented the codification of an emergent accountability regime that demanded "results" in return for federal dollars sent to local districts. Requiring testing of students, NCLB rewards districts where students demonstrate proficiency in particular subject areas and punishes "failing" districts. At the state level, legislatures have introduced caps that restrict the amount of money local communities may raise and spend on education, and state education agencies increasingly have adopted common standards for pedagogy. At the local level, site-based school management and, in some large cities, mayoral takeovers have circumscribed school-board governance. Private interests have developed charter school plans that place a local school under the management of a private entity. These interests also have been advanced by vouchers that enable district residents to take tax dollars that would have gone to their local district and use these funds to enroll their children in privately operated schools. Nevertheless, even as they negotiate a complicated field of constraints, school boards continue to serve crucial roles in the decentered system of U.S. education, making decisions about curriculum and instruction, personnel, and finances that affect the daily classroom experiences of students and impact the interests, values, and goals of local communities. Moreover, citizens repeatedly have affirmed the principle that local community members should continue to exercise primary responsibility for directing the education of their community's children.[11]

This book examines school-board deliberations in three medium-sized Wisconsin school districts: Beloit, Elmbrook, and West Bend. Although these districts enroll roughly the same number of students, they differ in terms of socioeconomic status and diversity. Based on two years of fieldwork, which occurred from fall 2009 through summer 2011, this book considers how the school boards in these districts deliberated about issues regarding finances, curricular and extra-curricular activities, personnel, and the composition of student bodies. As I highlight over the course of this book, these boards' deliberations raised themes of ideology, scarcity, expertise, and trust. Exploring how these themes informed particular deliberative episodes, this book elucidates processes of deliberation and decision-making at the local level, outlining a vernacular policy discourse that illuminates policymaking as an everyday activity undertaken by laypeople.[12] This stands as a counterpoint to the idea of policymaking as an activity distant from citizens' daily concerns. This book also illustrates how, in making consequential public decisions, ordinary folks build and sustain both complementary and contesting visions of community. School-board deliberations collectively chart a common future—even as board members may disagree over the shape of this future. And they do not necessarily resolve these disagreements productively. As I consider school-board deliberations as local instantiations of processes of democracy and education, readers may find themselves encouraged and discouraged, hopeful and forlorn.

Public Policy, Meaning-Making, and Deliberation

School-board members do not prepare lesson plans. They do not fix furnaces in school buildings when the heating system breaks down. When a sick student shows up in the nurse's office of a local school, board members do not sit, thermometer in hand, ready to take the child's temperature. And yet school-board members make decisions that affect all of these actions and more. They maintain contact with the daily operation of schools in their districts through their deliberation about district policy. Indeed, board members' primary mode of action unfolds through deliberation and other modes of communication. They communicate with their peers, district administrators, and others to craft district policies. They co-author subcommittee reports, prepare memos on district issues, and exchange phone calls and e-mails with people in the district. Through mediated and face-to-face communication, they converse with constituents and respond to media inquiries, maintaining a sense of their board's responsiveness to community concerns. Through communication, board members seek to guide their district, interact with various people and organizations within the district, and represent their district to the community and other outside audiences like state-level policymakers.

Far from peripheral, their communicative connection to district policy broaches the heart of policymaking as meaning-making. Board policy may serve as a framework for understanding disparate district activities like hiring decisions and curricular initiatives. Policies may order and prioritize various programs and practices, signaling significance and sketching a future direction for a district. For the community, board policies may express shared values and goals, or, when community members perceive a conflict between their values and goals and the board, controversy may erupt.

District policy may send messages to state and national policymakers about the successes and failures of a district and the extent to which a district follows state and national directives. In sum, board members make meaning by making district activities—in classrooms, administrative offices, and elsewhere—coherent and understandable and by conferring comparative value on these various activities. And school-board members are not alone in this respect—all policymakers participate in acts of meaning-making in their deliberations, speeches, op-ed essays, reports, and more.

Discerning meaning at the heart of public policy may threaten ostensibly orderly visions of policymaking as a linear movement from identifying a problem, to developing and assessing potential solutions, to choosing and implementing an optimal solution. Deborah Stone calls this view of policymaking the "rationality project," which envisions a "production model, where policy is created in a fairly orderly sequence of stages, almost as if on an assembly line."[13] Exemplified through such prominent methods as cost-benefit analysis, which presumes the commensurability of diverse interests, a production model highlights "rational" decision-making in the hope of transcending particular interests to maximize the general welfare. Silent about its selection of evaluative criteria, the rationality project denigrates language as "a distortion of rational thinking." Stone counters that people "think with and through language," such that any effort to dismiss language constitutes a "strange conceit" that elevates expert assessments and denigrates citizens' views.[14] Similarly, Frank Fischer explains that policy studies emerged in the United States in the mid-twentieth century as a technocratic project that aspired to generate greater efficiency in policymaking. According to Fischer, researchers operated with the belief that "better information would lead to better solutions." He retorts that a fuller scholarly contribution to policymaking requires an "understanding of the discursive struggle to create and control systems of shared social meanings."[15] Recognizing meaning refigures policymaking as a messy, multidirectional, valued process enacted through the discourse of diverse participants.

A focus on meaning-making does not eclipse the material dimension of public policy, which involves the provision of money, goods, and services to target populations to achieve particular outcomes, such as an educated citizenry that performs its democratic roles and/or obtains productive employment in society. In education policy, money historically has moved from federal and state governments to local school districts, although federal money has paled in comparison to state support of local education. Local districts have generated their own, historically substantial funds through property taxes, levies, and other means. Governments at various levels have not traditionally supplied money directly to students and their families, yet recent voucher plans effectively initiate money transfers from state governments to families in a district. The goods and services associated with education policy primarily consist of helping students to achieve competency in various subject areas and to develop critical ways of thinking. Local districts also provide various counseling services to students, free and reduced meals to qualifying students, extra-curricular clubs and sports, and more. All of these monies, goods, and services obtain a standing and constitution apart from the deliberations of school boards.

At the same time, the material dimension of education policy operates within discursive networks that create, negotiate, and redefine the meanings of the provisions of education policy. In this spirit, David Zarefsky, one of the first rhetorical scholars to write book-length studies of public policy, holds that "the *meaning* of [political and policy] events depends upon how they are characterized in public discourse." Zarefsky maintains that "people participate actively in shaping and giving meaning to their environment. What any element in that environment 'is' will depend on what it 'means.'"[16] Perhaps more so than other policy areas, education evidences a strong and comparatively conspicuous connection between meaning and environment; we would encounter great difficulty in imagining, say, the teaching of addition or reading without acknowledging the role of meaning, since both entail understanding of symbol systems. Outside the classroom, different visions of the values and goals of education invoke powerful and sometimes competing meanings, such as (and this often appears as a choice) whether education ought to serve vocational or democratic aims. Conflicts over meaning also join disagreements outside the classroom with pedagogy occurring within its walls, such as debates over the appropriate standards and methods for teaching history and science. Deliberations about education policy, then, extend Dewey's prescription for educating by means of a student's environment by bringing together multiple environments in which people create and negotiate meanings to make decisions to benefit students and their communities.

My focus on the connection between policymaking and meaning-making arises from my background as a scholar of rhetoric, which, in its contemporary academic configuration, consists of the study of discourse as a social force. Rhetorical scholars appreciate the power of discourse to shape people's understanding of the nature of public problems and the solutions that people propose to redress them, sketch the opportunities and constraints on human action, delineate the various roles of different levels and agencies of government as well as other public and private actors in addressing problems, and craft individual and collective identities of target populations, policymakers, and others. Through discourse, people articulate their commitments and obligations to one another, their guiding values and principles, their alliances and antagonisms. Zarefsky maintains that viewing "public policy as a problem of rhetoric, then, is to focus on the creation and exchange of symbols through which issues are perceived, defined, addressed, and resolved."[17] To the extent that public policy brings together multiple people and contexts, the circulation of discourse and meaning exceeds any particular exchange.

Foregrounding analysis, rhetorical studies of public policy approach instances and circulations of public discourse as texts that scholars may analyze to elucidate their rhetorical dynamics as well as their connections to immediate and wider contexts. The rhetorical policy text shares with other rhetorical texts a processual character—functioning not as a stable, static entity but expressing multiple, sometimes contradictory meanings that emerge as qualities of movement. Yet the policy text raises particularities of authorship, temporality, and polysemy.[18] Multiple authors—sometimes hundreds, even thousands—compose policy texts. If this book focused on the implementation of a national reform like NCLB at the federal, state, and local levels, it would reference numbers of interlocutors approaching these totals. Even as I focus on local deliberations, my analysis considers the participation of board members, administrators, and community members. Multiple authorship constrains the participation of any one single advocate, who must negotiate his or her participation with others. Neither the superintendent nor a board majority in a district can assert a policy initiative and a preferred meaning unchallenged.

Temporally, public policy unfolds as an ongoing negotiation of text and context—what serves as text in one moment of an ongoing policy debate may shift to context in another. For instance, a board decision to maintain existing property-tax rates will inform subsequent fiscal deliberations as context, as board members may need to cut programs to sustain this decision. Moreover, perceptions of time may motivate deliberations about public policy as well as function as an appeal during policy deliberations. Exemplifying the former, a school board may initiate deliberations over curricular changes because of a concern about students' readiness for an upcoming round of state tests. Over the course of these deliberations, exemplifying the latter, a board member may argue against drastic changes by pointing to steadily rising test scores over time. Policy debates may exhibit multiple temporalities, too. A reduction of state aid, for example, may draw board members' attention to their district's financial fortunes more quickly than long-term shifts in local property values.

Public policy deliberations constitute polysemous texts, since interlocutors may understand their objects and interactions differently.[19] A rhetorical approach to policymaking as meaning-making seeks to elucidate how participants and audiences may understand their deliberations as well as how a critic's readers should understand these deliberations. While these understandings may diverge, we should remain cognizant of the purposeful character of the policy text. In this spirit, John Murphy endorses efforts to explicate polysemy in texts, but urges rhetorical scholars to remain mindful of the "strategic aspect of rhetoric": "the potential of rhetoric to persuade people to make contingent choices in specific situations—its ability to shape the world's appearance such that we make this move rather than that choice."[20] As rhetoric serves instrumental and constitutive functions, policy polysemy manifests as multiple authors try to persuade their co-authors to accept their positions.

This book focuses on meaning-making through deliberation as a particular mode of communication. Toward this end, I define deliberation as an encounter among interlocutors who engage in a process of considering and weighing various perspectives and proposals for what they regard as issues of common concern. My focus on school boards indicates that I am referring to political and public deliberation, but I do not use these modifiers to recognize that much of the contemporary scholarship in rhetoric and communication and other fields has addressed deliberation's democratic potential. By defining deliberation as a process, I refer to an encounter that occurs over time, whether one hour, two weeks, or several years in duration. What happens earlier in this encounter influences what occurs later, such as the ways in which interlocutors' initial framing of issues informs their evaluation of potential solutions. My definition also calls attention to weighing. Identifying "careful weighing" as "the heart of most definitions of deliberation," Stephanie Burkhalter, John Gastil, and Todd Kelshaw maintain that deliberation entails "the performance of a set of communicative behaviors that promote thorough group discussion."[21] Their explication broaches the epistemic promise of deliberation to produce better decisions than solitary reflection. Although I share this view, I have refrained from modifying "weighing" with "careful" because I believe that the phrase may imply that actual encounters always fulfill this promise.

By mentioning perspectives and proposals in my definition, I wish to include a wider range of communication styles and orientations in deliberation than a strict propositional model. Advocating a democratization of deliberation, Derek Barker, Noëlle McAfee, and David McIvor urge scholars to widen an unnecessarily narrow conception of deliberation as "a rational discourse ideal of consensus reached through free and uncoerced public discussion." They call for a reframing of scholarly inquiries regarding the role of deliberation in democratic governance to account for "emotion, storytelling, and other varieties of communication."[22] In this spirit, I include perspectives to suggest that interlocutors may offer valuable and diverse contributions to deliberation that go beyond narrow means of resolving disagreements. As Iris Marion Young notes, perspectives may introduce varied questions and experiences into discursive encounters.[23] My definition references common concerns, but I do not understand these concerns as determined a priori or indicating strict separations of public and private. Interlocutors negotiate the content of common concerns through their deliberations. Over time, issues formerly considered private, such as domestic violence, may obtain a public standing.[24] Moreover, by referencing interlocutors' judgments of common concern, I situate deliberation in context to appreciate, as William Keith holds, that theories of deliberation must treat discourse "as issuing from actual people in a time-, place- and institution-bound context."[25]

My definition embraces "rowdy" deliberations as well as peaceful interactions, seeing both as potential enactments of local democracy and policymaking. Formulating this approach, Robert Ivie holds that "rhetorical deliberation is often a rowdy affair, just as politics is typically messy." Ivie explains that a "rowdy" conception of deliberation maintains "a productive tension between cooperation and competition" and does not privilege "any single perspective to the exclusion of all others."[26] This conception affirms a robust practice of deliberation as operating independently of strict procedures. Further, my definition recognizes that deliberation may lead to agreements among interlocutors as well as productive articulations of disagreement. Disagreement in deliberation does not necessarily signal error—a series of wrong turns en route to a preferred outcome. As Charles Willard suggests, we do not need to treat disagreement as indicating "an imperfection in a relationship, an obstacle to group harmony and goals."[27] Understanding our disagreements with one another may promote decision-making and collective problem-solving as well as helping us to discover a shared set of values. My definition envisions deliberation as an enactment of Dewey's vision of creative democracy. Accepting a range of styles and addressing various issues, deliberation enables people from diverse backgrounds to articulate their desires, coordinate their actions, and make their environments meaningful.

Fieldwork and Local Policymaking

Deliberations about local policymaking occur in innumerable locations across the United States and the globe. However, analyzing these deliberations may raise the logistical challenge of accessing them. Unlike many national and international policy deliberations, local deliberations often do not appear in publicly accessible archives and databases. Scholars interested in a U.S. president's speeches and statements on education policy, for example, may find every public statement of every modern-day president recorded in the *Public Papers of the Presidents of the United States*, as well as texts of major speeches in newspapers like the *New York Times* and on various websites. Similarly, scholars often can find congressional debates and the advocacy of prominent organizations in government and nongovernment archives. Bolstered by regular media coverage, national and international deliberations occur with a wider public awareness and availability of the proceedings. Like any scholarly inquiry, studying these deliberations presents challenges, but accessing primary materials often is not a major problem. The meetings of school boards and other local governing bodies do not receive the same archival treatment, as there exists no local equivalent of the U.S. Government Printing Office, which publishes print and electronic versions of presidential speeches and statements, congressional hearings and floor debates, and more. A scholar interested in local policy deliberations has to go out and find them.

My initial foray into fieldwork in Wisconsin school districts began as part of an effort to illuminate a local aspect of a prominent national and international trend toward calls for research-based decision-making in a wide range of policy areas. Mentioning "research" more than one hundred times, NCLB legitimated this approach for education policy and practice, situating research evidence as the appropriate basis for decision-making in curriculum and instruction, teacher training, and more.[28] For example, the law seeks "to enhance the early language, literacy, and prereading development of preschool age children, particularly those from low-income families, through strategies and professional development that are based on scientifically based reading research."[29] In this context, as Vivian Tseng, a senior officer for the William T. Grant Foundation argues, "the research community needs a stronger understanding of how practitioners and policymakers engage research. This understanding should include their definitions of research, their perceptions of its relevance and quality, their preferred modes of communication, and the forces that influence their use of research."[30] Private foundations like William T. Grant and government agencies have played key roles in supporting scholarship on the use of research evidence in policymaking. Pursuing this line of inquiry, I co-led a Wisconsin-based study supported by the William T. Grant Foundation called the Research on Education, Deliberation, and Decision-Making (REDD) Project.[31]

Serving as research sites for the REDD Project, Beloit, Elmbrook, and West Bend comprise three similarly sized districts (enrolling roughly seven thousand students) that vary in terms of diversity and socioeconomic status. Serving a working-class city along the Wisconsin-Illinois border, Beloit contains the highest levels of diversity but also the highest levels of economically disadvantaged households. For the 2010–11 school year, 73 percent of Beloit students were identified as economically disadvantaged, and over half of all students were minorities. By contrast, Elmbrook, which encompasses some of the upper-middle-class suburbs west of Milwaukee, serves a financially stable and comparatively homogeneous population. For the 2010–11 school year, only 11 percent of the students were identified as economically disadvantaged and 20 percent of the students were minorities. An "exurban" community northwest of Milwaukee, West Bend constitutes a district in transition. For the 2010–11 school year, 32 percent of its students were economically disadvantaged while only 10 percent were minorities. Yet both figures represent substantial increases in the last ten years: since the 2000–2001 school year, the number of economically disadvantaged students has increased from 12 to 32 percent, and the number of minority students has increased from 4 to 10 percent.[32] From September 2009 to May 2011, REDD team members attended school-board and other committee meetings in the three districts. Over the course of the fieldwork, REDD team members attended over two hundred meetings across the districts. The specific focus for the REDD project consisted of analyzing board members' and other participants' use of research and non-research evidence during their deliberations over policy issues. We considered both the frequency and function of this evidence in deliberations within the three districts.[33]

Providing the materials for this book, the REDD Project offers insights for how field methods may complement textual analyses of public discourse.[34] Fieldwork generates opportunities to bolster discovery alongside interpretation as a means of producing knowledge of policy discourse.[35] In this spirit, Phaedra Pezzullo holds that fieldwork offers scholars an opportunity to "study public discourse that is not yet recorded, a situation in which textual analysis is impossible."[36] When studying well-known and accessible texts, scholars may presume some familiarity among audiences regarding content and focus their critical energy on articulating an interpretation that facilitates a more nuanced and/or alternative understanding of this material among their audiences. If I were to conduct an analysis of President Obama's education initiatives, for example, I would focus less on generating awareness of his statements and more on offering an analysis of his statements that illuminates their function and significance. Yet this critical endeavor depends on the texts being known. From this starting point, textual criticism may productively defamiliarize the familiar, offering audiences a new understanding of public discourse. Reapplying this dynamic, fieldwork may complement textual criticism by defamiliarizing the familiar bounds of public discourse, widening audiences' understandings of who may deliberate about public policy, how they may deliberate, and where these deliberations may occur. Discovering "new" texts for analysis may reconfigure our understanding of policymaking generally.

As interpretation implicates ethics in scholarly judgments, discovery carries ethical weight by identifying discourses as warranting analysis. Just as particular studies may inform ongoing intellectual conversations, objects of study may circulate among scholarly communities, adding to discourses about particular topics (e.g., the rhetoric of education) and inviting further inquiry. Patterns of circulation broach the politics of canons, which endorse some texts as timeless and worthy of repeated engagement and others as transitory and deserving minimal attention.[37] Pezzullo holds that utilizing textual criticism and fieldwork may "affirm the importance of cultural performances unrecognized by mainstream culture and, in the process of interpretation, offer a record of them."[38] Pezzullo's reference to recognition invokes both scholarly and lay audiences. Both may come to see previously unfamiliar discourses as contributing to the conduct of public life. Moreover, multiple audiences imply various positions for (not) recognizing the significance of discourse. From the perspective of a local community, a school board may not appear as outside the awareness of "mainstream culture." To the contrary, board members often serve as leaders in their communities, and, as my case studies suggest, community members often appreciate the significance of board deliberations. Critical discovery, then, may widen this local pattern of circulation for other audiences.

Once locally circulating materials have been accessed, fieldwork offers textual critics an opportunity to understand the local contexts and cultures contributing to the production of discourse. Traditionally, rhetorical scholars have turned to histories and news accounts to understand contexts and cultures. While these methods hold value, unexplored discourses often may occur in underreported contexts, and they may engage unfamiliar cultural practices. For this reason, Gerard Hauser advocates field methods as a complement to textual analysis to learn about "local knowledge, concerns, meanings, modes of arguments, value schemes, logics, and the like shared among ordinary people."[39] Further, fieldwork may enable insights about context and culture that other methods cannot provide. Michael Middleton, Samantha Senda-Cook, and Danielle Endres observe that rhetorical field methods allow "critics to experience rhetorical action as it unfolds and offers opportunities to gather insights on how rhetoric is experienced by rhetors, audiences, and critics."[40] If scholars rely exclusively on already available texts, we necessarily encounter rhetoric after it has occurred, studying its record but not its embodied performance.

As textual critics learn about local contexts and cultures, we may gain new perspectives on the concepts we study. Dwight Conquergood writes that fieldwork may offer new insights on ostensibly familiar and well-studied concepts. He holds that rhetorical scholars may reflect on their assumptions to understand the "cultural constructedness of key concepts such as 'reason,' 'the rational,' 'the logical,' 'argument,' 'evidence,' and so forth."[41] In the pages that follow, I foreground themes of ideology, scarcity, expertise, and trust—concepts that I have explored to varying degrees in my previously published work. However, in this book, as I connect these concepts to particular events in Beloit, Elmbrook, and West Bend, both the concepts and the cases inform one another.[42] Yet I could not have made these connections without employing field methods to conduct, in Aaron Hess's terms, "a close reading of cultural activities, which is necessary for gaining the participant or insider perspective for the examination of vernacular organizations or local publics."[43] To be clear, this book is primarily a work of textual analysis, as transcripts of meetings and interviews serve as its basis. I also have relied on newspapers (many of them local) and state databases to build the contexts for my cases. Still, I have written about these discourses with an enriched understanding of the local district cultures that informed their production. Further, my understanding of context also has been illuminated by fieldwork.

Deliberative Themes, Deliberative Practice

School-board deliberations and policymaking manifest an everyday quality to public affairs by addressing pocketbook issues like taxes and local
concerns like the conduct of neighborhood schools and the development
of community youth. Local education policy connects people to policies, as
people often see their schools as symbols of their communities. The values
that people associate with these symbols may vary from community to community, but school-board deliberations may evidence common dynamics
and themes. The larger lessons that emerge from deliberations in Beloit,
Elmbrook, and West Bend constellate around themes of ideology, scarcity,
expertise, and trust. Multiple themes sometimes informed deliberative episodes across the districts, but I have focused on them successively to provide
analytic and conceptual clarity. As board members negotiated tensions common to deliberations elsewhere, their successes and failures offer insights
into the ways we may understand the function of ideology, scarcity, expertise, and trust for theories and practices of deliberation.

To provide some background for my analysis of local deliberations, in
the first chapter I discuss the networked character of education policy in
the United States. The federal government did not play a prominent role
in education policy until the passage of the 1965 Elementary and Secondary Education Act. In the ensuing decades, federal interest shifted from
opportunity to accountability, as increasing federal prescriptions regarding
finances, standards, testing, and performance have delimited the deliberations of local school boards. However, no single actor controls education
policy. Rather, school boards operate in a network of local, state, and federal
actors that craft education policy. School boards function as "strong publics"
that combine opinion formation and decision-making authority. Their decisions shape everyday instruction in the classroom and the conduct of public
education.

I begin my analysis in chapter 2, where I highlight the theme of ideology as I consider board deliberations in West Bend over an application from
a group of high school students to establish a local Gay-Straight Alliance
(GSA) chapter as a school-sponsored club. Initially, at a May 2011 meeting,
a majority of board members rejected this application. However, the board
reversed course after attorneys representing the students filed a discrimination lawsuit in federal court. Contra calls for procedural neutrality, I argue
that the GSA controversy reveals the force of engagement for negotiating

ideological differences in public deliberation. Enacting a counterpublicity—
a contesting mode of publicity that advanced alternative interpretations of
students' needs, interests, and identities—GSA advocates pressed tensions
in board members' ideologies between fiscal and social conservatism.

In chapter 3, I focus on scarcity in my analysis of deliberations in Beloit over taxes and school budgets. Already struggling economically, Beloit
felt the impact of the 2008–9 recession especially sharply. Unemployment
reached the highest rate in the state, and home foreclosures and other signs
of economic misery pervaded the community. Scarcity both constrained
board deliberations and circulated as a theme in board deliberations. Recognizing suffering in the community, board members disagreed about the
role that school funding should play in reviving economic fortunes. Some
board members called for retrenchment, while others held that the district
needed to invest in education to foster economic success. Addressing these
issues, board members did not behave as the strict rational actors imagined
in the state education funding formula. Rather, they considered a range of
factors in making their decisions.

I turn to expertise in chapter 4, examining deliberations in Elmbrook
over the district's participation in a metropolitan integration program
with the city of Milwaukee called Chapter 220. Facing declining student
enrollments and other budgetary pressures, board members developed sophisticated financial forecasting tools that identified Chapter 220 as an economic loser. However, these tools also constrained people's visions. Board
members and others spoke with precision and confidence about the costs
of Chapter 220, but they fumbled when trying to assess the value of diversity. Turning to anecdotes and the testimony of Chapter 220 families, board
members discerned a "soft" benefit to diversity. This case demonstrates the
constitutive relationship between expert methods and objects of study: the
Elmbrook board members measured what they knew, and they knew what
they measured.

In chapter 5, I consider the role of trust in deliberation. This chapter
constitutes a shift from the previous case studies as I analyze interviews
conducted with board members and administrators from across the three
districts. Interviewees cited trust as central to their deliberation and decision-
making. Building on these materials, I develop a model of deliberative trust
as a relational practice. From this perspective, trust does not function in
deliberation as an all-or-nothing phenomenon that determines a priori the
success or failure of deliberation by its presence or absence. Interlocutors
may transform relations of trust through their interactions, strengthening

or weakening levels of trust in deliberation. As a relationship, deliberative trust functions not as an attribute of one participant or another, but as a quality that may emerge in the interactions of participants—the discursive relationships they mutually construct.

Drawing inspiration from John Dewey's vision of a Great Community, in the conclusion I argue for the continued relevance of local, democratically oriented policymaking bodies as actors in an education policy network. Even as local bodies like school boards have their flaws, they empower local individuals and communities by facilitating participation in the conduct of education policy. Participation both fulfills an aim of justice and enables people to develop a sense of themselves as capable agents. Further, local participation offers important perspectives on state and national developments. Local officials alone cannot overcome a market-oriented accountability regime—for this also requires leadership at state and federal levels—but they can contribute to the realization of a Great Community by asking different questions and envisioning different futures, namely, by reflecting on the ways that schools can reconnect democracy and education so that students may act as capable agents in their communities.

I

NETWORKED PUBLICS, NETWORKED POLICIES

Deliberations about primary and secondary education in the United States occur in a wide range of forums populated by diverse participants. Neighbors at an informal backyard barbeque may consider the pros and cons of a proposal to close a district elementary school. Teachers at an elementary school may devote a portion of their lunch period to weighing the successes and failures of a recently implemented reading-instruction program. School-board members may agree or disagree with one another as well as with state legislators about prospective changes to statewide student achievement tests. National figures may favor policies that situate the country's public education system within a global economy that demands skilled workers and technological innovation for national prosperity. These deliberations and others typically proceed independently, as interlocutors interact with some awareness of their participation in larger education discourses but without an effort to draw together distinct deliberative episodes. Nevertheless, these episodes unfold in relation to one another, as decisions reached in one forum may influence deliberations elsewhere. A national commitment to economic competitiveness through education may motivate action from a state legislature, or local opposition to a school closing may forestall a school-board vote on the issue.

Involving different participants, topics, and modes of engagement, deliberations over education policy illustrate the operation of a networked public sphere.[1] Encompassing online discussions of education occurring on blogs, personal webpages, and other Internet forums, a networked public sphere nevertheless refers fundamentally to a pre-Internet understanding of social networks as "webs" of interaction and relationships that bring together diverse social actors. A networked public sphere suggests that deliberation does not reside in a singular site of public discourse but circulates among a multitude of overlapping and intersecting sites dispersed in space and time. In this spirit, Gerard Hauser writes that "the contemporary public sphere has become a web of discursive arenas, spread across society and even in some cases across national boundaries." He explains that "our direct daily encounters with others who share our discursive spaces may be local, but our awareness of association with others who are part of this dialogue extends to locales and participants who are strangers."[2] In a network, we may hold indirect, complicated relationships with people several sites removed from our primary places of engagement. Along these lines, Michael Warner maintains that the public sphere sustains a "stranger sociability" insofar as it does not delimit participation in advance and treats strangers as "already belonging to our world."[3] Strangers belong not because we necessarily sense an affinity with them or see strangers as potential allies, but because we recognize their standing as interlocutors. While some networks may operate with a hub-and-spoke design, the multiplicity of the public sphere evidences a decentralized network, including people officially charged with crafting public policy and others who may articulate views about and seek to influence policy.[4]

At alternative moments in U.S. history, different actors operating in an education network consisting of local, state, and national sites have exerted varying degrees of influence over the shape of public policy. For much of the early history of the nation, local committees maintained control over their district schools. As historian Carl Kaestle explains, district-school committees operated with the primary goal of providing children in the community with "rudimentary instruction at low cost under firm community control."[5] Satisfaction with this arrangement and resistance to property taxes stalled efforts to establish statewide systems of education. By the mid-nineteenth century, reformers associated with the common school movement sought to increase the role of state governments in public education. As Kaestle notes, "The evils of district control became a major theme of state school reports."[6] Reformers pressed for the consolidation of smaller districts and introduced state supervisory and regulatory mechanisms, such as state education agencies, funds, and superintendents of common schools.

Around the turn of the twentieth century, many reformers shifted their attention once more—this time to professionals as the appropriate stewards of education. Seeking to "remove 'politics' from educational decision making," as William Reese observes, many Progressive Era reformers exalted expertise as the legitimate basis for policymaking. Reformers in cities and towns pushed for the consolidation of existing school boards, which sometimes consisted of more than thirty members, to smaller boards of fewer than ten members. Further, they looked to centralize power in the office of the superintendent. Political scandals convinced many reformers that ward-based school politics propagated a system whereby local power brokers used public schools as sources of personal gain and political favors. Some reformers also believed that school systems had become too complicated for laypeople to control. Perhaps unsurprisingly, and articulating a view that circulates today, city superintendents argued that "only experts, and not lay-people on school boards, could keep apprised of the latest pedagogical ideas through wide reading, professional correspondence, and association with other urban leaders."[7] These reformers saw themselves as reformulating the relationship between democracy and education from local participation by citizens to creating well-managed schools for citizens.[8]

The federal government did not involve itself significantly in primary and secondary education until the 1960s, when President Johnson advocated for passage of the 1965 Elementary and Secondary Education Act (ESEA). Demonstrating respect for local control, ESEA provided modest funding for school districts that enrolled disadvantaged students while leaving policy decisions to state and local governments. President Johnson argued that the nation offered most of its children a solid education but that poor students in rural and urban areas lacked sufficient resources. Statements of defer-ence notwithstanding, ESEA initiated a trajectory of greater federal involve-ment in education policy, as reformers began to sound alarms about the quality of education experienced by all primary and secondary students. An accountability regime arose in the 1980s and 1990s that demanded stan-dards and testing to measure student success. This movement culminated in the passage of the 2001 No Child Left Behind (NCLB) Act, a bipartisan piece of legislation that mandated annual testing in core subject areas and tied federal funding to student performance on these tests. NCLB refigured the historically local character of education policy in the United States by placing the federal government in an unprecedentedly prescriptive role.[9]

Across historical waves of reform, the school board as a form of local governance has survived. School boards do not operate in the present day as embodied links to a small-town past in which yeoman farmers governed themselves. Historian David Tyack holds that "by and large the changes in school governance have narrowed the discretion and confined the powers of local school districts." Tyack does not wish to "romanticize local control of schools," but he worries that contemporary reforms have ignored local school boards, which teach important democratic lessons—good and bad—by engaging theory and practice. In earlier eras, school boards and local governance enabled "public spaces where citizens of all ages learned and practiced democracy in a familiar setting."[10] Yet we need not discuss this pedagogy in the past tense. Even in an accountability regime, local governance proceeds—school boards continue to serve as sites of democratic engagement. As Diane Ravitch notes, in the face of market-oriented demands for change, "school boards insist on deliberation."[11] When we consider education policy through the perspective of a networked public sphere, we may recognize school boards as engaging in deliberation and decision-making in a field of constraint. Federal policy delimits and informs the deliberations of local school boards, but boards still make decisions that shape the everyday operation of the classroom and the conduct of public education.

In this chapter, to provide some background for my analyses in subsequent chapters, I consider this networked relationship between federal policy and local deliberation. Focusing primarily on the public discourse of President Lyndon B. Johnson and President George W. Bush, I first address the development of federal policy on primary and secondary education from the mid-1960s through the passage of NCLB. Promoting federal financial support for education, President Johnson foregrounded the key policy term "opportunity," advocating a basic level of federal support to unleash powerful ameliorative forces in communities. In contrast, President Bush emphasized the key policy term "accountability," holding that educators and administrators should not be granted federal resources without oversight. Next, I address the contemporary operation of school boards, arguing that they function as "strong publics" that combine opinion formation with decision-making authority.

From Opportunity to Accountability

In the decades preceding the passage of ESEA, proposals for federal support of primary and secondary education confronted three obstacles: race, religion, and federal control. In terms of race, policymakers had disagreed about whether to provide federal funding to segregated schools. Passage of the 1964 Civil Rights Act resolved the question of funding and race, because Title VI of the Act prohibited federal funding of any program engaged in illegal discrimination: "No person in the United States shall, on the ground of race, color, or national origin, be excluded from participation in, be denied the benefits of, or be subjected to discrimination under any program or activity receiving Federal financial assistance."[12] Resistance to desegregation continued in many locales in the South and elsewhere, but the Civil Rights Act removed the possibility of Congress underwriting de jure segregation in the nation's schools.

A similar question concerning whether Congress should extend funding to private schools offering religious instruction presented a difficult challenge to advocates of federal support. A legal basis for negotiating the separation of church and state had appeared in the 1947 Supreme Court decision *Everson v. Board of Education of Ewing Township*, which famously invoked Thomas Jefferson's metaphor of a "wall of separation between church and state" in the majority opinion's interpretation of the Establishment Clause of the U.S. Constitution. The case was initiated by a resident of Ewing, New Jersey, who sued the school district to stop its practice of reimbursing parents for the cost of busing their children to public or private schools. Even as it insisted on a wall of separation, the Supreme Court, by a 5–4 majority, upheld the town's reimbursement policy, likening the provision of transportation to such essential services as police and fire protection. According to the majority, albeit not without charges of inconsistency from dissenting justices, governments legitimately could climb the wall separating church and state when their actions served a public purpose, evidenced neutrality, and did not interfere with the free exercise of religion.[13] Justice Black argued that the First Amendment "requires the state to be a neutral in its relations with groups of religious believers and nonbelievers; it does not require the state to be their adversary. State power is no more to be used so as to handicap religions than it is to favor them."[14] Audiences interpreted the decision as restricting funding for such items as teacher salaries and capital expenses but permitting funding for services that would more directly benefit children.

No act of Congress or decision by the Supreme Court could answer the question of federal control, which some policymakers and other advocates feared would emerge as a deleterious consequence of federal funding. Allaying this fear constituted one of President Johnson's primary challenges. In part, his administration sought to answer this challenge by designing ESEA to distribute the majority of its funds according to a formula based on the number of poor children in a district, recalling *Everson* by tying aid to children rather than institutions or structures.[15] This approach promised to avoid potentially contentious debates over whether the federal government would participate in local decisions about staffing and curricular issues. Moreover, offering an inducement to policymakers, this formula significantly expanded the number of districts across the nation eligible for federal funds. Eventually, 94 percent of all school districts in the United States would receive federal funding under Title I.[16]

President Johnson confronted the fear of federal control in his public advocacy for ESEA by highlighting "opportunity" and subordinating the role of the federal government to state and local authorities. In a January 12, 1965, message to Congress urging passage of ESEA, he announced a national goal of *"Full Educational Opportunity."*[17] Intimating reciprocal actions, opportunity emphasized the individual student's responsibility to take advantage of available educational resources and the government's responsibility to provide these resources. Drawing on a spirit of innovation, opportunity comported with the forward-looking, optimistic mood of Johnson's Great Society programs.[18] Opportunity offered students a chance at success, but opportunity could not guarantee an outcome. Foregrounding this key term, Johnson resisted a view of life circumstances as static and unyielding; he conveyed a confidence that young people would seize opportunities they encountered, just as previous generations of Americans had used education to improve their lives.

Full educational opportunity could be obtained because education appeared to be an inexhaustible resource. Johnson held that children should "get as much education as [they have] the ability to take."[19] In this phrasing, education constituted something tangible and cumulative that could be possessed by a student. Under this guise, a student entered school as a tabula rasa to be filled with knowledge imparted by teachers and books. Indeed, acquisition constituted the student's primary task; not everyone could acquire the same amount of education, but students should absorb as much education as their ability permitted. Moreover, urging children to obtain levels of education commensurate with their abilities implied that a sufficient quantity of this resource existed for all students. Opportunity thus avoided a zero-sum politics of scarcity in which educational resources directed toward one group of children would arrive at the expense of another. Tied to Johnson's optimistic envisioning of a plentiful future, opportunity required individual effort for its realization, but opportunity did not require collective sacrifice nor did it foster potentially divisive competition.

As Johnson saw it, the problem arose from a lack of universal access to the excellent education resources that existed in the nation. In this spirit, Johnson told the story of two educational systems: one representing the best of America, the other appearing in shambles. Johnson pronounced that "America is strong and prosperous and free because for one hundred and seventy-eight years we have honored that commitment [to education]."[20]

More Americans in the mid-1960s attended schools at the primary, secondary, and postsecondary levels than at any previous period in the nation's history. And yet, beneath this tremendous success lurked a "darker side to education in America": dropout rates in some areas reached intolerably high levels, and youth unemployment and crime jeopardized the nation's future. In the first system, education worked well: teachers taught, students learned, and everyone benefited. This first system, which enrolled the majority of schoolchildren, required no intervention; left alone, it would continue to bolster the nation. The solution lay in making this first system of education the only system of education for all children.

The second system failed students because it lacked resources—the resource of education itself was unevenly distributed across the nation. Johnson maintained that "the burden of the nation's schools is not evenly distributed. Low-income families are heavily concentrated in particular urban neighborhoods or rural areas. Faced with the largest educational needs, many of these school districts have inadequate financial resources."[21] Just as poorer communities struggled with limited resources to educate their children, the children in these communities began schooling with an education deficit that quickly grew. Johnson observed that "the child from the urban or rural slum frequently misses his chance even before he begins school. Tests show that he is usually a year behind in academic attainment by the time he reaches third grade—and up to three years behind *if* he reaches the eighth grade."[22] As Johnson's reference to "chance" suggests, poor children did not have an opportunity to attain an education.

The federal government could best serve students by effectively facilitating a national distribution system of educational resources. In this role, the federal government would defer to established authorities by facilitating the extension of sound educational practices from the first system to the second. Johnson insisted that "federal assistance does not mean federal control." The federal government would not usurp the authority of state and local officials; it would not participate in decision-making about curricular, staffing, and other issues. Justifying a role in distributing resources, Johnson approvingly quoted the late Senator Robert Taft's argument that although "education is primarily a state function . . . the Federal Government has a secondary obligation to see that there is a basic floor under those essential services for all adults and children in the United States."[23] Appearing immediately after his disavowal of federal control, Johnson's reference to the well-known conservative Republican Taft served to bolster his claim that the federal government would undertake a subordinate role. Keeping with traditional practices of American education, this limited role purportedly removed education policy from the province of partisan politics.

The federal government needed to establish a "basic floor" because re- source disparities among states and localities meant that smaller units of government did not possess the capacity to redress this issue. Johnson held that "this is a national problem. Federal action is needed to assist the States and localities in bringing the full benefits of education to children of low-income families."[24] Johnson did not question decision-making at the local level; rather, he appreciated that a lack of resources constrained local decision-making. The federal government could provide the financial resources required to distribute educational resources equitably across the nation. In this way, likening the federal role in primary and secondary edu- cation to providing a "basic floor" underscored the essential role of educa- tion for all Americans, situating education as part of an individual's basic needs and also part of a national infrastructure. Making resources more widely available, a basic floor deferred to states and local communities to use these resources as they wished. A basic floor would provide a minimum threshold of funding—no more, no less. With the federal government adopt- ing a background role, the primary energy and agency for education reform remained with educators, researchers, and other social actors who were al- ready at work to deliver an excellent education to all students.

In the years after the passage of ESEA, policymakers and citizens alike lost confidence in the ability of educators and local decision-makers to im- prove education. During the 1970s and 1980s, a growing chorus of crit- ics called for changes in curriculum and instruction. In 1983, the National Commission on Excellence in Education issued a blistering report titled *A Nation at Risk*. Noting that the report captivated public attention, Patricia Albjerg Graham maintains that *A Nation at Risk* turned "dissatisfaction with the academic performance of most American children [into a] national political issue."[25] Highlighting a sense of danger at the outset, the report ad- opted an alarmist tone. On the opening page, the Commission held that "if an unfriendly foreign power had attempted to impose on America the me- diocre educational performance that exists today, we might well have viewed it as an act of war."[26] Surveying the landscape of American education, the Commission found watered-down curricula, fewer course requirements, less homework, easier exams, and underprepared teachers. The Commis- sion recommended strengthening high-school graduation requirements, developing more rigorous and measurable standards, returning to basic subjects, bolstering teaching, and raising expectations. The rhetoric of *A*

Nation at Risk betrayed a shifting political culture toward education policy in the 1980s, as themes of opportunity circulated amid an emergent economic discourse enabling standards and outcomes.[27]

In this climate, reform swept across many states. Capitalizing on this energy, President George H. W. Bush, who campaigned as an "education president," convened a summit of the nation's governors in Charlottesville, Virginia, in 1989. During the summit, the governors voiced support for a voluntary system of national education goals. For his part, Bush concluded that "the American people are ready for radical reforms. We must not disappoint them."[28] Although his proposal to develop a set of national standards failed in the Congress, some governors continued to press for reform. Having participated in the 1989 Charlottesville summit as governor of Arkansas, President Clinton had demonstrated a commitment to national standards upon entering office.[29] In 1994, his administration successfully pushed for congressional passage of Goals 2000, which called for the creation of voluntary national standards and offered grants to states for developing such standards. Former Secretary of Education Richard Riley reflected that an unprecedented "statutory framework defines the federal role as one of supporting and facilitation to improve all schools for all children."[30] Goals 2000 evidenced the growing policy consensus around standards and testing as the keys to education reform.

Building on the momentum of standards-based reform, NCLB intensified the federal role in primary and secondary education by moving from voluntary to mandatory mechanisms.[31] Tying federal funding to student performance, NCLB required annual testing of many students in core subject areas. To remain in good standing, schools needed to demonstrate "adequate yearly progress" toward a goal of 100 percent student proficiency by 2014. Schools that failed to meet "adequate yearly progress" faced increasingly strict penalties, including potentially replacing instructional staff and restructuring school governance. NCLB also required that "highly qualified"—usually meaning licensed or certified—teachers populate every classroom in the nation's public schools. A bipartisan group of legislators supported these mandates, with Representative George Miller (D-CA) and Senator Edward Kennedy (D-MA) playing key roles in the House and Senate, respectively, intervening at crucial moments when a bill seemed in jeopardy. The conference report passed the House (381 to 41) and Senate (87 to 10) with overwhelming bipartisan majorities.[32]

Championing the key policy term of accountability, President George W. Bush positioned himself and other federal policymakers as the ultimate authorities to whom schools, teachers, and students must answer. He announced that "my focus will be on making sure that every child is educated."[33] He promised that "once failing schools are identified, we will help them improve." Bush insisted that "we want success," yet he stipulated that "when schools are willing to accept the reality that the accountability system points out and are willing to change, we will help them."[34] Distinguishing "we" from "schools," these statements made clear who set the expectations for improved performance and who needed to meet them. Local schools could not participate in crafting these expectations; their agency consisted of measuring up or suffering the consequences if they failed to do so. At times, Bush's invocation of a "we" demanding accountability expanded to include parents and citizens, but he consistently included federal policymakers and, at key moments in his public statements, excluded local schools from this role. Along these lines, "accountability" sustained a vertical line of authority in contrast to the horizontal relationship facilitated by opportunity. Whereas opportunity justified a basic floor upon which students and schools could act, accountability placed individuals at different levels of authority and prescribed a reporting system to transmit information up the hierarchy.

Believing that improved performance from all students required strong leadership, President Bush explained the failure of education in recent decades through a lack of leadership. Bush insisted that "all of us in positions of responsibility must set the highest of high standards for every child."[35] The very call to adopt the "highest of high standards" through NCLB implied that state and local policymakers had not done so previously. Although local officials did not issue the demand for accountability, they could exemplify the qualities of strong leadership in specific cases, and the president periodically praised school principals for doing so. At a visit to one elementary school, Bush praised the efforts of the principal and underscored the importance of local leaders setting "the highest of high standards. Leaders that understand that every child can learn and refuse to accept excuses when they don't. . . . That's what a leader does."[36] Accountability connoted the strength and determination that Bush discerned in leadership. In effect, accountability promised to enact at a national level what exceptional principals had achieved at a few local schools. Moreover, diagnosing the problem as one of leadership retained Bush's focus on outcomes rather than inputs. While President Johnson likened the federal government's role to distributing resources more widely, Bush cautioned that "we must focus the spending of federal tax dollars on things that work. Too often, we have spent without regard for results."[37]

To hold others accountable, leaders needed accurate information, which testing would provide. Along these lines, Bush explained that "by accountability I mean testing children to determine whether or not children are learning."[38] Enabling this determination, testing functioned as an information resource that gauged student performance. As Bush maintained, "Without yearly testing, we don't know who is falling behind and who needs help."[39] The audiences for this information—the "we" who need to know—appeared primarily as the adults responsible for raising children, instructing them, and formulating education policy: federal policymakers, education officials, and parents. Even though students took tests, Bush did not situate students as an audience for the test results. Indeed, recounting his own daughters' complaints about test-taking in Austin, Bush shared his reply: "We, the adults, want to know whether or not you're learning."[40] Bush implied that without testing such knowledge would be unavailable. For instance, asserting the need for annual rather than periodic testing, Bush urged his audiences to consider that a "child may pass the third grade reading test; he or she gets in the eighth grade and lo and behold, fails the eighth grade test. And the parent says, 'Who do I hold accountable? What happened?'" This example implied that other sources for monitoring student progress did not exist, or that parents were unaware of alternatives. Bush answered the question of accountability with another question: "Where did the system let me down?"[41] Responsibility for student failure resided in the "system," and testing helped policymakers and parents assign blame.

While student testing constituted a familiar (and sometimes anxiety-inducing) classroom activity, Bush constructed accountability as a consequential test for teachers, too. Bush saw part of his task as "convincing teachers of the importance and power of accountability." Presumably, the power of persuasion would produce sound audience judgments: "A good teacher welcomes accountability, because a good teacher understands that measurement is the kernel for success." Bad teachers would fear and resist reform: "If you haven't been held accountable, and all of a sudden somebody starts holding you accountable, it's going to create a certain sense of anxiety."[42] As these quotes suggest, in Bush's view, accountability would inaugurate an important period of introspection and decision for the nation's teachers: lacking courage, some educators would be forced by the sanctions in NCLB to leave the teaching profession; heeding Bush's call, other teachers would renew their pledge to their important vocation. In these ways, Bush conveyed a strong sense of moral obligation in discussing accountability. He asserted that "every child can learn, and that ought to be indelibly etched into our national conscience, that every single child in America has got the capacity to learn and we should accept nothing less."[43] Expecting anything less than "educated" children—forsaking accountability—would violate the nation's collective conscience.

As federal policymakers articulated clear expectations, President Bush insisted that state and local officials should determine the best means for achieving successful outcomes. In this way, Bush imagined a relationship among levels of government that highlighted federal agency at the beginning and end of the process of education reform, while foregrounding the agency of state and local governments to chart the best path between these two points. In this spirit, Bush asserted that "the agents of reform must be schools and school districts, not bureaucracies."[44] Although they could not set goals, states and localities retained a flexible agency in trying to achieve them. Accountability comported with public frustration with education in the decades before Bush took office. Since the 1983 release of *A Nation at Risk*, policymakers and citizens alike worried that a failing educational system had slowed economic growth, threatened the United States' international standing, and harmed families and the nation. Policymakers could no longer defer to educators and local decision-makers to produce positive outcomes.

School-Board Governance

Even as he envisions a linear process of policymaking, President Bush articulates a flexible relationship between the federal government and other levels of government. Policymaking defies linear visions, as various actors and agencies of government may participate at different moments and in different ways, revisit prior decisions, and resist decisions made by others. But President Bush rightly notes that accountability does not eliminate local control—if we understand "control" as a power to direct action.[45] Educators and other local officials may bemoan the pervasiveness of student testing, for example, but they still look to school boards and superintendents to set directions for their districts. Local control disappears only if we imagine responsibility for education policy as an all-or-nothing proposition, which would contradict the long-standing decentered character of U.S. education policy.

Situated in specific locales, school boards exert an authority that draws on relations among levels of government. Addressing the legal standing of local school districts, Richard Briffault explains that primary and secondary education in the United States exhibits a "tension between the 'black letter' rule of local school district subordination to the state and the practice—and occasional legal recognition—of local school district autonomy."[46] The legal subordination of local districts reflects the special interest of state governments in providing citizens with a public education, which reflects "an unusual departure in American constitutionalism" from typically limiting the power of governments at various levels to "affirming government obligations to provide a public service."[47] Like most states, Wisconsin affirms the provision of public education in its state constitution. Article X of the Wisconsin Constitution opens with the declaration that "the supervision of public instruction shall be vested in a state superintendent and such other officers as the legislature shall direct." The creation of district schools appears later in Section 3 of Article X, which indicates that "the legislature shall provide by law for the establishment of district schools."[48] As this statement makes clear, the legislature serves as the agent in establishing a public school system for the citizens of Wisconsin, while local school districts appear as the objects of legislative action.

At the same time, in key cases, federal and state courts have highlighted local control when adjudicating responsibility for education policy. Briffault observes that some courts, "particularly the U.S. Supreme Court, have found significant normative value in entrusting some measure of control over public education to local school boards."[49] In important cases on funding inequities and desegregation, the U.S. Supreme Court has turned to local control to halt state- and region-wide corrective measures. In the 1973 decision *San Antonio Independent School District v. Rodriguez*, the Supreme Court ruled against plaintiffs challenging gross funding inequalities among school districts across the state of Texas, discerning a legitimate state interest in local control.[50] In the 1974 case *Milliken v. Bradley*, the Supreme Court overturned a lower-court order for interdistrict busing to remedy segregation in the Detroit Public Schools. While the lower court saw suburban school districts as essential components of a successful integration plan, the Supreme Court held that such a plan would violate the autonomy of suburban districts.[51] In Wisconsin, the state supreme court has found that the state constitutional mandate to establish district schools grants local districts some autonomy.[52]

While local school boards operate with some degree of independence as local governing bodies, they nonetheless differ from other institutions of local government. Perhaps most conspicuously, whereas city councils and county boards address a range of local issues, school boards focus their deliberation and decision-making on education. This sharpened focus reflects the importance that Americans attach to education. However, it also may convey a false sense of clarity about school boards' purposes and policies. Education presumably delineates a bounded area of governance, yet, as Karen Tracy notes, "'education' is not an easily delimited issue; it is best conceived as a gloss for a messy tangle of concerns about children, schools, learning, civic conduct, money, and moral issues."[53] A focus on education does not absolve school boards from answering questions about what should appear on their agendas.

In contrast to many other elections for public office, school-board elections proceed as nonpartisan affairs. In a nationwide survey of school-board members, Frederick Hess reports that nearly 90 percent of respondents indicated that they participated in nonpartisan elections.[54] According to Jennifer Hochschild, the nonpartisan character of these elections offers voters few "reliable clues about which candidates may share their own views."[55] Further, school-board elections frequently occur on different days from higher-profile national and state elections. Noting that fewer than half of his respondents were elected on the same day as national or state elections, Hess concludes that "rather than being held when voters are already going to the polls for more visible elections, board elections are held at times when the body politic is more inactive."[56] A legacy of Progressive Era reforms designed to depoliticize schooling, these factors contribute to low turnouts in school-board elections, where typically less than one quarter of eligible voters cast a ballot. However, in cases where highly publicized and/or controversial issues shape elections, voter turnout spikes.[57]

School-board members interact regularly with their district superintendent, who works full-time to oversee the operations of the local public schools. Crucial to setting a productive district climate and facilitating efficacious decision-making, this relationship often appears vulnerable to conflicting interpretations of roles and power struggles. In part, the complexities of this relationship arise from the different types of accountability experienced by board members and superintendents. While most school boards—more than nine in ten—consist entirely of elected members, nearly all district superintendents in the United States hold appointed positions, and most school boards—including every school board in Wisconsin—hire their own superintendents.[58] Board-superintendent relations, then, enact a dynamic in which board members hire someone they presumably regard as capable of directing their district's schools, yet nevertheless as elected officials bear the public responsibility for success of their district's schools.

School-board members often do not attract widespread attention from their constituents until the latter become dissatisfied with district policies.[59] A superintendent's standing often rises or falls with board turnover, contributing to the gallows humor among superintendents that "the board that hires you is not the board that fires you."[60] In Elmbrook, the superintendent Matt Gibson served for seventeen years until his retirement in 2012—a tenure lasting more than three times the national average—while Beloit and West Bend experienced turnover in their superintendents by the end of the two-year period of REDD fieldwork.[61]

Boards and superintendents often conflict in their interpretations of their respective roles. A superintendent may object to a board's oversight as micromanagement, while a board may object to a superintendent's direction as steamrolling. Attempts to articulate a strict delegation of responsibilities—such as assigning policymaking to boards and administration to superintendents—may appear impractical, as the interdependence of boards and superintendents frustrates clear boundaries. More productively, as Deborah Land observes, boards and superintendents may develop their respective roles "as best suits them and continually evaluate and reassess the arrangement."[62] To some extent, this situational approach both depends on and fosters good relations, which also may be bolstered by cooperative approaches to decision-making.[63] Investigating what she terms "micromanaging" and "collaborative" approaches to decision-making, Meredith Mountford explains that people's approaches typically rely on their conceptions of power. Micromanagers define power as controlling others to obtain a desired outcome, whereas collaborators define power as working with others to achieve a desired outcome.[64] Similarly, grounding good relations in "the basic principles of educational and democratic theory," a survey of four successful school districts appearing in the practitioner-oriented *School Administrator* journal identifies as two keys to good board-superintendent relations "mutual respect for the talents and expertise each has to offer" and a willingness to refine roles.[65] In the REDD interviews, both board members and superintendents sometimes voiced complaints about what they regarded as the domineering approaches of others.

Just as local communities assumed responsibility for public education for much of the nation's history, so, too, did they serve as the primary funding source for local schools. Even after the widespread establishment of state education agencies by the turn of the twentieth century, the burden for financing public education still rested primarily with local communities. In 1930, for instance, local communities still provided more than 80 percent of the funds for their public schools. And local communities continued to provide more than half of these funds as the nation headed into the 1970s. Before federal policymakers focused their attention on public education, the biggest shift in education funding in the twentieth-century United States came from the states. In the early part of the twentieth century, states provided only 16 percent of the funding for primary and secondary education. By the end of the 1970s, this figure increased to 46.8 percent—a nearly threefold increase.[66] Nationwide, this level of state support effectively has plateaued, although wide variations exist among states. In Wisconsin, for the 2008–9 school year, the state provided 44.3 percent of school-district revenues, while local sources accounted for 43.7 percent of these revenues, although variations among local districts existed here, too.[67] Increases in state support for education occurred partly in response to legal challenges to funding inequalities among districts within states, which found success in state courts (as opposed to federal courts) beginning in the 1970s.[68]

Prior to the passage of ESEA, the federal government provided modest funds for primary and secondary education. At the beginning of the 1960s, the federal government contributed 4.4 percent of the total revenues spent on primary and secondary education, which nevertheless represented an increase from its minuscule contribution of 0.3 percent of revenues for the 1919–20 school year. By the end of the 1960s, the federal share nearly doubled, to 8 percent, and it kept growing during the 1970s. However, Ronald Reagan's election in 1980 halted this trend, as he pushed for cuts in federal funding of public education. Reagan objected to the federal role in primary and secondary education, advocating unsuccessfully for the elimination of the U.S. Department of Education during his first term. Federal spending on primary and secondary education did not recover until the early 1990s as Bill Clinton took office, remaining constant until it increased during the last few years of the Clinton administration.[69]

NCLB utilized federal funding as a carrot and stick. Schools and districts that failed to make progress on student achievement would suffer its penalties. As a carrot, NCLB increased overall federal spending on education, which motivated some initially reluctant Democrats in Congress to support the legislation.[70] While federal spending remained a small percentage of the overall revenues for primary and secondary education, NCLB nevertheless motivated states to respond to calls for accountability. Against claims that state objections to standards and testing would lead them to opt out of federal funding, Patrick McGuinn retorts that "states are hard-pressed to turn down the millions (and often hundreds of millions) of dollars in federal funds that they each receive annually."[71] While any budget cut hurts, a 9 percent budget cut, which represented the federal share of funding in the first few years after the passage of NCLB, would prove substantial and potentially harmful to many students.[72] At the same time, to maintain perspective on the federal role in the funding of primary and secondary education, I should note that at no point from the passage of ESEA to the implementation of NCLB did the federal share of funding exceed 10 percent of total revenues. Only one year into the Obama administration, with the 2009–10 school year, did federal spending cross this threshold to account for 12.7 percent of total revenues for primary and secondary education.[73]

Though their numbers have declined from earlier eras in U.S. public education, school boards remain, in Karen Tracy's phrase, prevalent sites of "ordinary democracy." Numbering over 160,000 before the twentieth century, school districts—the locales for school-board deliberation and decision-making—declined precipitously as a result of consolidation over the course of the twentieth century to 15,780 in 1972.[74] This number has remained relatively constant, as the Census Bureau estimates that roughly 14,500 school districts operate in the contemporary United States.[75] When we consider that school boards typically have between five and eight members, this represents considerable opportunities to practice ordinary democracy—both for board members and others who attend meetings.[76]

According to Tracy, "ordinary democracy is what happens" in local settings. Eschewing idealistic conceptions of democracy, Tracy advances an approach that "begins with existing institutions and describes what is occurring in them."[77] And she does not always find mild-mannered, polite conversation. To the contrary, Tracy's observations lead her to develop a concept of "reasonable hostility," which she defines as "an expression of anger that most people would judge reasonable." Like Robert Ivie's "rowdy" deliberation, Tracy's reasonable hostility recognizes that people may experience a range of emotions when engaging others, and these varied emotions may contribute productively to the exploration of different perspectives and positions. No universal standard of conduct spans innumerable local practices of ordinary democracy—reasonable hostility invokes "a situated, socially rooted standard of judgment."[78] Building on ordinary democracy's focus on varied local practices—which Tracy pursues through a study of the Boulder, Colorado, school board—my approach seeks to mediate theory and practice by considering how concepts of ideology, scarcity, expertise, and trust may illuminate deliberation and decision-making by the school boards in Beloit, Elmbrook, and West Bend.

Even during those rare meetings where dozens of community residents attend to express their views on a district issue, school-board members retain a special role as local community members charged with crafting district policy. Tracy characterizes school-board members as "politicians with a small 'p,' or, perhaps better, citizens with a capital 'C.'"[79] In the language of public sphere theory, school boards function as "strong publics." Nancy Fraser distinguishes "strong publics" from "weak publics," defining the latter as "publics whose deliberative practice consists exclusively in opinion formation and does not also encompass decision making." In contrast, strong publics combine "both opinion formation and decision making."[80] They serve as sites where participants may engage one another to develop collectively perspectives and positions that each might not hold individually and to act on these perspectives and positions in charting a common future course. Fraser offers this distinction in an essay critiquing Jürgen Habermas's historical account of the bourgeois public sphere, which interpreted its separation from official state power as a critical distance useful for evaluating the actions of government. While Habermas endorses this separation, Fraser counters that it excuses diminished forms of accountability between representatives and their constituents.

As strong publics, school boards negotiate an environment distinct from the legislatures to which Habermas entrusts decision-making and the self-managed institutions (e.g., self-governed workplaces, child-care centers) that Fraser cites as examples of strong publics. Whereas the strong publics imagined by Fraser operate with a high degree of autonomy, school boards operate in an education policy network. And yet, they do not function simply as local legislatures. To be sure, as Tracy suggests, they exhibit a pronounced local orientation. Board members often interact with—and sometimes are accosted by—fellow community members at the grocery store, dry cleaners, and elsewhere. Because they spend significant time in state or national capitals, state and federal policymakers experience unscripted, informal interactions with their constituents as less of a daily routine. Further, as one board member wistfully shared with Tracy, state and federal legislators often have staffs who serve as buffers between themselves and their constituents.[81] Community members typically may contact board members directly via e-mail or phone, while constituents trying to contact legislators through these channels more likely will reach staff and/or receive a pro forma response.

As they engage in opinion formation and decision-making, school boards combine people and roles in distinct ways. Although board members cast votes on policy, superintendents interact with boards as key interlocutors.

The superintendent has no analogue among state or federal legislatures, where staffs serve as representatives for elected officials. By contrast, a superintendent often participates in decision-making during board meetings and, especially in cases of a long tenure, a superintendent may lead a board on some decisions. Community members do not vote at board meetings, nor do they engage board members as decision-making partners, but they often speak at board meetings without invitation and as a recognized speaker, whereas speakers at meetings of state and federal legislatures often participate as officially invited witnesses at committee hearings. When ordinary citizens engage members of state and federal legislatures, they do so effectively as laypeople addressing professionals. School-board members, on the other hand, serve effectively as "citizen-policy makers."[82]

School-Board Policymaking in an Accountability Regime

Influence among sites in a networked public sphere does not always proceed directly, with interlocutors in one site awaiting decisions from others before acting to implement these directives faithfully. Interlocutors in a particular site may view deliberations occurring elsewhere as consequential for their own interactions, but the variously situated discourses of a networked public sphere also function indirectly to create a context for action. This is especially the case for policies like education that actors engage at various levels, gainsaying unqualified declarations of a loss of local control. Such a diagnosis wrongly implies that in an accountability regime local actors simply implement federal initiatives as federal policymakers envisioned them. Board members in Beloit, Elmbrook, and West Bend periodically addressed the frequent testing required by NCLB and decisions by state government that they regarded as constraining the board's flexibility in decision-making, but at no point during the REDD fieldwork did board members engage in extensive deliberation about how to comport their decision-making with NCLB, nor did they seek to anticipate the possible implications of a reauthorization of NCLB during the Obama administration.

Sometimes, board members and administrators in these three districts explicitly and extensively considered federal policy. In West Bend, they deliberated about whether federal law and policy would reverse the board's initial rejection of the Gay-Straight Alliance chapter's application for recognition as a school club. Board members sought the opinions of district staff and outside experts. Although board members did not agree about how a federal challenge would unfold, they all framed their arguments about potential outcomes in relation to federal institutions. As board members in Beloit looked to set a tax levy and a budget that balanced student needs and the needs of an economically struggling community, some board members bemoaned the district's place in a testing regime that emphasizes scores. Board members regarded this emphasis as unfair, because students in the district encountered obstacles to learning unfamiliar to many students in prosperous districts like Elmbrook, which excelled in an accountability regime. Elmbrook's deliberations about ending its participation in the Chapter 220 integration program reflected the board's savvy in negotiating the incentives of accountability. Board members recognized that in a regime that privileges test scores, the district's participation in Chapter 220, which fostered goals of equity but also cost the district revenues, went unrewarded.

Beyond these specific engagements, an accountability regime contributes to a wider context of policymaking for actors at the local level. Accountability instructs local policymakers to focus on outcomes rather than processes. A focus on outcomes defines success in terms of particular measureable thresholds and promotes board decisions that may maximize short-term testing gains over long-term student benefits. Accountability thus undervalues the capacity of interlocutors in deliberation to respond to contingent developments over time. Further, accountability reshapes views of what counts as knowledge and how local policymakers may measure knowledge. If accountability connotes results through testing, then knowledge takes shape as divisible, quantifiable, and reproducible bits of information—fungible units transferred from teacher to student to answer sheet. A strong emphasis on accountability as testing threatens to disqualify types of knowledge that do not render themselves to easy reproduction in standard form. Reflecting connections between method and object, quantifiable measurement indicates ontological standing. Following this logic, boards may seek to build curricula, programs, and services that submit to this method. Accountability also encourages boards to approach education policy as a marketplace, with districts and schools acting as businesses competing for students and families as customers. Yet transfiguring education from a public good to a private consumer product does not proceed without losing some of its ostensibly less profitable aims and, potentially, its connection to democracy.

2

IDEOLOGY, COUNTERPUBLICITY, AND
THE GAY-STRAIGHT ALLIANCE

By many accounts, Washington County, Wisconsin, is a conservative place. County residents regularly vote for conservative politicians in local, state, and national elections. In the 2008 presidential election, for example, even as Barack Obama carried the state of Wisconsin by a double-digit margin over his challenger, John McCain, Washington County voters preferred the conservative McCain by an almost two-to-one margin, providing McCain his highest percentage of support among counties in the state.[1] As for local politicians, State Senator Glenn Grothman, whose district includes most of Washington County, signals his unwavering fiscal conservatism by driving a car adorned with the license plates "TAX CUTR." As a co-sponsor of a bill that repealed Wisconsin's 2009 Equal Pay Enforcement Act, Senator Grothman drew national attention—and censure—for justifying repeal by asserting that "money is more important for men."[2] Beyond the streets of Wisconsin, national media have attended to Washington County. In 2010, considering factors such as voting patterns, various laws, religious attendance, and "intangibles" like "a long conservative history, an ingrained military culture, prominent right-wing politicians," the conservative *Daily Caller* website ranked Washington County as one of the hundred most "conservative-friendly" counties in the United States.[3] The entry about Washington County called attention to a recent controversy in the county seat of West Bend, where some citizens had called for the library to remove eighty-two books geared toward young adults that, in their view, promoted homosexuality and featured "raunchy sex acts."[4]

Illuminating prominent features of the ideological orientation of Washington County politics, these illustrations nevertheless threaten to conceal as much as they reveal. No community is ideologically homogeneous. And even policymakers and citizens who share particular ideological commitments may disagree about specific policies and ways to apply general abstract beliefs. Nor are individuals' ideological orientations necessarily internally consistent. David Zarefsky has noted that people may draw on seemingly opposed ideological elements in forming their political views. Zarefsky observes that "people may be fiscally conservative but socially liberal, for example. Or they embrace the future while feeling nostalgia for the past."[5] At the individual and collective level, different elements of a presumptively coherent ideology may produce tensions that invite reflection and deliberation, supporting and/or frustrating reconciliation of newly discovered disparate elements. People may support multiple values and policy goals—such as fiscal conservatism and law and order—but bolstering one, such as hiring more police officers, may weaken the other. Moments of controversy may expose ideological tensions, providing advocates with opportunities to challenge reigning ideological orientations.[6]

Understanding these dynamics requires negotiating meanings for the term "ideology" itself. As Terry Eagleton observes, scholars across a range of intellectual traditions have advanced divergent—and sometimes conflicting—definitions of ideology. These definitions range from an expansive sense of ideology as a general process of producing ideas, values, and beliefs in social life, to a narrow sense of ideology as the efforts of a dominant social group or class to propagate false or deceptive ideas, values, and beliefs to maintain their privilege and protect their interests.[7] Avoiding the ends of this conceptual spectrum, my use of the term "ideology" refers to strategic sets of claims, values, and beliefs that advocates may use to build collectives, forge alliances, highlight differences, and challenge alternatives. This definition distinguishes ideologies from worldviews per se, and it avoids the association of ideology and falsity. People may speak falsely in defense of an ideology, but they need not do so. Instead, this definition foregrounds the political dimension of ideologies, underscoring the connections among people's values and beliefs and the positions and policies they advocate and support in the public sphere. In diverse societies—perhaps in any society—this means that actors often contest ideologies as they practice public engagement. In this way, my approach resonates with what Chantal Mouffe has characterized as the agonistic operation of the public sphere. Expressing skepticism over the possibility of deliberation to eliminate disagreement, Mouffe argues that an agonistic view of the public sphere, one which sees conflict as irreducible and potentially productive, seeks to "keep the democratic contestation alive."[8] On school boards and elsewhere, people may continue to disagree even after they have deliberated and reached decisions—and yet these disagreements need not weaken the force of a decision.

In spring 2011, tensions and contestations within and among ideologies appeared in full force in Washington County. During the 2010–11 academic year, a group of students filed an application with the West Bend school district, which serves many students in Washington County, for the status of school-sponsored club. Typically, administrators handled such applications without much fanfare. But this group was different. The students sought official recognition for a Gay-Straight Alliance (GSA) that had been meeting informally at the West Bend high schools. As part of a national network of GSAs, the prospective club members hoped to "combat bullying and harassment through education" and provide "an emotionally and physically healing learning environment for people of all genders and sexual orientations."[9] Despite a favorable recommendation from the administration, during its May 2011 meeting the West Bend school board rejected the application. As they had promised during the meeting, the GSA's attorneys quickly filed a discrimination complaint in federal court, charging that the board had violated the Equal Access Act. With a lawsuit looming, the board reversed its decision during its June meeting. Even so, dissenting board members voiced their strong disapproval, and the board president, Randy Marquardt, who switched his vote to form the new majority, complained that he had been "bullied" into approving the GSA application.

The GSA controversy drew on potentially conflicting elements of the board members' ideologies. The threat of losing the lawsuit and having to pay their attorneys' fees as well as the fees of the GSA's attorneys challenged their fiscal conservatism, especially when two sets of attorneys advised the board that the GSA likely would prevail in court. The GSA's composition and mission threatened the social and religious conservatism as well as the heteronormative notions of family and society held by many board members, even though the GSA application made no mention of marriage or sex. Some board members who voted in favor of approving the application at both board meetings still struggled to accept the group. Despite calls from district staff, attorneys, and even their colleagues, board members did not separate their personal values and experiences from their putatively public roles. Moreover, GSA advocates and allies enacted a counterpublicity—a contesting mode of engagement—that pressed this tension, exposing its faults and calling some members of the board and community on their homophobia and discriminatory policies. Their counterpublicity engaged the prevailing ideology articulated by many board members, refiguring it and opening spaces for critical reflection. In doing so, GSA advocates achieved recognition for their members and others. In these ways, interactions between the

board and GSA advocates demonstrated the need for the safe space generated by counterpublics and illuminated their promise.

Analyzing the GSA controversy in West Bend, this chapter explores dynamics of ideology in deliberation. Focusing on the role of religion in public
deliberation, I develop a conceptual framework in the first section to argue
that interlocutors may adjudicate differences among diverse ideological orientations not through varied attempts at neutrality but through the kind
of contestation enacted in counterpublicity. To establish a context for my
analysis, in the next section I discuss the rise of a new conservative majority
on the West Bend school board in the two years before the GSA controversy.
A conservative governing philosophy had guided the previous board, but
the new majority believed that past members had been too deferential to the
administration, and they pursued a more robust social agenda. I begin my
analysis by considering how a combination of district policy, state law, and
federal law served as an effectively localized public reason, but that varied
interpretations of these materials revealed the limits of a putatively neutral
ground. In the next section, I examine the ideological tensions that arose
between participants' perceived public roles and their personal experiences
with the GSA and beliefs about homosexuality. In the final section of my
analysis, I explore how the GSA enacted a counterpublicity that pressed
the ideological tensions in West Bend to obtain recognition as a school-
sponsored club from a recalcitrant school board.

Engaging Ideology in Deliberation

The West Bend GSA controversy offers lessons about the function of ideology in public deliberation, especially the religious views informing the social
conservatism that some board members and other participants expressed
as reasons for rejecting the application. The controversy demonstrates that
scholars should not regard religion as something that devout advocates
must avoid or sympathetic advocates must render in neutral language, but
rather as claims that interlocutors may engage through deliberation itself.
As Dave Tell trenchantly recommends, we should judge "religious discourse
as secular discourse: it should be evaluated in terms of what it proposes,"
which means neither excluding nor privileging religious advocacy over
other modes.[10] In associating religion and ideology, I do not wish to suggest
that religion necessarily constitutes an ideological perspective. Rather, religion serves ideological functions, which may be positive and negative, when

articulated as part of a constellation of political beliefs that inform political positions and strategies. In this way, some of the board members in West Bend voiced a particular interpretation of religion as part of their political ideologies.

Considering the place of religion in the public sphere, some scholars have discerned no place at all. Legal theorist Robert Audi insists that "one has a *prima facie* obligation not to advocate or support any law or public policy that restricts human conduct, unless one has, and is willing to offer, adequate secular reasons for this advocacy or support."[11] Drawing a distinction between religious congregations and ecclesiastical organizations, philosopher Richard Rorty expresses his hope that "ecclesiastical organizations will eventually wither away." While presumably preserving congregational discourse, this distinction does not preserve a public role for religion in debates over politics and policy, since Rorty restricts congregations' proper role to helping members "find meaning in their lives" and assisting them in "their times of trouble."[12] On political matters, Rorty believes that religious people should refrain from drawing on their religion to justify policies. Referencing contemporary homophobia in the United States, he endorses the position that "if the churches would stop quoting Leviticus and Paul on the subject of sodomy, would stop saying that tolerance for homosexuality is a mark of moral decline, and would stop using tax-exempt funds to campaign for repeal of pro-gay ordinances and statues, there would be fewer gay-bashers around."[13] Not all churches espouse these views, but, for churches that do, Rorty leaves unanswered the question of how to stop them. A vague hope in social progress will not achieve this goal, nor will a wish that churchgoers adhere to norms of politeness in deliberation. The GSA controversy shows the power of counterpublicity to engender change by contesting religiously justified positions that marginalize, oppress, and do violence to others. The GSA advocates may not have persuaded all board members to disavow prejudice, but they did expose tensions in the board's deliberations and the GSA achieved its desired policy outcome.

Demonstrating a more tolerant attitude toward religion, John Rawls has famously articulated the proper role for religion in the public sphere—as well as other ideologies—in his concept of public reason. In *Political Liberalism*, Rawls distinguishes public reason from "reasonable comprehensive doctrines" (RCDs). Whereas RCDs function as worldviews, public reason is available to all members of a polity, consisting of "substantive principles of justice," "principles of reasoning," and "rules of evidence."[14] While RCDs potentially divide people, public reason serves as a common ground. RCDs are particular; public reason is universal. Rawls believes that public reason may negotiate the irreducible pluralism of contemporary democratic societies. And he obliges citizens to use it, affirming a "duty of civility" that calls on citizens to explain to one another "how the principles and policies they advocate and vote for can be supported by the political values of public reason."[15]

While Rawls does not dismiss religion like Rorty, his affirmation of civility prescribes a similarly circumscribed role. However, in the paperback edition of *Political Liberalism*, which was published only a few years after the original, Rawls reconsiders his views. Noting the ameliorative force of the Abolitionists and the civil rights movement in the United States, Rawls revises his views on civility to permit RCDs to be "introduced in public reason at any time, provided that in due course public reasons, given by a reasonable political conception, are presented sufficient to support whatever the comprehensive doctrines are introduced to support." He explains that "both the Abolitionists' and King's doctrines were held to belong to public reason because they were invoked in an unjust political society, and their conclusions of justice were in accord with the constitutional values of a liberal regime."[16] While offering a subsidiary place for political invocations of religion and other ideologies in public deliberation, this revised view does not adequately account for the role of ideology in deliberation. First, it sustains an untenable divide between RCDs and public reason, suggesting that people's moral frameworks may be compartmentalized according to deliberative contexts. In contrast, I maintain that interlocutors tend to regard their moral outlooks as organic wholes. We may recognize contradictions among our beliefs, and deliberative engagement may prompt a reconsideration of our views, but we do not espouse the "modular" orientation that Rawls demands. Second, Rawls's position invites a post hoc evaluation of ideology, looking for public reasons to arise *in due course* to support particular worldviews. This after-the-fact approach does not enable us to understand how ideology may operate in a particular moment, when the passage of time has not ratified the justness of a movement.

While agreeing that institutional decision-making bodies such as parliaments and courts should justify their actions in secular terms, Jürgen Habermas retorts that citizens should not have to express themselves in secular language when they participate in the public sphere. Habermas, whose early work drew interdisciplinary scholarly attention to the public sphere,[17] has focused on the question of religion in some of his more recent writings. Rather than Rawlsian civility, Habermas calls for an "institutional translation proviso," which does not proscribe religious reasons, but "calls for the epistemic ability to consider one's own religious convictions reflexively from the outside and to connect them with secular views."[18] He sees translation as a cooperative task, urging secular citizens to "open their minds to the possible truth content of those presentations [of religion] and enter into dialogues from which religious reasons might well emerge in the transformed guise of generally accessible arguments."[19] The secular counterpart to religious reflexivity consists of a "form of postmetaphysical thinking" that preserves a distinction between faith and knowledge while operating with a more expansive form of reason that admits religious doctrines as part of the genealogy of reason.

Habermas suggests that finding a place for religion in the public sphere may bolster deliberation. He maintains that religions hold "semantic potentials capable of exercising an inspirational force on society *as a whole* as soon as they divulge in their profane truth contents."[20] Religion may serve as a resource for meaning-making and identity construction. Secular citizens may recognize their own normative truths when engaging their religious interlocutors. Religious advocates may articulate wider moral intuitions. Through deliberation, religious and secular citizens may engage in cooperative learning. In this spirit, Calvin Troup highlights the deliberative potential of religion because "churches and religious people are so deeply involved in political life."[21] And Mark Steiner outlines different modes of religious engagement, which may be more or less capable of the reflexivity that Habermas urges from religious citizens.[22] At the level of analysis, Martin Medhurst illustrates this reflexivity in a study of a speech that candidate Mitt Romney delivered about his Mormon faith during the 2008 U.S. Republican presidential primary. Praising Romney for explicating the relationship between religion and freedom while critiquing Romney for not defending secularism, Medhurst effectively illustrates what translation would entail.[23]

If Habermas's translation proviso offers resources for scholars to analyze expressions of religion in the public sphere, what does it offer advocates who advance or respond to religiously justified positions in public deliberation? For Craig Calhoun, Habermas moves beyond untenable notions of linguistic neutrality, but he does not fully recognize that such encounters exceed rationality. Calhoun explains that "by pursuing rational mutual understanding, we open ourselves to becoming somewhat different people."[24] He calls for the formation of bonds of civic solidarity according to which people perceive that they owe one another reasons for their political statements and views. According to Cristina Lafont, Habermas's call for translation may end up restricting deliberation by placing excessively demanding epistemic requirements on interlocutors. Lafont worries about the possibility of discovering translations in cases of genuine conflict between secular and religious reasons. And, she maintains, secular citizens who reject the truth of religious claims may not be able to engage in a cooperative process of translation, thereby feigning agreement if they do. Lafont holds that "in such cases they have no alternative but to be disingenuous and come up with alternative reasons that are independent of their authentic beliefs in order to participate in public deliberation."[25] On this point, Andrea Baumeister contends that Lafont goes too far. Baumeister objects that secular citizens should not accept religious reasons uncritically, but "engage with religiously grounded contributions in an attempt to recover those aspects that are potentially morally significant and assist in transposing these into a language that is accessible to all."[26] Yet she does see potential problems with translation. Baumeister asserts that appeals to the divine may be what pious citizens regard as the most compelling quality of religious reasons. Moreover, the "partial and tentative" character of translation may render religious language as "the other."[27] Even though they disagree about the cognitive requirements of Habermas's translation proviso, Lafont and Baumeister agree that neither avoidance nor neutrality can adequately address the deliberative role of religion in pluralistic societies. Instead, they both call for engagement, intimating the sense of contestation that counterpublics may productively engage in deliberative controversy.

Counterpublics may attend both to specific issues that arise in debates over religion in the public sphere as well as to the contexts in which interlocutors debate these issues. In contrast, Rawls's public reason and Habermas's translation proviso operate implicitly with a hub-and-spoke model of institutional and vernacular publics and assume that interlocutors encounter one another on equal ground. In terms of (in)equality, just as relations of power and symbolic and material inequities inform secular discourse in the public sphere, they may inform public expressions of religious faith. Baumeister notes that hierarchies of power within religious communities may negatively affect members' ability to deliberate about religious doctrine. She calls for greater secular engagement with religious communities to increase the religious freedom of marginalized members and inculcate a critically reflexive attitude among religious citizens.[28] Baumeister is right to call attention to inequalities within religious communities. And, a few times during the GSA controversy, community members appealed to religious values to support the GSA's application. But counterpublics may facilitate

engagement within and across religious and secular communities. Sometimes, people may be marginalized because of their religious views, but
other times a dominant morality—expressed most forcefully in West Bend
by board member Dave Weigand—may marginalize and oppress people
who cultivate alternative identities and beliefs. Counterpublics may arise
in these situations to expand discursive space and to redress symbolic and
material inequalities. The ameliorative force of counterpublicity constitutes
a crucial quality, since entrenched interests sometimes may assert claims of
exclusion to extend their privilege.[29] Instead, as Daniel Brouwer observes,
counterpublics seek *"recognition of resource disparities among social actors."*[30]
Engaging publics variously affected by religious discourses, counterpublics
provide a "safe space" for people who are marginalized and promise to expand the discourse of wider publics, exemplifying, as Brouwer notes, "a dialectic of inward and outward address."[31]

This movement belies the hub-and-spoke model intimated by Rawls and
Habermas, who maintain that various vernacular publics converge at common institutional sites. Along these lines, Rawls asserts that "there are many
nonpublic reasons and but one public reason."[32] Yet school-board members
are not institutional actors in the same sense as members of state and national legislatures. School-board members do not have dedicated staffs
assigned to them. They do not physically remove themselves from their
communities to meet, deciding policy in state or national capitals. They do
not conduct policymaking as a full-time occupation, and they are paid virtually nothing for their efforts. Operating fully within the community for
whom they make policy, school-board members blur lines of vernacular and
institutional publics. When they express or respond to religious statements,
they do so simultaneously as public officials and ordinary folks, as citizen-
legislators. We cannot, then, rely on clear boundaries, insisting that neutrality ultimately must reside within the state. The West Bend school board
did not exhibit neutrality during the GSA controversy, even when members
tried to adopt an official pose. Perhaps counterpublicity would have exposed
fault lines in a more consistently maintained neutral stance. Instead, GSA
advocates enacted counterpublicity as they engaged ideological tensions in
the school board's deliberations about their application.

Seeking to overcome exclusions, counterpublics may sustain exclusions.
In West Bend, the most significant exclusion arose when no student members of the GSA spoke on their own behalf. Instead, their lawyers represented the group during the presentational portions of the meetings as well
as the question-and-answer session, while adult community members spoke

in favor of the GSA during the audience participation portions of the meetings. Perhaps these arrangements can be explained partially by procedural concerns. The impending lawsuit may have led the GSA members, whose officers prepared the group's application, to favor their attorneys as their primary representatives during the formal parts of the meetings. But the absence of the GSA members' voices—especially during the audience participation portion, even though GSA members attended the meetings—was a real exclusion. This weakened but did not fatally undermine the counterpublicity enacted during the meeting. Even though this particular exclusion could have been avoided, Rita Felski warns that some exclusions may inevitably arise in counterpublics. Felski notes that feminist counterpublics sometimes have operated with "a suspension of other forms of difference." She maintains that they "cannot simply transcend existing power structures but [are] deeply implicated within them, and that the exclusive focus upon gender politics can serve to obscure other, equally fundamental structural inequalities."[33] Moreover, unless we adopt an essentialist view of the identity of counterpublic members, which the GSA's own advocacy resists, we need to admit potential alliances among people who may be directly affected by exclusions and others who may be indirectly affected and find such exclusions objectionable. Exclusion alone cannot constitute a counterpublic—participants must recognize exclusions and resolve to overcome them.[34]

A New Board Majority, a Reconfigured Ideology

"If you're a moderate Republican in West Bend, you're a liberal," said past West Bend school board president Joe Carlson, as he bemoaned a lack of moderation and cooperation in the city and on its school board. When the GSA advocates presented their case to the school board, they encountered opposition from a new majority of members mostly elected to the board within the previous two years. This new majority advanced a reconfigured conservatism for the school district. While past boards monitored spending carefully, some in the community felt that the new board had sacrificed education in its unyielding insistence on frugality. Carlson drew upon traditional business values to counter that "good businesspeople focus on return on investment, not spending alone."[35] In addition, some community members criticized what they saw as an unrelenting, narrow-minded social agenda being pushed by the majority on the school board. Carlson and others discerned a new political culture in town. In this section, I provide context for my analysis of the GSA controversy by addressing the rise of the new majority on the West Bend school board.

On September 28, 2009, over seven hundred people crammed into the Badger Middle School gymnasium in West Bend to attend the school district's annual meeting. Many in the crowd were angry, and they let the board know it. They had attended to protest the board's plan to raise the district's tax rate by 12.1 percent—a figure that struck many in the economically stagnant community as obscene.[36] Addressing a rowdy crowd, superintendent Patricia Herdrich tried to defend the district's plan. Herdrich explained that the West Bend school district consistently ranked among the most fiscally conservative in the state. She observed that "we are among the lowest spending school districts in the state, and we are the lowest spending in the region." And yet, increasing enrollments, which grew at the sixth-highest rate in the state, placed additional pressures on the district. Herdrich maintained that "each year for the last fifteen years, we've reduced programming for students while we're serving more children within the system."[37] From this perspective, the tax increase—totaling roughly twelve dollars per month for the average home owner in the district—represented a modest effort to keep pace with population growth in Washington County, which had increased nearly 40 percent since 1990.[38]

Most attendees rejected this reasoning. They shouted down the proposal in an advisory voice vote, as their anger and frustration resonated throughout the gym. Rather than identifying with the board and administration, attendees appeared to express greater sympathy with the views of community members like Helen Neal. Neal asserted that "I'm from a neighborhood where my neighbors are either losing their jobs or were taking pay cuts or were being given furloughs. We can just afford our homes. If you give us a 12.1 percent increase, many of us will lose our homes. That's the end, that's the bottom line. And we can't take it any more."[39] For Neal and others, arguments about frugality and increasing enrollments could not overcome their feelings of economic insecurity.

Over the next month, board members and top administrators fretted over the proper tax rate. Board president Joe Carlson insisted that the board would "pay attention to what took place in the annual meeting," but he reaffirmed the board's commitment to meeting the needs of the district's students.[40] In an e-mail quoted in the local newspaper, Superintendent Herdrich wrote that "the decisions will be wildly unpopular."[41] She was right. On October 26, over eight hundred residents packed the West Bend Field House to watch the board unanimously approve a 10.9 percent increase. In a crowd filled with supporters and opponents of the increase, some people carried signs demanding "NO CUTS!" and "Yes to 10.9%," while others vociferously objected.[42] Among the opponents, future board member Bart Williams called for no increase, insisting that there is "plenty of fluff, waste in the budget."[43] But even board members who had pledged no tax increases during their campaigns went along with the 7–0 vote. Tim Stepanski, who would survive to become part of the May 2011 anti-GSA majority, feared for his seat.

The battle over the tax levy concerned not only finances but also whether the board listened to its constituents and whether district leaders adopted a condescending tone in their interactions with the community. For some community members, these qualities constituted a district culture they wanted to change. West Bend *Daily News* columnist and popular local blogger Owen Robinson wrote shortly after the October meeting that the community should draw three lessons from the board's decision to increase the tax rate by 10.9 percent. First, the board ignored the will of the voters. Second, the board guarded relevant information rather than sharing this information with the community. Third, while citizens opposing the increase "did everything right," the school board "gave the voters the ol' one-finger salute." Reminding his readers of the elections the next spring, Robinson explained that "the taxpayers don't currently have a representative on the School Board and the time to fix that will be in April."[44] In an October letter published in the *Daily News*, future board president Randy Marquardt recounted that as he "sat and watched as our School Board was inundated with numerous pleas from the 'no cuts' crowd as well as a few from overburdened taxpayers," he knew the "fix was already in on the tax increase." He held that an "unholy alliance" among Democrats in the state capital and the teachers' unions forced even the fiscal conservatives on the board to approve the levy. Although he did not declare his candidacy, Marquardt insisted that "courageous stands need to be taken."[45]

In January 2010, Randy Marquardt and Dave Weigand announced their candidacies for the West Bend school board. Outspoken critics of the board, Marquardt and Weigand ran a coordinated campaign for two seats up for election. Among a primary field of six candidates, Marquardt and Weigand advanced to the April general election along with the two incumbents to present a clear choice to voters between what the challengers regarded as the status quo and a renewed commitment to fiscal constraint.[46] On his campaign blog, Randy Marquardt posted that "the taxpayers need an advocate to watch out for their interests during this crucial time."[47] Weigand sounded similar themes, and both candidates talked about the need for school-board members to listen to the community. Weigand identified himself as "a true conservative who believes in local input into matters of policy, and I support less intrusive government."[48] Owen Robinson framed the election as a choice between incumbents who have been "strong supporters of tax increases" and challengers who "are more willing to look for ways to work within the existing means of the district's finances."[49]

Both Marquardt and Weigand were affiliated with a local organization called Common Sense Citizens of Washington County, which had become a significant political force since its formation after the 2008 presidential election, fielding candidates for various local offices. A testimonial from Marquardt appeared on the group's website, praising Common Sense Citizens as a "public watchdog and advocate on behalf of the average taxpayer."[50] Some community residents derided Common Sense Citizens as stoking local anger and perpetuating resentment that had been "manufactured, nourished and sustained by billionaires with a financial stake in preventing any movement for political or economic change."[51] Common Sense Citizens served as the local chapter of Americans for Prosperity, a national conservative political organization founded by Oklahoma energy baron David Koch, one of two billionaire brothers who became infamous in some parts of Wisconsin and celebrated in others for backing Governor Scott Walker's successful campaign to eliminate collective bargaining rights for public employees. Rejecting this characterization, Common Sense Citizens President Scott Schneiberg described his organization as "a grassroots group of 'Regular-Joe' common-sense, tax-paying U.S. citizens who have decided to find the time to make an impact on the futures of our towns."[52] In the April general election, the common-sense candidates, as Marquardt and Weigand referred to themselves, won.[53] Marquardt proclaimed that their victory meant "voters chose the conservative vision—to operate the school system within the limits of our means."[54] The *Daily News* framed the results as "conservatives flexing their muscles at polling places."[55]

Although taxes constituted the major issue in the campaign, religion became a focal point in the candidates' responses to a questionnaire. Prepared by the Eagle Forum of Washington County, a local chapter of the national organization founded by well-known conservative activist Phyllis Schlafly, the questionnaire asked candidates whether they would support the "teaching of alternative theories of origins such as Intelligent Design and Creationism as an alternative, or in addition to, the theory of evolution to students in science classrooms." Marquardt indicated his support for an alternative curriculum, while Weigand expressed his view as "be[ing] FOR teaching the TRUTH about evolution."[56] For some, these responses proved that Marquardt and Weigand would pursue a controversial social agenda if elected to the school board. *Daily News* columnist Mark Peterson charged that Marquardt and Weigand "would weaken the science curriculum and drag the school district into federal court." Tweaking the candidates' affiliation with Common Sense Citizens, Peterson wondered, "How much common sense does it demonstrate to endorse candidates who publicly assert that their religious beliefs should intrude into the school curriculum[?]"[57] In a letter to the editor, Marquardt shot back, accusing Peterson of an "anti-religion bias." Accepting the existence of evolution, Marquardt countered that its explanatory power as a theory of origins carried no greater weight than Intelligent Design. Further, he rebuked Peterson, widely regarded as a "liberal" among the newspaper columnists, as an intellectual elitist: "Belief in God and his creation is rather normal down here, as is upholding moral principles, free enterprise and personal responsibility."[58]

That fall, religion moved into the spotlight when the school board considered an application from Bruce Dunford, pastor of the First Baptist Church, to establish a charter school called the Crossroads Academy. Citing financial and curricular concerns, West Bend district administrators objected. They worried that the school, which sought funding to enroll up to one hundred students, would drain scarce district resources. As for the curriculum, Assistant Superintendent Ted Neitzke described it as "a standard parochial curriculum, with evangelical leanings and a fusion of Christian literatures . . . without multiple religious views offered." He added that the Crossroads consultants had mentioned that "intelligent design would be part of their curriculum and offerings."[59] Mike Sternig, longtime principal of the local Holy Angels School, dismissed the Crossroads Academy as, "simply speaking, a startup parochial school looking for taxpayer funding without any substantial investment of its own."[60] Arguing for Crossroads, Marquardt contended that his reading of the history of American education indicated that "parents have the right to determine what school is best for their children. It's just that we don't give them the choice anymore."[61] Weigand's advocacy for the Crossroads Academy drew an ethics complaint. A month before the board vote, Weigand submitted a guest column to the *Daily News* supporting the Academy.[62] The complaint, which the board ultimately dismissed, charged that this column violated his obligation not to prejudge matters deliberated by the board.[63] Some people wondered whether a third board member, Tim Stepanski, should have recused himself from the vote, since he was a deacon at First Baptist Church. By a 4–3 vote, the school board rejected the Cross-roads proposal during its November 2010 meeting.[64]

Just before the GSA controversy began, the spring 2011 election produced a new conservative majority on the West Bend school board. Bart Williams joined Marquardt, Weigand, and Stepanski to form a four-vote majority. Like Marquardt and Weigand, Williams was affiliated with Common Sense Citizens. Williams campaigned for the school board the previous spring, but he withdrew from the primary so that conservatives could focus their efforts on winning the two available seats without splitting votes among three candidates. In a letter to the editor explaining his withdrawal from the race, Williams maintained that "Randy and Dave know district residents deserve maximum value and effectiveness from their generous support of our schools," and he "welcome[d] their common-sense, financially respon-sible approach."[65] With no other "common-sense" candidates available in 2011, Williams jumped in the race and stayed. His 2011 campaign included a "24-point action plan" for the district, including promises to balance the "budget while respecting families/taxpayers" and to "continue the positive, conservative progress made on the board in the last two years."[66]

My analysis focuses on the deliberations at a committee meeting and two board meetings. Both the committee meeting and the first board meeting oc-curred consecutively on May 9, 2011, in the gymnasium of McLane Elemen-tary School. The committee meeting addressed the staff's recommendation to approve the GSA application, the district criteria for school-sponsored clubs, and a presentation by one of the GSA's two attorneys. Deliberation about these items continued at the board meeting, with a greater focus on the lawsuit and presentations by both GSA attorneys, as well as statements from four community members divided evenly in support of and opposition to the GSA. Deliberation at the May board meeting concluded with a 3–3 vote on the GSA application (Bart Williams had been excused for travel), which meant that the application failed. Dozens of community residents attended these meetings, mostly in support of the GSA, with many wear-ing rainbow ribbons to symbolize their support. All seven board members attended the June 13, 2011, meeting, which occurred in the Badger Middle School cafeteria, as well as dozens of mostly GSA-supporting community residents. The June meeting began with a presentation from the adminis-tration indicating that the district likely would lose the lawsuit. Four com-munity members—again, evenly divided—addressed the issue, followed by deliberation among board members, concluding with a 4–3 vote to rescind their May vote. Deliberation about a new motion to approve the GSA ensued, including an extended dissenting statement by Dave Weigand. Although present at the June board meeting, the GSA attorneys did not speak. Randy Marquardt cast the deciding fourth vote both to rescind the May decision and to approve the GSA application.

Law, District Policy, and Public Reason

At a national level, John Rawls presents a clear picture of the content of public reason: basic rights, liberties, and opportunities consistent with constitutional democracy. Along these lines, Rawls names the Supreme Court as the exemplar of public reason.[67] What would a localized public reason look like? What materials would constitute its core? Local policymakers may need to deliberate about basic issues, like the full participation of all students in curricular and extra-curricular activities, but unlike a national court, they cannot rely exclusively on founding documents, precedent, and scholarship. National laws would apply, as illustrated by the references of the GSA's attorneys, but local policymakers would need to consider ostensibly neutral materials that address local issues. In West Bend, the most obvious candidate was the school board's own policy on extra-curricular clubs, which district staff specified in response to the GSA application. In this section, I examine their use of this effectively local public reason, which combined district policy with state and federal law, and how their very usage demonstrated the limits of a putatively neutral ground.

Before receiving the GSA application in the 2010–11 school year, the West Bend school district did not have a specific policy for approving extra-curricular clubs. The district addressed the issue generally in Board Policy 370, which, in its opening paragraph, read, "The School Board endorses a quality athletic and co-curricular program to serve the interests of all students. The District shall not discriminate in student participation in athletic programs or activities or facilities usage on the basis of sex, race, national origin, ancestry, creed, pregnancy, marital or parental status, sexual orientation or physical, mental, emotional or learning disability."[68] Although the policy contained inclusive language, the absence of any corresponding criteria for clubs enabled uneven enforcement of the policy. Indeed, the GSA had sought recognition as a school-sponsored club repeatedly, but encountered an ad hoc series of denials by principals and other district staff without the input of the school board. This treatment prompted the GSA to hire attorneys, who filed a discrimination complaint with the district charging that the absence of any criteria simply allowed administrators to approve or deny clubs arbitrarily.

In his appearances before the school board, GSA attorney Waring Fincke stressed that the administration's positive recommendation to the board promised to conclude an "eight-year-long request for GSA recognition and sponsorship." He recalled that the group had been denied recognition on "numerous occasions, both at the high-school level . . . [and] by past superintendents, past curriculum and instruction superintendents." Yet the bases of these denials remained unclear: "We've been given different reasons at different times . . . which led to my request for what are the rules, nobody could tell me, it was a moving target."[69] Fincke intimated that personal discomfort and prejudice influenced the prior decisions. While denying that the GSA had been treated differently than other student groups, district administrator Kathy Zarling held that the application prompted the district to clarify its criteria, which the district staff believed the GSA had met.[70] Recounting the process leading to the favorable recommendation, Zarling explained that "we discovered that the procedures for club approval or recognition weren't written down, so I worked with the high-school administration to clarify that process and put it into writing."[71] Her response shows that standards for deliberative judgment do not exist as already operative criteria to which advocates may appeal, but as purposeful frames crafted partly in response to the advocacy of individuals and groups.

Zarling and her associates developed four criteria for school-sponsored clubs: "curricular tie, national/state affiliation, student appeal, volunteer advisor approved by site administration."[72] The explicit reference to "sexual orientation" in the nondiscrimination clause of Board Policy 370 left board members little room to object to the nature and composition of the GSA under the guise of neutrality. In comparison, these four criteria enabled board members to disagree with the staff recommendation while maintaining their adherence to district policy. Three board members agreed with the recommendation, including Kris Beaver, who stated that "we set forth the criteria, and they met the criteria."[73] But others voiced concerns, such as whether thirty students, which the GSA application identified as the number of students with definite interest in the club, qualified as sufficient student appeal. Randy Marquardt wondered what distinguished these thirty students from "certain cliques and differences . . . kids who like playing computer games, or are overweight, or whatever." He asserted that "there's lots of different things that set people apart and, you know, make them susceptible to bullying."[74] Reminding Marquardt that district policy specifically mentioned "sexual orientation" in enumerating students who should not be discriminated against, Fincke also retorted that, based on the proportion of LGBT people in the general population, the number of students attending GSA meetings likely would be significantly higher than thirty. A recognized group would draw students who were unaware of the informal meetings and potentially embolden other students to attend.

The "curricular tie" criterion drew the most attention from board members. In her presentation to the board, Zarling explained that the district staff believed that the GSA connected with materials that students encountered in their psychology and sociology courses. Questioning this connection, Dave Weigand asserted that the GSA would undermine the health curriculum, where, in his view, students learned about "traditional marriage as defined by law," referencing a successful 2006 ballot referendum that amended the state constitution to recognize as legally valid only marriages between one man and one woman.[75] Zarling responded that the relevant connection arose not in health but sociology, where students learned about "traditional and non-traditional families." To this, Weigand objected that "we teach a number of things in sociology or psychology that we wouldn't make a club on that. If we taught about WWII and the Nazis, we wouldn't necessarily use that as a reason for, a substantial reason for having a club."[76] In stark terms, Weigand disclosed his view of the GSA: they represented a bad, threatening group motivated by a perverse ideology. Even if we grant that Weigand did not intend a strict equivalence between the GSA and Nazis, the negative association remained. Weigand appeared to extend his judgment about the nature of the group to its application, contravening the district's nondiscrimination policy. The criteria for school-sponsored clubs did not serve as a means for making a decision but a means of justifying his decision.

Bart Williams, who did not attend the May board meeting, insisted that not only did the GSA lack a curricular connection but that its activities would disrupt the education of all students. At the June board meeting, he dismissed the group as "a distraction from what our true mission is in this district." Williams worried that "the GSA is asking for multiple days and weeks to recognize this thing, recognize that thing."[77] He especially objected to GSA members' participation in a national Day of Silence at the high schools to raise awareness of bullying and harassment.[78] Some, but not all, participating students signaled their protests by wearing tape over their mouths. This irked Williams, who asserted that "wearing duct tape over your mouth during the classroom is a distraction." He amplified this point through a series of illustrations: "Would you go out and vigorously exercise in gym class with your mouth duct-taped over? . . . Try to play a wood instrument or brass instrument with duct tape over your mouth. . . . How about this—being called on to give a complex answer to a math question, a science question, an English literature question." The Day of Silence prevented necessary interactions between teachers and students and placed "a disproportionately higher burden on the rest of the students who have to answer the questions."[79] With each illustration, Williams grew angrier. Williams did not offer his remarks as caricature but genuine concern. The district criteria focused his objections but they did not modulate his tone.

The GSA attorneys elevated law over policy, maintaining that their clients did not have to meet the district criteria, since state and federal law required the district to treat all students equally. State law on school-sponsored extra-curricular activities, which likely provided the framework for district policy, clearly prescribed equal treatment of all students in any school-related activity. Wisconsin's Pupil Nondiscrimination Law mandated that "no person may be denied admission to any public school or be denied participation in, be denied the benefits of or be discriminated against in any curricular, extra-curricular, pupil services, recreational or other program or activity because of the person's sex, race, religion, national origin, ancestry, creed, pregnancy, marital or parental status, sexual orientation or physical, mental, emotional or learning disability." Each item enumerated in this list constituted a protected class, and the law directed school boards to "develop written policies and procedures to implement this section and submit them to the state superintendent."[80] The law also required districts to establish procedures for hearing discrimination complaints, which the GSA attorneys initiated, indicating that negative judgments at the district level could be appealed to the state superintendent.

Threatening and eventually filing a federal lawsuit, the GSA attorneys based their legal arguments on the 1984 Equal Access Act (EAA). Serving as a federal nondiscrimination law for student groups, the EAA prohibited public schools receiving federal assistance from denying access to or discriminating against students seeking to conduct meetings because of the "religious, political, philosophical, or other content of the speech at such meetings."[81] Although Congress originally passed the EAA to protect students' religious speech, GSAs and their allies across the United States increasingly have used the law to challenge recalcitrant districts.[82] In all but one case, courts have ruled in favor of GSAs, even when school districts have tried to eliminate extra-curricular clubs entirely to avoid recognizing GSAs.[83] Todd DeMitchell and Richard Fossey note that "even massive student and parental protests" have not persuaded courts to rule against GSAs.[84] Despite this nearly unanimous body of case law, some West Bend school board members expressed a willingness to fight the GSA in court. Their confidence in victory in the face of contrary evidence demonstrated the power of their ideology in shaping their approach to the issue and their understanding of a likely outcome.

In both May meetings, the GSA attorneys adamantly outlined the potential consequences of a lawsuit. Stating that "this group of students constitutes a protected class under the constitution and laws of Wisconsin and the United States," Fincke maintained that denials at the district level would lead to further "discussion in federal court, where we will prevail."[85] Dan Patricus, a second attorney representing the GSA, explained that school boards denied less than 1 percent of all GSA applications across the United States. When the groups have sued the school boards in federal court, "in all but one occasion, the boards of education have lost." Further, in these cases, the boards have been ordered to pay their own attorneys' fees as well as the plaintiffs' fees. In some cases, the bill totaled $500,000. Patricus concluded that "in my twenty-six, twenty-seven years of practicing now, I have rarely seen a body of case law that's been this crystal clear."[86] Board member Todd Miller urged his colleagues to consider that "you're about to spend a lot of taxpayer dollars on legal fees."[87] Despite these warnings, as well as reminders of their campaign pledges of frugality, three board members voted against the GSA. Dave Weigand made his view of the group known. Tim Stepanski believed that the district's anti-bullying policies already addressed the needs of the proposed club. And Randy Marquardt questioned the curricular link. With these three members voting no and with Williams out of town, the GSA application failed on a tie vote.

Only after the attorneys filed their suit did the legal and financial arguments become pressing for at least one board member. At the start of June board meeting, Superintendent Neitzke underscored the potential dollar and time costs of a lawsuit. He noted that "two separate law firms have indicated that it's more likely than not that the GSA would prevail on the merits of the lawsuit." Community members like Joy Schroeder echoed these views. She asserted that the "taxpayers do not want to have to pay for a legal procedure that would take money away from the quality of education."[88] And Randy Marquardt seemed swayed. When Dave Weigand complained that he had been "sandbagged out" of the review process and that other attorneys would reach different conclusions, Marquardt responded that "just because you didn't get the answer you want does not necessarily mean that it wasn't considered."[89] Marquardt engaged in his own considerations, referencing the legislative history of the EAA as a protection for religious speech,[90] and he determined that the district would lose. Either the district would have to eliminate all extra-curricular groups, or it would have to accept the GSA. In justifying his decision, Marquardt effectively turned to public reason, stating that "the law does not apply selectively" and that "the answer to speech you don't like is more speech, not less."[91] If social conservatives disapproved of the GSA, they would have to engage the group.

The continued advocacy of the GSA and their allies, represented most forcefully in the lawsuit, forced Marquardt to make a choice—one that he made grudgingly. Marquardt had been forced to choose between his fiscal conservatism and his social conservatism. He chose money, disagreeing with his anti-GSA colleagues only on the likely outcome of a lawsuit. Weigand exhorted Marquardt to fight: "Let this case go to the Supreme Court. . . . We will win there. Let's do this for the kids and families of West Bend and across the nation."[92] Weigand wanted the May majority to stand firm on their social values; he insisted that finances should not trump morality. Marquardt shared this morality but not Weigand's prophecy. Even though he felt attacked by the GSA and their allies, Marquardt could not risk voting "no." He retorted that when Weigand addressed the law, "you're starting to fall apart. And, you know, you cannot—just because you believe something strongly—change the legal argument."[93] The GSA controversy exposed and pressured tensions in Marquardt's ideology. In this case, he could not reconcile his different beliefs into a coherent whole. Moreover, even though Marquardt and Weigand shared fiscal and social values, they weighed these values differently when confronted with the GSA's advocacy. Typically allies on the school board, their particular interpretations of a larger ideology led them to opposing votes.

Personal Values, Public Roles

Randy Marquardt spoke in a public language when he announced that he would switch his vote to approve the GSA, but his announcement was not free of personal revelations. He shared that he had been subjected to "very, you know, vile and insulting statements" from GSA supporters since the May vote. He expressed "discomfort" with the idea that a group could compel board action with a lawsuit. He disclosed that he had been "stewing" over the decision for weeks. Marquardt felt aggrieved—and he let the people attending the June board meeting know it. These qualities of his statements demonstrate that Marquardt did not translate his parochial views into a neutral public language when he referenced liberal notions of equal treatment under the law and the marketplace of ideas. Rather, as he struggled to negotiate the tension between his personal views and what he regarded as his public duties as a school-board member, Marquardt articulated alternative aspects of his ideology. Through articulating this tension, rather than adopting a neutral language or translating doctrinal beliefs, Marquardt engaged ideology in deliberation. And he was not alone. Both opponents and supporters of the GSA articulated ideological tensions as they addressed the issue.

From the perspective of administrators and attorneys, board members confronted a straightforward task. In the May committee meeting, as board members and the GSA attorneys debated the need for the club, Kathy Zarling urged everyone to "keep focused on the criteria, because there's a lot of conversation that is occurring, and although important, the final decision will be based on: does it meet the criteria?"[94] Dan Patricus argued that the GSA "may be against your personal ideology, it may be against the personal ideology of the folks you're going to hear today, but, at the end of the day, it's not about any of those things, it's about one thing—it's about the law. Whether you agree with it is irrelevant."[95] Their directives reflected their particular areas of expertise, policy and law respectively, but Zarling and Patricus conveyed the same underlying message: avoid personal biases and stay on neutral ground.

Yet others could not maintain this exclusive focus even when they referenced the law. Weigand tied his heteronormative view of the family to the law when he asserted that "endors[ing] the GSA club would be asking me to deny the values of my faith and violates my religious freedom."[96] In this statement, religious absolutism and liberal tolerance comingle. Weigand repeatedly drew together these seemingly countervailing traditions, but perhaps the most illuminating instance appeared as he argued with Marquardt and fellow board member Rick Parks about the competency of the law firm hired to provide an outside analysis. Parks, recounting his experience in working with law firms as an insurance executive, praised the firm as one of the best in the state. Weigand charged his colleagues with bias: "We already knew what we were looking for, and they confirmed what we were looking for." A "truly unbiased" opinion required having one's client's "best interest at heart." Critiquing the firm, he insisted that "unless they have a heart for the issue, they may be overlooking things."[97] Associating law and heart, Weigand conveyed multiple meanings. For pious listeners, this statement may have invoked notions of the "heart of Christ," which some Christians see as a symbol of divine love that inspires believers to social action. In more secular or nondenominational terms, "heart" connotes compassion and care. Insisting that a fuller examination requires a "heart for the issue" intimates that (passionate) commitment rather than disinterest produces reliable knowledge. Even supporters of the GSA might have viewed this association favorably insofar as it dismissed a purely rational approach to the issue.

Supporters of the GSA also blended personal and public appeals in their advocacy. At the May board meeting, community member David Shew invoked "respect" and "civility" as qualities represented by the GSA and needed in society. Demonstrating that religion appeared on both sides of the debate, Shew reminded board members of the vision of Dr. Martin Luther King Jr., the pastor who advocated for more just laws on decidedly religious terms. But the most personal part of Shew's message appeared when he talked about his son Nicolas, the GSA president. He expressed pride for his son, describing Nicolas as a passionate person and the GSA as a passionate group. The Shews had gotten to know the kids who belonged to the GSA, "who come into my house . . . we get lots of them who come over and play video games and spend time with them, and they all have that same sense of compassion and care." Nicolas's mother, Christy, who also spoke at the meeting, explained the origins of the West Bend GSA as the work of a young woman motivated by a "call to love your neighbor as yourself, to justice, to be a voice to those who needed a voice, [not] to make a political statement."[98] From home, to pulpit, to public square, the multiple references in the Shews' statements resonated richly across personal and public lines, demonstrating that the propositional content of a message may not be extracted cleanly from its expression, as translation may suggest.

While the Shews appeared to embrace their son's involvement in the GSA, board member Rick Parks, who voted in favor of the GSA application at the May and June meetings, struggled in his dual role as father of a GSA student and board member. In his statements across the three meetings, Parks alternated between formal statements reflecting his position as a board member and business executive and personal reflections as a father and community member. At the May committee meeting, Parks began his comments by discussing possible reasons why board members might recuse themselves from decisions. He identified financial interest and a predetermined opinion as proper grounds, but suggested that his discussions with the superintendent indicated that familial involvement in an activity did not require recusal. Quite the opposite, he learned from the superintendent that "we like to have, you know, people on the school board who actually know something about a particular activity." Then, without disclosing his son's sexual orientation, and noting that his son was seated in the audience, Parks announced that his son was a member of the GSA. Parks promised that his son's membership "absolutely" would "not [be] a deciding factor on however I will vote on this later tonight."[99] From an analytic perspective, this statement strains credulity. Even if his son's membership would not serve as *the* deciding factor in Parks's decision, it likely functioned as *a* deciding factor, which Parks's statements at other moments evidenced. However, the significance of this statement lies not in its accuracy, but in its marking of the obligation that Parks felt to claim a neutral ground and the difficulty he experienced in doing so.

As he expressed his position on the GSA, Parks treated his son's membership as a resource for sharing information about the group. His efforts produced an awkward, forced, stilted discourse that represented an odd exchange between father and son. Parks shared "um, a discussion I had with him, as a member of this group, over the weekend, because I had an opportunity, essentially, to interview a member. And what I, a few things that I was interested in finding out, um, and we've kind of tap-danced around some of these." Parks asked his son what happened at the meetings, and he learned that the GSA functioned as a "support group," where members affirmed one another, comforting kids who suffered bullying and harassment. Parks paraphrased his son to say that "we talk with the—we help them; we give them a hug. Um, so that's what he told me. That's his report."[100] Twice, Parks referred to his conversation with his son as a "report," which resonated with the formal tone of a disinterested board member. But he seemed uncomfortable using this tone, especially when asking his son about "recruitment": "I asked, you know, from my standpoint, how does the group, um, promote the gay lifestyle as superior to the straight lifestyle. How do they essentially try to move people over their way? And he looked at me with that look that only a, you know, high school student can look at you, like, duh, what are you talking about?" Parks seemed embarrassed by this exchange, as if he asked a question to which he knew the answer but felt obliged to ask anyway. And his tone shifted as he relayed his son's response. Reflecting on his own youth, Parks recalled that "ever since I was a little boy I always knew some people that, um, we didn't call them gay or whatever back in my day, it probably wasn't very—it probably didn't speak very well for us when we said it at the time, but it's always been there, it always will be there, and our children always have had to deal with this."[101] As he engaged in these reflections, Parks sounded less like a board member reporting on an interview and more like a parent admitting his own mistakes and trying not to repeat them.

Shortly thereafter, at the school-board meeting that followed, Parks replayed this same dynamic. He initially made no mention of his son, announcing that he had reached an "unbiased decision" by considering district policies and state and federal law, as well as the need to prepare students to enter a diverse workforce and the military. But Parks shifted ground when Marquardt wondered if anyone wished to share final comments before the vote. Parks explained that he had known the students involved with the GSA for most of their lives, "since five or six years old, and they're good kids, I mean, these are, these are not kids that I see as revolutionary, or somebody who is going to cause havoc in our schools." Expressing fondness for the students, he recalled that "these kids come to my house, and they have access to my refrigerator, and that's the ultimate compliment when someone can come into your house and go to your refrigerator." When a fellow board member joked about the cost of such access, Parks quipped, "That's true. It's almost like going to federal court."[102] In this riposte, Parks invoked the varied factors that informed his decision. He considered the law, but he also rendered a judgment on the goodness of the GSA members gleaned from his familial and neighborly experiences with them. Parks considered a wide range of reasons that drew on various roles.

One board member articulated a cleaner separation of his personal beliefs and public role, but in doing so he engaged less with the ideas and values of the GSA than did the conflicted Parks. Kris Beaver strongly supported the GSA, spending more time than any other board member in responding to the objections of the majority. Beaver repeatedly asserted that the GSA had met the district criteria and thus merited approval. He characterized the debate as "a fairness issue," which, in his view, trumped personal beliefs. Beaver maintained that "I disagree with the homosexual lifestyle, but I also don't believe that people should be prejudiced against just because they are gay, lesbian, transgender."[103] In this statement, Beaver heeded the directives of Zarling, Fincke, and Patricus. He set aside his personal beliefs in favor of a law- and policy-based decision. And while his favorable vote contributed to a just outcome, his neutrality did not carry the ethical force that Rawls and Habermas associate with their proposals. Beaver's reference to a "lifestyle" belittled the experiences and sufferings of LGBT youth, effectively suggesting that they had chosen a marginalized position. This characterization resonated with Marquardt's equivalence of GSA members with students who play computer games. Further, this insult appeared superfluous, since it did not advance his fairness argument. Yet, perhaps because he attached his disapproval to a commitment to following law and policy, Beaver did not encounter the scrutiny of a GSA opponent like Weigand. In effect, the presumptive neutrality of Beaver's nondiscriminatory view cleansed his dismissive comment about homosexuality and absolved him of engaging the other. Beaver's position disclosed a weak tolerance for difference, but it did not affirm GSA members as full-fledged participants in their school communities. In contrast, Parks's struggle to reconcile his sense of duty with his personal experiences constituted a meaningful engagement with the other and, perhaps, a change in views.

The GSA and Counterpublicity

Although school-board members occupy a more intersectional position than their state and federal counterparts, whose policies increasingly have circumscribed district decision-making, they nevertheless act as official decision-makers on education policy in their local communities.[104] Engaging these officials, GSA advocates articulated a counterpublic discourse in an institutional forum.[105] Addressing this kind of interaction, Jürgen Habermas delegates the functions of informal and institutional publics clearly, charging the former (exemplified in individual and collective advocacy) with discovering problems and the latter (modeled in the debates of legislatures) with deciding among available solutions to public problems.[106] Yet the GSA controversy demonstrates the constitutive engagement of advocate and institution: the GSA pressured local policymakers to pursue an agenda item that some had not recognized and forced a decision that a majority reluctantly accepted. Moreover, the GSA deployed the institutional mechanism of a lawsuit in combination with advocacy to achieve their desired end.

In her well-known essay on counterpublics, Nancy Fraser explains that they serve as places for participants to "formulate oppositional interpretations of their identities, interests, and needs."[107] In West Bend, the meetings over the GSA demonstrated the pressing need for these alternative discursive arenas. Some board members and community residents repeated disabling stereotypes of gays and lesbians, and they attributed illicit motives to the GSA. Having already associated nontraditional families with the Nazis, Weigand questioned the psychological profile of gay and lesbian youth.

Professing goodwill toward the GSA, he offered that "there also [are] a lot of psychologists, psychiatrists that would be able to help them, um, to choose to get out of that lifestyle."[108] Groans and "boos" arose from the audience as he made this jab, responding, perhaps, to his degradation of homosexuality as pathology. In Weigand's reference to "help," homosexuality appeared as a disease that needed to be cured. Like Beaver, Weigand's use of the term "lifestyle" also belittled the students affiliated with the GSA, intimating that their own choices may have led to the bullying they suffered.

If homosexuality constituted a choice, then board members carried a responsibility to help students make good decisions. Weigand insisted that homosexuality represented a harmful lifestyle that led to other "risky behavior" and a lower life expectancy for young men. He contended that "we have a responsibility to protect the children that come into these, these rooms and walls . . . to protect them from harmful activities, from a lifestyle that is harmful to them both emotionally and physically."[109] Community resident Rick Schwanns echoed these sentiments, claiming that "this lifestyle will eventually lead them into drugs and harm and I believe they need to be encouraged to do the right thing, to, in my view, a heterosexual lifestyle—husband, wife, kids."[110] Schwanns specified a preferred path for students in West Bend: not only did they need to avoid homosexuality, but they needed to marry and procreate, reinforcing the ideal of the heteronormative family. Both his and Weigand's references to protecting children from harm underscored what they regarded as the danger and threat of homosexuality, which, in their view, acted as a gateway to depravity.

The school board and other adults in the community had to protect their children because the GSA sought to lead them astray, "recruiting" ostensibly straight students into the gay lifestyle. Raising this point amid scattered audience laughter, Weigand asked directly, "How would you recruit?" Fincke responded by telling the board about an incident he witnessed involving a student who had never attended a GSA meeting: "I saw a kid, fourth period, walking down the hall who got called a bad name. . . . Why don't we go reach out to him and talk to him and bring him along." Fincke quipped that this represented the "kind of recruiting that I think will go on." Returning to the connotation conveyed in Weigand's question, Fincke charged him with repeating a falsehood that "homosexuals recruit other people to be homosexual, and it's just a myth, it doesn't happen. It is not a chosen lifestyle; it's who someone is." Invoking the harms suffered by LGBT youth, Fincke continued that "nobody is going out to recruit people to a class of people who are going to be discriminated against, who are going to be bullied, who are going to be harassed."[111] Weigand did not reply, but, at other moments, opponents of the GSA asserted the recruitment charge more forcefully. Community resident and future board member Vinney Pheng insisted, "They gotta recruit, I say again, recruit. It's not a hold hands, kumbaya, we-support-you-type organization. They gotta recruit."[112] Pheng's insistent tone cast recruitment as a matter of self-preservation: a lifestyle depended on it.

In the eyes of their opponents, GSA members appeared as predators and the ostensibly heterosexual student body served as their potential victims. Community activist and conservative blogger Ginny Maziarka spied an "infiltration of homosexual ideation into the classroom setting," charging the GSA with "build[ing] an environment that would potentially be unfriendly and even dangerous to other students, and undercut parental and family values."[113] Pheng accused GSA members of "targeting the vast majority of underage students."[114] Words like "infiltrate" and "target" cast GSA members as secret operatives pursuing a nefarious plot to turn the upstanding youth of West Bend into deviants. Insofar as they supported the GSA, ostensibly straight high school students appeared oblivious to the dangers, welcoming operatives into their midst under the guise of an inclusive learning community. Whereas LGBT youth supposedly chose a risky lifestyle, non-GSA students also faced a decision: they could make choices that would ensure their "healthy" development, or they could welcome or even join the GSA, and thereby expose themselves to pathology. Yet, as children, they could not face this choice alone, since they did not fully appreciate the consequences. The adults charged with their education needed to instruct them on the proper path. GSA opponents believed that the board needed to stand strong because children had not yet learned to make healthy decisions.

Accusations of "recruiting" enabled GSA opponents to question the group's motives. They alleged that rather than educating students about bullying and harassment, GSA members sought to seduce students into illicit acts. Pheng dismissed the GSA as a "sex club," holding that members could not enact their group identity without engaging in physical action: "You can think what you want. Until you commit that act, you're neither heterosexual or homosexual. . . . So if you're telling somebody that they are gay, they have to perform the act."[115] Pheng implied that people could not construct their identities through symbols alone; adopting a sign as a marker of self did not suffice to constitute identity. Symbols engendered subsequent physical action, as people acted in accordance with the markers they chose. By enabling students to affirm their identities, the GSA effectively promoted their pathological promiscuity. Maziarka maintained that a club "with ties to sexual behaviors" should not be geared toward minors.[116] In this vein, Weigand charged that the GSA contravened the district's official policy of abstinence. He alleged that "anti-bullying is just a front. I, for one, am not fooled by it." According to Weigand, despite its profession of inclusiveness, "this group does not exist for those who would classify themselves as being straight." To the contrary, Weigand claimed, "their true agenda [is] to promote a same-sex lifestyle."[117] Sex was the basis of the GSA—recruiting for sex, engaging in sex, and promoting the superiority of same-sex relationships.

Confronting stereotypes and prejudice at the meetings themselves, supporters elucidated how the GSA facilitated counterpublic moments of inward association as members constructed their own interests and identities as well as outward contestation as they engaged wider publics. Intimating interests and identities, community resident Joy Schroeder observed that "gay people are called names, threatened, and physically assaulted on a regular basis. . . . They deserve to have a safe place to go where they are not only tolerated but accepted and respected." Schroeder appreciated the power of language to create a positive sense of self in communication with others. She characterized the GSA as "a club for young people to be able to talk, talk about their emerging sexuality, to understand what is going on with their own feelings, what may contribute to healthy relationships, to learn how to stay safe, and how to encourage their classmates to foster a safe learning environment."[118] Schroeder's reference to "classmates" signaled a moment prior to GSA members engaging with an other, when they learned from each other how to conduct such engagement efficaciously and safely. Other GSA supporters echoed this language, reiterating the need for "safe space" and emphasizing the urgency of LGBT youth developing positive identities. Christy Shew, for instance, highlighted a primary purpose of the GSA as "connect[ing] people who sometimes feel like they're out there all alone."[119] By interacting with similarly situated others, GSA members could recognize that others shared their suffering and that working together they could enact change.

Change necessitated engaging classmates who perpetuated bullying, remained ignorant of its cruelty, and/or watched acquiescently as others suffered abuse. The Day of Silence protests represented one mode of engagement, generating mixed responses from fellow students. While some students reflected on the meaning of the protests, others verbally abused—and, in one case, punched—protestors. Fincke reported that when protestors were teased in classrooms, some teachers failed to respond appropriately. Even as they encountered recalcitrance, GSA members enacted their outward-directed roles as, in the words of Christy Shew, "a voice for justice . . . an advocate."[120] When GSA members spoke, they sought to "raise the visibility of this discussion," as Fincke explained. He observed that GSA members "have some very specific ideas of the kind of language that is hurtful that isn't mentioned in [district] policy. And I think it's time to air out words like 'fag' and 'gay' and other derogative, pejorative terms, um, and, you know, have discussions about those in all school, um, assemblies, and say this is not going to be tolerated."[121] Among themselves, GSA members had discussed the experiences of being bullied—their own experiences and/or those of friends and classmates. These internal discussions had readied them to express their views to wider audiences consisting of administrators and classmates. GSA members had developed ideas for reformulating policy, and they also wanted to talk informally about how words could inflict pain—how schoolyard taunts and even casual dismissals ("that's so gay") lingered, making them question themselves and feel isolated from their peers.[122] GSA members fully embraced the inward-outward dialectic of counterpublicity as they sought to change the policy and culture of their schools.

Fincke's references to "policy" and "assemblies" evidenced the entwinement of counterpublic and institution in the GSA controversy. GSA members could propose amendments to policy that would resonate with their experiences of bullying in West Bend, but they could not rewrite policy. They could talk to assembled students about the power of words to hurt, but they could not call an assembly. They needed action from school-board members to achieve their goals, even if board members would have preferred not to act. Daniel Brouwer notes that interactions of counterpublics and institutional actors present threats and opportunities for all parties. Discussing the congressional testimony of the AIDS activist organization ACT UP, Brouwer explains that "ACT UP fears co-optation by merely appearing in the forum; on the other hand, the threat of a disruptive violation of the discursive norms of the hearings might rightly set the representatives on edge." This tension presents an opportunity, since counterpublic "participation instigates a critical publicity and provides a mechanism by which members gain access to stronger publics."[123] In West Bend, the school board constituted the "stronger public"—the institutional decision-makers.

As they engaged the school board, GSA advocates stood firm in their promise to involve other institutional actors—namely, federal judges—if necessary to obtain official standing as a school-sponsored club. The GSA's opponents felt threatened by the group's legal tactics, redirecting the issue of bullying toward the GSA itself. During the May board meeting, Randy Marquardt spoke indignantly about the GSA's efforts to compel the board to decide against its preferences: "I don't like the precedent of a group of people coming before us and essentially saying 'do this or else we're going to make you spend a whole lot of legal fees.' . . . It's, you know, being told to do something or else, and that's not the way, um, this is supposed to work." Marquardt analogized the GSA application to other issues decided by the board. He imagined a disgruntled vendor whose contract proposal had been rejected by the district: "What if a vendor came in and, you know, was, you know, not low on a contract or something and said, you know, give me this contract or I'm going to take you to court and, you know, drive up legal fees?"[124] Like his association of LGBT youth with students who played video games, Marquardt's analogy devalued the issues that the GSA hoped to address: deciding whether to support a group that educated students about bullying and harassment amounted to a decision about which vendor to employ for repairing a school building, or supplying snacks in the school cafeterias, or some other mundane issue. Further, by stipulating that the vendor had not been the low bidder, he recast the GSA application as deficient, ignoring the favorable recommendation of district staff. In June, as Marquardt announced that he would switch his vote because he believed that the district likely would lose in court, he complained that "I think that all of us have been bullied and harassed by the supporters of the GSA." Weigand did not switch his vote, but he likened the GSA's actions to blackmail.

Both board members objected to a perceived loss of agency: their positions as board members meant that they should decide district policy. In this view, the role of people appearing before the board should have consisted of providing reasons and information to inform board decisions. The GSA was supposed to behave as a "weak public," which engaged solely in opinion formation, against the "strong public" of the school board, which possessed decision-making authority.[125] GSA advocates acknowledged that their tactics might upset the board, but they remained unapologetic. Dan Patricus asserted that "this isn't a threat. This isn't the students being bullies. You will leave these students with no option." Despite these denials, references to a lawsuit did amount to a threat, insofar as we define threat as an interlocutor promising a negative consequence (filing a lawsuit) if others did not agree to an outcome (approving the GSA application).

This observation raises questions about the legitimacy and fairness of the deliberations themselves: as a threat, did the lawsuit disqualify the advocates who supported the GSA? Did the threat (and filing) of a lawsuit stand outside of deliberation? My answer to these questions is an adamant "no," which is a position, I suspect, that theorists like Rawls and Habermas likely would not share. Habermas, for instance, famously asserts that no force should influence argumentation except for the "force of the better argument."[126] From one vantage point, the lawsuit filed by the GSA's attorneys fails this test, since Marquardt clearly would have preferred to uphold the board's May decision to reject the GSA application. Indeed, Marquardt's analogy to the hypothetical litigious vendor indicated that he regarded the May decision as the better policy choice. On this view, the lawsuit exerted a coercive force over Marquardt, but it did not engage his free exercise of reason. However, this assessment incorrectly assumes a level playing field on which all interlocutors experience power and privilege similarly. Counterpublics generally do not emerge in these contexts, and the GSA advocates specifically did not engage the school board on a level playing field. The GSA advocates lacked the institutional authority of the school board; they confronted a district culture that, in significant respects, exhibited hostility to the needs, interests, and identities of GSA members. In this situation, they used the resources available to them, which included exploiting opportunities that arose as they engaged the ideologies of board members. The lawsuit served as a deliberative tactic that pressured tensions within the anti-GSA board members' ideologies of fiscal and social conservatism.

Rather than curbing deliberation, the lawsuit generated deliberation by the school board and the community. Without the lawsuit, the school board's consideration of the GSA application would have been limited to its two May meetings, during which board members opposed to the GSA utilized the district criteria for school-sponsored clubs not as a neutral public reason but as justifications for their opposition. Producing an additional board meeting, the lawsuit furthered deliberation in terms of its duration and conduct. Regarding the latter, the lawsuit forced board members—even anti-GSA board members like Dave Weigand, who did not change his vote in the June meeting—to consider the relative weight and relations among their social and financial commitments. In this way, the lawsuit did engage board members' reason; they had to reason through their various—and potentially conflicting—commitments. The lawsuit may have forced board members to engage in processes of reasoning they otherwise would have wished to avoid, but placing interlocutors in this position sometimes may be necessary for counterpublics seeking to achieve change.

Exploiting Ideology, Sustaining Counterpublicity

The *Daily Caller* may have ranked Washington County among the hundred most "conservative-friendly" counties in the United States, but the West Bend GSA controversy demonstrated that "friendly" did not mean the county was monolithic in its views. Although they encountered some harassment, GSA members also received support from other students when they participated in the Day of Silence protest at their high schools. Community members supported them by writing letters to the editor, showing up at board meetings, and wearing rainbow ribbons. Two local attorneys risked rebuke and lost business by pursuing a high-profile case. And three board members voted in favor of the GSA application at the May and June board meetings. Among those who consistently voted no and the vote-switching board president, the GSA exploited tensions in their ideology that belied a coherent articulation of belief.

The alternative interpretations that board members and others offered of district criteria did not render the criteria useless but signaled that the criteria—effectively a localized public reason—operated differently than a public reason or translation proviso would suggest. Rather than constituting a common ground that interlocutors reasoned from, the criteria served as shared points of reference facilitating contestation. Public reason, which Rawls links to an "overlapping consensus" of belief, or a translation proviso, which Habermas associates with a cooperative learning process, envision interlocutors reaching a mutual accord. Interlocutors did not follow this model in West Bend. Instead, they employed the criteria as a means of connecting—not to overcome difference but to voice disagreement in a delineated field of engagement while connecting policy positions to ideological beliefs.

By connecting their personal experiences and beliefs to their perceptions of their public roles, board members did not abrogate their official responsibilities but illustrated the various resources from which ideological engagement draws and the tensions that ideologies often exhibit. Yet tension does not indicate error—tension serves as an inventional resource, a means for bolstering advocacy and motivating assent even in seemingly foreboding circumstances. In an important sense, policy change cannot come from entirely outside a decision-making body and its constituents. The long history in the United States of local communities defying judicial orders about education—desegregation, most notably—demonstrate that communities possess ample resources to resist change.

Ideological tensions provided opportunities for advocates to promote change from within their communities even as they employed all of the available means of persuasion, including utilizing the threat of a lawsuit. The school board approved the GSA, but it would not have done so without sustained counterpublicity that pressured ideological tensions for ameliorative change, demonstrating that the GSA deployed the inward-outward dialectic of counterpublicity deftly. Achieving recognition as a school-sponsored club represented an important gain, a crucial symbolic victory with material consequences. This achievement promised sustained momentum as the West Bend GSA continued its counterpublicity in the schools and the community.

3

SCARCITY, DISTRICT FINANCES, AND DIFFICULT DECISIONS

Money matters for school-board deliberations. Collecting and spending money—by levying taxes and determining budgets—constitute some of the most potentially contentious and consequential subjects that school boards address. Deliberations and decisions about revenues and expenditures influence personnel and curricular matters, student experiences and outcomes, and family budgets, including the budgets of families who do not have children attending district schools. Even as they may disagree about specific tax rates and budget priorities, board members, district administrators, and community members agree that financial commitments to education may make people and businesses more or less likely to live and operate in a community, thus influencing the market value of homes and enterprises. To the extent that money signals resolve and enables action, financial decisions may match or miss boards' expressed commitments to particular educational values and goals. In terms of public awareness, financial decisions may make board members, who sometimes serve as comparatively unknown public officials, visible in their communities, affecting local constituencies differently and generating support and opposition from various individuals and groups. Even as state and federal officials increasingly have used money both as reward and punishment for succeeding or failing to meet their directives, local communities retain the primary responsibility for funding their schools, both in terms of the money districts actually collect from residents as well as the amounts of state and federal aid triggered by board decisions.[1]

The pronounced localism of American education means that local community wealth significantly shapes district deliberations about money. Since local property taxes serve as a foundation for educational spending, wealthier communities have greater resources available than poorer communities and greater flexibility in their deliberations and decision-making. Legal challenges to property-based funding and state laws designed to redistribute tax dollars among districts in a state have made some progress in reducing the gap in spending between rich and poor districts, but, as I explain below, these changes have not eliminated differences, nor have they accounted for the comparative resources and costs of education—both inside and outside of schools—in different communities.[2] Further, state equalization aid formulas cannot undo perceptions in some poorer communities that they have little to spend—even when the state offers incentives for spending. On this basis, Stephen Macedo writes that a combination of residential patterns, zoning practices, and school funding has produced "local communities and schools divided by class privilege." People may not actively discriminate, Macedo concedes, but "local politics as currently organized make all of us into stakeholders in undemocratic exclusion and perpetuation of inequality."[3] As Douglas Reed has documented, Americans support educational equality in the abstract, but they resist policies that threaten local control and privilege.[4] Inequalities across districts have drawn significant scholarly and popular attention, including the pathbreaking 1966 Coleman Report as well as exposés like Jonathan Kozol's bestselling 1991 book *Savage Inequalities*.[5]

This decentralized system of educational funding leaves unaddressed the chronic condition of scarcity confronting school boards in communities like Beloit. Although not a large city, with a population of roughly thirty-seven thousand people, Beloit has endured prolonged economic hardship. As the U.S. economy collapsed in winter 2008–9, prompting commentators to liken the disastrous economic situation to the Great Depression,[6] many Beloit residents struggled to meet basic needs for themselves and their families. By April 2009, the city's unemployment rate reached an astounding 17.7 percent, the highest in the state, and among the highest rates in the nation.[7] In 2010, still the highest in the state at 16.3 percent, Beloit's unemployment rate was more than twice as high as Brookfield, one of the main communities served by the Elmbrook school district, and more than five points higher than the unemployment rate in West Bend.[8] Indeed, more than one in five people in Beloit lived in poverty, a figure that increased to one-third of all families with children under the age of five.[9] The city's schools felt this deprivation acutely. For the 2010–11 school year, more than three-fourths of all the students in Beloit schools—77 percent—qualified for free and reduced lunch, which, again, represented one of the highest levels of need in Wisconsin.[10] In absolute and relative terms, Beloit residents lacked money, which constituted a material and symbolic constraint for school-board members as they deliberated about taxes and budgets.

Just as money constituted an important topic of deliberation, its relative scarcity in Beloit influenced the conduct of board deliberations. Board members perceived the district as trapped in a situation whereby a pressure to improve student performance collided with a sense that it lacked the resources of more successful districts. Further, board members themselves did not escape economic hardship—they, too, reported lost jobs, increased debt, and limited incomes. The sense of scarcity informing their deliberations sharpened choices, complicating material compromises possible in a more propitious environment and highlighting differences rather than shared interests among various constituencies. Scarcity also magnified spending decisions about specific budget items and increased the salience of short-term fiscal gains that may have produced long-term (financial and other) costs.

In this chapter, rather than focusing on a particular incident, I examine budget and tax deliberations in Beloit across the two years of fieldwork, which arose as a sustained topic of debate in eighteen board meetings, committee meetings, and public hearings. In these forums, board members and administrators agreed that the district should cut its budget in response to economic distress and reduced state aid, but interlocutors sometimes disagreed strongly about the magnitude of the cuts and the necessity of tax increases to maintain important programs and services. I argue that participants' experience of scarcity circumscribed their deliberations topically and temporally. Even though the state incentivized higher tax rates and spending in poorer communities with increased state aid, board members saw this move as too risky, fearing that the community had little money to contribute. In this way, participants did not behave as the rational economic actors favored in idealized visions of markets. Scarcity also foregrounded the relative power of constituencies in the district, as board members and administrators especially resented the union-based power of teachers, which protected them against salary and benefit cuts. Dissociating themselves from teachers, board members and administrators saw taxpayers as their primary constituents, even as they disagreed about taxpayers' interests.

I begin this chapter by exploring the relationship between deliberation and scarcity, explicating scarcity as a material and perceptual force. Next, I provide a brief history of national legal challenges to unequal school financing as well as school funding formulas in Wisconsin. My analysis of tax and budget deliberations in Beloit begins by considering how supporters of various tax rates and budget cuts invoked economic hardships in the community to justify their positions. Whereas supporters of lower taxes and higher budget cuts cast their position in terms of community belt-tightening, participants favoring higher taxes and lower budget cuts urged community investments in education. Yet these competing economic arguments did not translate into strict economic responses to the financial incentives embedded in the state funding formula, as the experience of scarcity trumped financial calculations. I then analyze participants' deliberations over proposed budget cuts, in which employee salaries and benefits played a significant role. However, while board members and administrators viewed teachers as powerful antagonists, they regarded the custodial staff sympathetically. My analysis concludes by addressing participants' efforts to communicate with the community.

Scarcity and Deliberation

School boards negotiating the unequal system of education funding encounter disparate contexts and exigencies when deliberating with and about resources. Boards serving wealthier communities operate with relatively greater flexibility than do their poorer peers. If unexpected needs arise or district circumstances change, they may have the resources to address these matters without too much upheaval for the majority of their students. Less dependent on state and federal resources, these boards can operate with a greater degree of autonomy in making some decisions. Boards serving wealthier districts may encounter lessened time pressures in assessing programs and weighing different scenarios. Poorer districts may operate with less flexibility in decision-making and less autonomy insofar as they depend on more funding from outside the district. These boards may exhibit a greater sense of urgency and, perhaps, even an ongoing sense of crisis when addressing fiscal matters. These differences raise the issue of the relationship between scarcity and deliberation. What resources, if any, do school boards need to deliberate productively? How does scarcity inform deliberation?

Unfortunately, while scholars of public deliberation have noted this dynamic, they have not fully investigated it. John Rawls, for instance, has called for a number of political and economic reforms to secure public deliberation: "public financing of elections"; a "certain fair equality of opportunity" in education and training; "a decent distribution of income and wealth"; "society as employer of last resort"; and "basic health care assured all citizens."[11] These conditions constitute an ambitious list, one that envisions a polity functioning far from the reality of the contemporary United States.

Indeed, in some areas, notably campaign finance and income and wealth, the nation has moved further away from fulfilling these conditions, as courts and legislatures have equated money with political speech and economic inequality has reached levels unseen for several decades.[12] Nevertheless, Rawls regards campaign financing, education and training, and financial stability especially as "essential prerequisites" for the efficacious operation of public reason. He holds that these conditions "are necessary for this deliberation to be possible and fruitful."[13] And a healthy democracy, in turn, requires deliberation.

Yet references to "prerequisites" and "necessary" conditions offer little guidance for assessing deliberative practices in the context of contemporary U.S. education policy. Since equal opportunity and financial stability demonstrably do not exist at the local level—and, perhaps, at the state and national levels, too—does this mean that genuine deliberation cannot happen until these conditions have been achieved? Whereas his reference to fruitfulness raises questions about the quality of deliberation, Rawls's reference to its possibility broaches the fundamental standing of deliberation. Absent opportunity and stability, must we regard actually existing school-board deliberations as illegitimate? And what role, if any, might deliberation play in changing this system? These quandaries suggest that the question of possibility appears as improperly framed. Rather, my analysis seeks to understand how scarcity influenced deliberations in Beloit. This approach does not devalue calls to redress scarcity, suggesting instead that understanding its impact may motivate positive change.

Emphasizing connections between theory and practice, communication scholars nevertheless have not considered extensively the relationship between material resources and deliberation. For example, Darrin Hicks identifies three goods that he views as necessary for interlocutors to engage one another equally: access, resources, and capabilities. Yet Hicks spends less than one page of an otherwise thoughtful and detailed exploration of the promises of democratic deliberation discussing the problem of inadequate resources. This lack of attention does not stem from a lack of awareness, as he notes that "the pervasive inequality of resources, such as time, money, and expertise, significantly distorts the deliberative process."[14] To rectify this situation, Hicks envisions varied efforts by legislators, judges, and activists to advance laws, policies, and programs that would sufficiently redistribute resources to guarantee people an equal opportunity to exercise political influence. Invoking the work of Amy Gutmann and Dennis Thompson, Hicks endorses the realization of a "basic opportunity principle," which he characterizes as "a standard for distributing health care, education, security, income, and work in such a manner that all citizens have the legitimate opportunity to enjoy a decent life."[15] Like Rawls, Hicks appreciates the connections among resources such as health, education, income, and public deliberation, but, unlike Rawls, Hicks avoids the question of possibility, recognizing instead that deliberation may proceed without sufficient resources. However, beyond noting the potentially deleterious impact that insufficient resources may have on deliberation, Hicks does not consider how interlocutors may address scarcity in their deliberations.

As both a contextual factor that may inform deliberation and an issue that may arise in deliberation, scarcity constitutes a material and perceptual force. Materially, in terms of school-district budgets and community resources, scarcity exerts force that manifests in a short supply of funds, which, in turn, produces a short supply of teachers, courses, books, and other resources. The material force of scarcity operates independently of the direct attention of a school board. Regardless of whether a school board considers its district budget, class sizes may increase, books and other materials may fall into disrepair, students may arrive at school hungry, and, in the community, household budgets may stretch to a breaking point. Material manifestations of scarcity enable comparisons of socioeconomic conditions between districts, which appear through such common measures as the proportion of a student population that qualifies for free and reduced lunch. As a perceptual force, scarcity refers to the dynamic processes through which people perceive the relationship between their needs and the ability of available resources to meet these needs. In addition to the average number of students in a class, or the age of a school's textbooks, perceptions of scarcity entail judgments about just how many students make a class too big, or just how many torn pages make a book too worn. As a perception, scarcity is something that people feel and think about.

Scarcity as material force and scarcity as perceptual force sustain a mutually informative relationship, and together they influence deliberation. Comparative material resources in Beloit, Elmbrook, and West Bend present each board with different constraints and opportunities, but these resources do not elicit uniform perceptions in each district. Had they adopted a comparative perspective, Beloit board members may have agreed that they could access fewer resources than could their counterparts in wealthier Elmbrook, but they nevertheless needed to make judgments about their district's budget in relation to resources available in Beloit. Board members could have measured household income, unemployment rates, and mortgage default

rates. They could have asked all of the families in Beloit to prepare an item-
ized list of all household expenses, but, still, the board needed to render a
judgment about the proper balance between their perceptions of the district's needs and the available resources in the community. In important
respects, board members' deliberations constituted efforts to negotiate the
material and perceptual force of scarcity.

As a force that operates through deliberation, scarcity challenges the view
of the interlocutor as an autonomous, rational actor imagined in traditional
models of deliberation. In his influential account of deliberative democracy, Joshua Cohen underscores the importance of interlocutors' autonomy,
which, in his view, means that an agent's preferences should not be determined by a person's circumstances.[16] On one interpretation, this affirmation
of autonomy represents an overly heroic view of agency as operating independently of context, such that individuals may form and assess preferences
without constraint. The rhetorical tradition challenges this view, recognizing a close connection between individual agency, context, and community.
In this spirit, Karlyn Kohrs Campbell explains that "agency is constrained
by externals, by the community that confers identities related to gender,
race, class, and the like on its members."[17] Acknowledging this point, the
problem identified by Cohen may have more to do with the degree to which
circumstances "determine" one's agency. Community and context constrain
agency, but they do not do so equally for everyone. Public sphere scholars
have elucidated how people may experience varying degrees of autonomy as
a consequence of relations of culture and power, such that participants who
obtain entry to discursive forums from which they were previously excluded
may be constrained by unstated norms and values that privilege particular
modes of engagement.[18] In addition to the constitution of identity, which
Campbell references, scarcity draws attention to constraints arising from
relations of power and resources. People who experience the material and
perceptual force of scarcity may feel greater pressure to make decisions that
they regard as flawed or harmful.

Interlocutors' rationality emerges in their ostensible ability to achieve a
critical distance from their preferences sufficient to assess these preferences
on their own terms and to compare them with preferences shared by others.
In this way, deliberation exhibits a capacity to engage diverse perspectives
by potentially transforming preferences, whereas aggregative models of
decision-making treat preferences as given.[19] While the latter remain silent
on the quality of different preferences, deliberation enables interlocutors
to evaluate different preferences and thus adds an epistemic dimension to

decision-making.[20] This quality arises from the "weighing" that characterizes deliberation.[21] As a verb, the term "weigh" denotes meanings of assessing, considering, valuing, and comparing.[22] These actions imply a process
of reflection by interlocutors, suggesting that examining the strengths and
weaknesses of one's views and their relation to other positions may lead
interlocutors to see their preferences from a different perspective. Weighing entails movement from particularity to generality, from knowing one's
views in isolation to recognizing a range of perspectives that encompass
one's own. Christian Kock and Lisa Villadsen maintain that weighing public issues "implies holding together all reasons and considerations relevant
to the issue—not only those of one's own that speak for a given policy but
also others that may speak against it."[23] Regardless of whether one discov-
ers all reasons and considerations, weighing presumably generates greater
awareness.

Scarcity threatens to close the distance and compress the time for weighing in deliberation. Interlocutors experiencing the material and perceptual
force of scarcity may refuse to step away from their preferences. Scarcity
may elicit the opposite dynamic: interlocutors may hold tight to their preferences for fear of losing what little resources they possess. Deliberation entails risk—the risk of changing one's views.[24] People experiencing scarcity
may judge this risk as too great to bear. Rather than widening one's perspective, scarcity may induce a tunnel vision that frustrates new understandings.
Moreover, while weighing need not proceed at a leisurely pace, it does, as
has been observed since the classical tradition, invoke a process that unfolds
over time. In the *Nicomachean Ethics*, Aristotle observed that people "deliberate a long time, and they say that one should carry out quickly the conclusions of one's deliberation, but should deliberate slowly."[25] To the extent that
scarcity produces a heightened sense of urgency among interlocutors, it may
lead interlocutors to believe that they lack sufficient time to weigh all options fully and equally. In these circumstances, the views of more powerful
and privileged interlocutors and their constituents may prevail.

School Financing in Wisconsin

Beloit's place in Wisconsin's school financing system represents a complex
mixture of community wealth, local property tax rates, and state aid. Since
the 1970s, in Wisconsin and other states, legislatures and courts have recognized that relying solely on property taxes to fund education reproduces

gross inequalities across districts; legislative and judicial remedies have helped to create an environment where district decision-makers must negotiate federal requirements, state incentives, and local pressures. Wisconsin distributes state aid through a formula that makes a laudable but incomplete effort to account for differences among school districts. To establish a context for my analysis, I address federal and state legal challenges to unequal school funding structures, Wisconsin school financing law, and public officials (both board members and administrators) and tax decisions in Beloit.

Despite professions of interest from Democratic and Republican presidents, as well as the passage of the landmark No Child Left Behind (NCLB) Act, the federal government provides only a small portion of the funds for primary and secondary education in the United States. For the 2008–9 academic year in Wisconsin, the federal government provided only 12 percent of the total funding, while property taxes and other local revenues accounted for 44 percent of the total funding and state aid also provided 44 percent of the total funding.[26] Even though local and state funding levels were equal during the 2008–9 academic year and comparable in other years, I have identified the local district as the primary source for education funding because decisions made by school boards across the state of Wisconsin, which the legislature has tried to influence through financial incentives and penalties, determine how the total amount of state aid gets divided among districts.

At the same time, state aid (and, to a lesser extent, federal aid) plays a crucial role in augmenting local funding for poorer districts, since a world without state funding would be one where property taxes reigned, rich communities thrived, and poor communities suffered even more than they do today. Consider two hypothetical districts with stark differences in property values. In district A, property values average $100,000 per dwelling, whereas in district B property values average $50,000 per dwelling. If both districts taxed their residents at the same rate of 5 percent, district A would generate $5,000 per dwelling and district B would generate only $2,500 per dwelling. The school board in district B would have to set its levy twice as high as district A—at 10 percent—to generate the same level of revenue per dwelling. We can see how these differences in wealth translate into differences in educational spending by noting that at the time when legal challenges to property-based funding arose in the late 1960s, plaintiffs filed suits to redress situations where richer districts spent as much as twenty times more per student than the poorer districts in their states.[27]

A wave of challenges to inequitable state funding systems began in California with the 1971 case *Serrano v. Priest*. This case dramatized differences in resources between the woefully underfunded East Los Angeles public schools and their counterparts in the middle-class, predominantly white suburbs. In its decision, the California State Supreme Court ruled that the state's education funding system violated the equal protection clauses of the state and federal constitutions. With this judgment, as Lesley DeNardis notes, "*Serrano* became to school finance reform what *Brown* [*v. Board of Education*] was to the civil rights movement, both as a rallying cry and a blueprint for action."[28] Moreover, since poorly funded schools served a disproportionate concentration of minority students, some advocates felt that school finance reform also could advance the cause of civil rights.

Over the next two years, advocates filed fifty-two lawsuits in state and federal courts, but a rebuke by the U.S. Supreme Court left states as the only remaining path for reform.[29] In the 1973 U.S. Supreme Court decision *San Antonio Independent School District v. Rodriguez*, by a 5–4 margin, a majority of justices sided with the state of Texas in a lawsuit challenging its inequitable school finance system.[30] Written by Justice Lewis Powell, who had served on the city of Richmond and state of Virginia boards of education prior to his appointment by President Richard Nixon, the majority opinion expressed a commitment to local control over education policy. Local control constituted a legitimate state interest, thereby permitting statewide inequalities. Further, the majority opinion rejected the idea that education represented a basic constitutional right, since the text of the Constitution made no reference to education. Whereas the plaintiffs argued for education as a basic right by underscoring its connection to recognized rights like speech and voting, the majority worried about a potential slippery slope. Moreover, as James Ryan notes, viewing education as a constitutional right would have required the Court to recognize the idea of positive rights, which entails the government providing something to citizens rather than the negative right of freedom from government constraint. Ryan explains that the U.S. Constitution "traditionally has been thought a charter of negative rights."[31] This explanation gains credence in light of another decision made during the 1973 term, *Roe v. Wade*, where the Court discerned a constitutional right to privacy in the absence of explicit textual evidence. In this case, the right to privacy met the definition of a negative right.

While *San Antonio Independent School District v. Rodriguez* brought federal challenges to education funding to "a screeching halt,"[32] advocates continued to fight for equal funding in state courts. Just a few weeks after this decision, the New Jersey Supreme Court ruled in favor of plaintiffs seeking to redress the state's unequal school financing laws. In state cases, advocates for equality could draw on explicit references to education in state constitutions. The Wisconsin Constitution addresses education in Article X, which was adopted as part of the original state constitution in 1848, calling for "the establishment of district schools, which shall be as nearly uniform as practicable."[33] Moreover, state-based challenges, which Justice Thurgood Marshall appeared to encourage in his dissent in *San Antonio v. Rodriguez*, may better comport with the decentralized U.S. education system by responding more directly to the distinct financing systems of different states.[34] Since 1970, every state has enacted some form of school finance equalization.[35] In some states, including Wisconsin, legislatures have not waited for court decisions before acting to redress unequal education funding.

Efforts in Wisconsin date back to the 1920s, when the legislature adopted a flat aid and a guaranteed tax base to supplement resource disparities among school districts. In 1949, as the legislature increased aid to school districts, policymakers also adopted a philosophy of state aid that sought to balance equity with property tax relief—potentially competing goals that continue to inform education funding. Major reform came in 1973, as policymakers introduced a tiered system that offered a primary flat level of aid to most districts in the state and a secondary level of aid based on the concept of "equalization," which seeks to ensure that districts taxing their residents at equivalent rates will raise the same amount of revenue.[36] If we recall the hypothetical districts A and B from above—where property values were $100,000 and $50,000, respectively—equalization would mean that if both districts levied a 5 percent tax rate, then the state would make up for the difference in property values so that both districts could generate revenues of $5,000 per average dwelling.

The most recent major reform in Wisconsin appeared in the mid-1990s, as policymakers shifted the funding system to a three-tiered formula.[37] Eligibility for the three tiers of funding depended on the average property values in each district and district spending per student: virtually all of the school districts in Wisconsin qualified for a minimal flat level of aid per student; most districts qualified for a second level of aid providing state funds as a percentage of costs up to a fixed amount per student, known as a "secondary guarantee"; and some districts with lower property values—including Beloit—received tertiary state aid as a percentage of costs above the secondary guarantee of spending per student. At the same time, policymakers imposed revenue caps that limited the amount that any district could spend on their students and thus capped increases in local property taxes. All districts in the state could tax and spend up to their allowable limits, but poorer districts would receive positive aid for increased spending above the secondary guarantee while richer districts spending above the secondary guarantee would experience a reduction in their share of state aid.

This system of school financing created incentives for increasing and decreasing spending by levying a different "tax price" on poorer and richer districts. Maher, Skidmore, and Statz define the "tax price" as "the cost to a school district of increasing spending by an additional dollar."[38] For districts with lower property values, the tax price of additional spending was less than a dollar, since additional state aid meant that local residents would not be fully responsible for paying for an increase in school funding. For higher-spending, higher-property-value districts, the tax price was greater than a dollar, since new tax revenues would be offset by reduced state aid. In this way, the current system of education funding in Wisconsin creates clear financial incentives for poorer communities like Beloit to spend money on education at rates comparable to wealthier communities.

In pursuing the goal of equalization, Wisconsin has made important strides in eliminating some of the differences in education funding that arise from differences in community wealth. For example, although equalized property values in Beloit during the 2010–11 school year were one-third of the property values in West Bend and one-fifth of the property values in Elmbrook,[39] the revenue differences in each district were not nearly as stark as these comparisons would suggest. Beloit actually reported higher revenues per student than West Bend, which likely arose as a consequence of the strident fiscal conservatism of the West Bend school board. Serving a wealthy community, the Elmbrook school board raised revenues of $14,487 per student, while Beloit raised $12,745 per student.[40] This difference of roughly 13 percent is significant in generating resources for education, but it is not nearly as significant as one produced through a system that would force localities to rely exclusively on property taxes. Further, when comparing the proportions of local property taxes and state aid that contribute to revenues, we see that local property taxes in Beloit accounted for 15 percent and state aid for 70 percent of revenue per student, while in Elmbrook local taxes accounted for 83 percent and state aid only 8 percent of revenue per student.[41] Taxpayers across the state of Wisconsin paid for a significantly higher percentage of the cost to educate children in struggling Beloit than in prosperous Elmbrook.

Yet looking solely at financial incentives and tax revenues presents a highly misleading picture of the disparate educational experiences of children in Beloit and Elmbrook. A 13 percent difference in revenues may be smaller than the differences in their respective property values, but this money matters in an austere climate for public education where local communities make line-by-line budget decisions about whether, say, to rehire a math teacher or continue to teach foreign languages. Further, the equalization formula in Wisconsin presumes that board members behave as rational economic actors who base their decisions fully on financial incentives while ignoring other information. However, in Beloit and other poorer communities, board members may not believe that they can take advantage of financial incentives if doing so imposes a greater financial burden on their constituents; incentives may not incentivize in difficult economic situations. Moreover, equalizing the ability to generate revenues from taxes may not equalize the costs or resources present in communities. Education scholars have long noted that poorer and/or non-native-English-speaking children cost more to educate than wealthier, native English speakers.[42] And Beloit has significantly higher percentages of these students—for example, seven times as many students qualifying for free and reduced lunch—than does Elmbrook.[43] Further, these comparisons do not reflect the countless material and symbolic advantages that children in wealthy communities possess over their poorer peers that bolster their academic performance: academic tutors; flexible parental job schedules; parents familiar with large organizational structures ready to advocate for their children's needs and interests; after-school activities that build children's confidence and develop important skills; multiple models for successful college attendance and rewarding careers; and more.[44]

In each of the two years of fieldwork, the Beloit school board voted to increase its tax levy by 6.6 percent.[45] These increases represented a compromise between board members like Shannon Scharmer and John Winklemann, who wished to see no increase, and others like Jessica Everson, Missy Henderson, and board president Michael Ramsdail, who favored higher increases. A fierce opponent of tax increases, Shannon Scharmer pursued her positions with fervor and focus. She asked questions of administrators and others delivering presentations to the board; she demanded additional information on key issues before agreeing to proceed with a vote. One of the longest-serving board members, Scharmer knew how the district operated, and she advanced her agenda unapologetically. Some people regarded Scharmer as an obstructionist, and while her actions sometimes warranted this judgment, she brought to light issues and concerns neglected by others. A mother of two children attending district schools, she remained committed to providing children in the district with a decent education. A dean of students at local Beloit College, John Winklemann had served longer than any other board member. Board members and administrators alike respected his detailed knowledge of district finances and the state funding formula. Whereas Scharmer defended her views in a confrontational style, Winklemann adopted a more reserved demeanor. He spoke often in meetings, perhaps more than anyone else, but acknowledged others' concerns, often proposing modifications to board motions to account for objections. Nevertheless, when it came to proposed increases in the tax levy, Winklemann did not vote for these motions, proudly recounting his record as never having voted for a tax increase during his time on the board.

A strong proponent of levying tax increases to avoid budget cuts, Jessica Everson spoke infrequently during board meetings. Everson's reticence arose in part from her visible frustration with Scharmer's loquaciousness, yet she countered with succinctness, not timidity. One of the youngest board members, Everson had two young children enrolled in Beloit schools. A retired social worker in the Beloit school district, Missy Henderson had gained a reputation as an ally of teachers and a proponent of education. Having lived in the community for more than forty years, Henderson's three grown children had attended the Beloit public schools and two grandchildren presently attended the district's schools. A regular contributor to board meetings, Henderson served as a passionate spokesperson for adequate funding. An African American and the youngest member of the Beloit school board at twenty-six, Michael Ramsdail graduated from Beloit College in 2006 and served as a pastor of a local church. As board president, he tended to encourage the participation of others before speaking, fulfilling his self-identified role as a facilitator. Yet Ramsdail did not shy away from expressing his positions on issues, especially when he felt strongly about something. He sometimes appeared frustrated with Scharmer's confrontational style and Winklemann's steadfast resistance to tax increases.

Of the two remaining board members, Tia Johnson agreed with the need for increases but preferred lower amounts, voting with Scharmer and Winklemann against higher increases, while John Acomb sought compromises among board members. The mother of a young child attending the Beloit public schools, Johnson was the second African American member of the

Beloit school board serving during the period of fieldwork. Johnson tried to build an alliance with Ramsdail on what she regarded as issues of special concern to minority students. In doing so, she sometimes introduced non-agenda items into board deliberations, and Ramsdail responded by ruling Johnson out of order. Her frustration with his leadership grew, and by the end of the fieldwork she had established an unlikely alliance with Scharmer, particularly on fiscal matters. John Acomb looked for a middle ground between anti-tax and pro-tax board members in 2009 and 2010. A moderate member of the school board, Acomb exhibited discomfort with conflict. He often delivered prepared remarks at the outset of controversial board deliberations. Interested in serving student needs, Acomb also articulated a desire to minimize bad publicity for the school board.

Among administrators, Superintendent Milt Thompson favored higher tax increases, but his institutional position of authority did not sway reluctant board members. An African American with long ties to Wisconsin education, Thompson had just joined the Beloit school district for the 2009–10 academic year, having served previously as an administrator in the Kenosha, Wisconsin, school district. Thompson brought passion and inspiration to a beleaguered district, raising people's hopes through his visions of a successful Beloit. Admittedly a "big picture" person, Thompson eventually frustrated some board members who complained about what they perceived as his insufficient attention to the pragmatics of policy implementation. Thompson and Scharmer increasingly engaged as antagonists during the two years of fieldwork, which some speculated had contributed to Thompson's decision to leave Beloit in spring 2011. Nevertheless, Thompson enacted some major changes in the district, including an overhaul of the grading system that required him to craft a coalition of board members, teachers, and parents. Further, Thompson was generally well liked and respected among board members and others in the district. The district's financial specialist, Jim Weise, executive director of business services, resisted making specific recommendations to the board, but he encouraged the board to consider combinations of tax increases and budget cuts in addressing district finances. Weise played a key role in meetings, providing nuts-and-bolts information about potential tax rates and budget cuts that complemented Thompson's big-picture contributions. With perhaps the best knowledge of the complicated state funding formula, Weise helped frame the board deliberations. He prepared extensive materials for most meetings and often delivered detailed presentations, outlining the potential effects of various tax rates and budget cuts.

Hard Times

No one needed to tell members of the Beloit school board that an economic recession had exacerbated suffering in the community. Board members knew about this condition—in fact, some of them experienced economic hardship directly. Yet board members regularly reminded one another of the economic woes present in the community. Their discussion of economic hardship marked the comparative willingness of board members to treat the economy as a trump card against any proposal to raise revenues or as an indication of their commitment to treat education, even in difficult times, as the only means that many poor and working-class people in Beloit had available to them to advance in society.

Across the meetings over the two years of fieldwork, as the board considered proposals for minimal, moderate, and substantial increases to the tax levy, Shannon Scharmer pleaded with her colleagues to "sincerely look at what our taxpayers are able to afford in the current economic conditions that our city is in." Scharmer presented an unequivocal, unambiguous answer: zero. She enumerated her reasons: "We have a 17 percent unemployment rate. We're the highest in the state. Our foreclosure rate is through the roof. Our number of at-risk students are in the top echelon throughout the state. What that says to me is the citizens in our city are hurting."[46] Scharmer cast available financial resources for Beloit households in a zero-sum frame— appropriating additional dollars for the school district would divert dollars from other needs, thereby harming the children that board members sought to protect: "How many more children are we going to have to provide for in our homeless children numbers? How much more are we going to have to expend to provide for these students that no longer have a home, who no longer have food? Because you know what, the more we tax, the less dollars they have to buy the clothing, to buy the food."[47] Scharmer saw families teetering on the edge of catastrophe—any tax increase, even a single dollar, would undermine their precarious financial condition. Her refusal to distinguish among comparatively smaller and larger tax increases revealed her no-tax-increase position to be as much a defiant gesture in difficult economic circumstances as a calculated assessment of people's ability to pay.

John Winklemann also turned to the economy to justify his opposition to tax increases: "The district has a, has a moral obligation to look at its community and say, you know, in tough times, it's not the time to push the edge."[48] His suggestion that the present did not constitute the "time" to raise taxes implied a measure of contingency. Weighing proposals against current circumstances, he implied that board members should wait for the right time to ask community members to pay more for local education. Yet his anti-tax record and his unwillingness to vote for his own amendments belied his gesture toward contingency. Unlike Scharmer, whose uncompromising anti-tax position seemed to arise from her belief that community members could not afford a penny more, Winklemann's position reflected an ideological rigidity. He opposed tax increases as a matter of principle in good times and bad.

Board members supporting tax increases to maintain programs and services often discussed their views, somewhat ironically, in the context of personal financial struggles. As Jessica Everson advocated tax increases, she explained that "I'm in a situation where, you know, and all families are people, reduced, my husband just lost his wages." Everson's jumbled delivery may have indicated the discomfort she felt in informing her colleagues of this situation, as their surprised and supportive responses suggested that they had just learned about it. Everson explained that she understood personally the difficulty of asking people to pay more, but she still supported this position, since "we're doing it for our kids, our community, to improve the graduation rates that everyone was complaining about earlier."[49] Like Scharmer, Everson tied her position to the economic recession, but rather than casting economic woes as a bulwark against tax increases, she saw tax increases for education as the solution to economic uncertainty. Depriving the school system of necessary funding would only worsen people's situations by making them less independent economically, since a well-paying job required a decent education. Moreover, whereas Scharmer diagnosed district finances in absolutes, Everson discerned degrees of magnitude in terms of what people could afford.

Board member Missy Henderson referenced income lost and income forsaken as she reiterated her support for a tax increase. She noted that her family's income had declined over the past eight years: "My husband hasn't gotten a raise in three years. . . . His end of the year bonuses [are] gone— that's reality, that's construction. We're happy he's still employed but we're working, ah, negative sixty thousand dollars from what we were eight years ago." Further, as landlords, the Hendersons had seen no increases in their rental incomes over the past few years even as the board had raised taxes in 2009 and would do so again in 2010: "We have always made the promise to our tenants that if they are good tenants we will never increase their rent, even if taxes go up." Effectively advocating for an increase in her business costs as a landlord, Henderson nevertheless insisted that "this is our community's future."[50] She weighed her business costs against the costs of a subpar education to her family and the community.

Few community members spoke during school-board meetings, but most of those who did speak supported increasing taxes even during hard times. Community member Bonnie Weeden referred to modest tax increases as "a no-brainer. If you don't, everybody loses. And I know it's hard and economic times are hard, but I just don't feel that we have that much of a choice." Likewise, community member Bill McGraft supported tax increases "even though Beloit has a community unemployment rate of 17 percent, 18 percent. There are families who are at 50 percent unemployment or 100 unemployment." Nevertheless, McGraft maintained that "education for the children is the single highest priority."[51] These community members (and others) appeared to endorse the view that major cuts to education, which no tax increases would necessitate, would exacerbate Beloit's economic insecurities. Everyone would lose, Weeden asserted, intimating that the key to prosperity for the whole community lay in an educated citizenry. They had no choice, she insisted, since the city had lost many of the blue-collar jobs that had provided steady incomes to its residents. Beloit lacked many of the resources of wealthier communities, but education remained a resource that the community could cultivate.

Investing in Education

Participants favoring modest budget cuts and increased taxes as the way to shepherd the school district through difficult economic times raised the banner of investing in education. As the word "investment" suggests, participants advancing this view cast their argument in financial terms: if an economic recession had strained household (and, importantly, state) budgets, then an adequately funded school system could potentially stabilize household finances and bring more money into the community. These possibilities arose through what participants regarded as a strong connection between property values and the quality of local schools, as well as the ability of good schools to retain current students and attract new students to the district.

Board members, administrators, and community members treated as common knowledge the notion that good schools bolstered property values and bad schools hurt property values. Jim Weise stated this view plainly: "In the long run, a strong school system is going to support the property values of the communities."[52] Others did not need to rely on Weise's financial authority to appreciate the connection between schools and property values. Community member Judy Christianson shared her own situation with the board: "It is so important that we support our schools because we just had an appraisal done on our house and we're totally shocked when it came in about forty thousand dollars less than our taxed, than our evaluation for our taxes."[53] Christianson likely asserted this connection in a more direct, causal way than Weise had intended, but her insistence revealed the power of this argument. Considering constituents' ability to make their monthly mortgage payments represented an important but partial assessment of household finances in Beloit. Board members also needed to consider other ways that community members might become financially trapped or lose their homes. Milt Thompson, too, affirmed that "property value is contingent upon having a quality education system, and it's not like you've been strapping it to them as far as taxes."[54] In establishing a commensurability between mortgage payments and property values, the language of investment enabled proponents of tax increases to weigh the comparative costs and benefits of different proposals. They saw tax increases as a modest investment that produced a considerable return: stabilizing property value.

Focusing on the relationship between good schools and student populations presented advocates with a means of shoring up district finances and generating new revenue. By enacting only modest budget cuts and increasing taxes, the school district could, at a minimum, retain students in the district who might be lured by course offerings and extra-curricular activities elsewhere. Thompson urged board members to balance "the desire not to raise taxes or to save money with the potential of creating a less rigorous educational program." Thompson warned of the negative financial consequences that could occur "if you bleed out more students because the parents want their child to take certain science courses that now are not gonna be available, or certain languages." He encouraged the board to consider whether "you are saving money only to lose the money through open enrollment for people that are gonna, that have the wherewithal to say, 'Then we're voting with our feet.'"[55] Thompson suggested that the district could not reconcile its balance sheets immediately as board members voted on proposals: the true cost of decisions appeared later. One community member, who did not identify herself, affirmed this view. She warned that "if we cut any more programs or we increase class sizes more than they are, we will lose students. We will lose them. I know families who have left because their kids were gifted and talented and weren't getting any programming." Urging the board to reverse this trend, this community member pledged to do her part: "As a taxpayer and a mother of three children, I will certainly support increasing the tax levy."[56] This community member (and others) understood that investing in education required a wider view of revenues and expenses.

Other meeting participants focused on the successes and failures of the school district in attracting new students. A prominent case concerned the employees of Kerry Americas, a U.S. subsidiary of an international food products corporation with operations spanning five continents. Maintaining warehouse and production facilities in downtown Beloit, the company announced plans in 2007 to close these spaces and build a new, larger facility on the outskirts of town near two interstate highways.[57] Made possible with state financial assistance, the announcement occurred with great fanfare, as the Wisconsin governor presented an oversized check to company executives during a widely publicized press conference in Beloit. State and local officials celebrated the retention of 300 jobs and the addition of 250 more jobs (once the facility opened) in Beloit. In June 2009, on a sunny summer day, Kerry opened the gleaming new corporate campus.[58]

For school-district officials, the celebratory mood soon vanished. As Jessica Everson observed, "We have Kerry coming in, we have five hundred employees of this building. I don't know anybody—I know one person that moved into this town. . . . People did not want to come to Beloit. They didn't want to send their kids to school here. They're in Rockton; they're staying in the Milwaukee area." Everson held that even if the city and state successfully recruited more companies, the board's financial decisions would not attract new students: "If we make these cuts, now these companies are going to keep looking at—and their employees aren't gonna want to move here."[59] Everson's comments resonated with at least one board member. John Acomb acknowledged hearing accounts of Kerry employees not relocating to Beloit, but he had previously discounted these reports as coming from people "who don't have firsthand information." In contrast, "what Jessie just said helped me to understand from a firsthand perspective that I haven't gotten before, that we've got a long way to . . . We've got to move our school district to a position of excellence, however much it takes, however long it takes, and whatever it takes." Yet neither Acomb nor any other board member save Everson proposed using the district's full taxing authority in 2009 and 2010.

Discussions of increases and decreases in student populations cast students and parents as consumers making market-based decisions about where to attend school. As good consumers, families shopped around, seeking information from various providers before making a purchasing choice.

These consumers carried out their purchases in two ways: by moving to communities with good schools and by sending their children to other schools, even if the families continued to reside in Beloit. Both types of purchases cost Beloit money. A decision to relocate or not to move into Beloit cost the city property taxes and other local household expenditures. For students that attended schools outside of Beloit, the school district lost money because, under Wisconsin's open enrollment plan, dollars followed students to the public schools they attended. In this environment, school districts needed to compete with one another for students, presumably improving themselves in the process. And yet, as with actually existing markets for other goods and services, this idealized consumer identity could not be obtained equally by everyone. As Thompson's reference to families' "wherewithal" implied, the choice and freedom ascribed to this consumer required material resources and a knowledge of educational structures typically possessed by more privileged families.

Spending and Incentives

As fieldwork began, Beloit suffered a series of economic and financial misfortunes. The economic recession, which affected the household income of community residents and the local economy, engendered its own anxiety and suffering, but the school district also faced a double sense of desperation as the recession affected state revenues and, in turn, state aid. For years, increased state aid had enabled Beloit to reduce its tax levy without significant losses in programs and services. When the threat and actuality of reductions in state aid appeared, board members struggled to come to terms with this new reality. Moreover, even though state incentives remained in place—Beloit would effectively receive two dollars of additional state aid for every dollar in new taxes it levied—board members resisted these incentives.

Wisconsin ties state aid to district spending. Beyond a minimal first tier of state aid, school districts receive state aid as a percentage of their spending per student. To make money in the form of aid, school districts need to spend money. Jim Weise delivered this message over and over during the two years of fieldwork—to board members, to other administrators, to community residents, to anyone who would listen. During a fall 2009 budget hearing, for example, Weise explained that "Beloit as a school district is rewarded for spending." He noted that at current spending levels, the state contributed 63 percent of each additional dollar that the district allocated toward education. This meant, too, that when the district did not utilize its full taxing authority or spent less than it had anticipated, the state withheld a similar percentage of aid for each dollar not spent: "If you decided you were going to spend a million dollars less this year, uh, the next year the state would say, 'That was a great job but we're gonna reduce your aid by 630,000 dollars.'"[60] In future years, the district would have to raise taxes over current rates to recover this lost state aid. As Weise discussed the state funding formula with various audiences, he confirmed that state legislators sought to incentivize particular decisions and disincentivize others: "So they actually reward you for making more expenditures if you are a poor district. They also penalize you if you don't make those expenditures."[61] State legislators cast board members and administrators as rational economic actors.

While the state funding formula benefited Beloit, it remained complex and difficult for people to understand, even for experienced board members and administrators. Weise conceded that community residents felt the impact of the dollars they paid in their tax bill more acutely than the dollars their contributions leveraged in state aid: "To spend a dollar, it only cost you thirty-six cents, so that's—it's hard for people to understand because . . . people are like, well, wait a minute, it's still costing me a dollar out of my own pocket."[62] Yet community residents did not fund the entire district budget directly out of their own pockets, only the portion they paid through the local tax levy. Still, the immediacy and directness of one's property taxes, which community residents in Beloit and elsewhere in Wisconsin receive as a bill like other consumer obligations, may have placed a greater premium on dollars paid rather than dollars leveraged, since only dollars paid come out of a household budget. State financial incentives and disincentives could not properly account for this dynamic.

Board members also expressed frustration with the state funding formula, especially during the second year of fieldwork when the board learned that the district, by a margin of $1.6 million, had spent less than its anticipated budget during the previous year. Weise explained that, as a consequence, the district would receive less state aid for the following year. When board members like Missy Henderson asked if the state had punished Beloit, Weise answered affirmatively. John Winklemann, in particular, appeared indignant: "Welcome to the world of the state of Wisconsin: school districts, if you save any money, you get [a] 22 percent increase in your taxes. Welcome to the world. If you lower your budget, you're hurt—22 percent increase in taxes." His reference to 22 percent identified the highest increase that the district could have levied in 2010—a percentage that no board member, save

Everson, supported. Still, Winklemann's point was that the district had suffered for its frugality. He likened the situation to the budgets of community residents: "We saved a million and something dollars—not beneficial. We lower our budget, we lower our—if I lower what I spent in my home life, that is most of the time beneficial because I either have more money to put to pay my house bills or somewhere, or I'm saving something."[63]

Like congressional policymakers who liken the federal budget to family finances, Winklemann's analogy rang hollow. The school district had not saved $1.6 million of its own money, but rather a combination of state and local money. And, by the reasoning of the state funding formula, money not "needed" in one district ought to be shifted to other districts with higher expenditures. Moreover, public budgets serve different functions than private family budgets. Addressing income, expenses, and savings, families craft budgets to maximize the first and third items while minimizing the second. In contrast, public budgets may serve larger purposes of spurring economic growth, increasing employment, or, in the case of education funding in Wisconsin, reducing the effects of differences in community wealth. The state had engaged in the very reallocation of resources that Winklemann attributed to families, but this move did not benefit Beloit. Not only did Winklemann's frustration appear misplaced, it was surprising, since he presented himself as an expert on the state funding formula. I suspect that his indignation expressed frustration with an ominous decrease in state funding levels as much as bewilderment about the mechanics of the formula.

For years, Beloit had benefited from increases in overall state funding levels, which kept property taxes relatively low. Indeed, as the state moved briefly to a two-thirds funding commitment for all districts in the state in the late 1990s and early 2000s, the school district had reduced its tax rate for fifteen consecutive years. Weise explained that "you've had tax reductions through those years because the state has always increased the amount of aid that they were able to give to districts, especially districts that in the equalization aid formula were positive tertiary districts, which you were." However, the economic recession had strained state finances: "Now, they are turning it around and they are reducing the amount of aid that they are able to give. The districts that gained the most are gonna lose the most."[64] In both 2009 and 2010, Weise urged the school boards to evaluate any increase to the tax levy over a longer time frame. He observed that present-day tax increases of the magnitude considered by the board still would keep tax rates below their levels from ten years ago.

In the fall of 2009 and 2010, the Beloit school board voted to increase
its tax levy by 6.6 percent. For 2009, this figure represented roughly the
midpoint between no tax increase and an increase utilizing the board's full
taxing authority. For 2010, this increase meant that the board used less than
one-third of its full taxing authority. Perhaps if board members were the
rational economic actors imagined by state law, they would have passed
higher tax increases. As investments, higher tax rates would have produced
handsome returns, leveraging two additional dollars for every dollar paid
by community residents. But board members refused a strict calculation
of investment returns. Some resisted tax increases generally. Others worried about community members' abilities to afford larger increases during a
recession. Instead, board members turned to the district budget to look for
places to cut.

Budget Cuts

An urgent tone and a hectic pace characterized budget deliberations in Beloit. The school board addressed the district budget year-round, but their
deliberations assumed greater weight in October, after the state had announced aid amounts, taxing authority, and spending caps and before the
deadline by which school districts needed to approve their budgets. In this
month especially, board members raised proposals and counterproposals in
efforts to build a majority of members around specific levy rates and budget
items. Throughout the year, board members examined the budget in detail,
often identifying specific line items they wanted the administration to justify or they wished to eliminate. Board members and administrators alike
recognized that the district had entered an era in which it would struggle to
maintain an efficacious and well-balanced school system amid dwindling
resources.

A key to meeting the fiscal challenges of increasing scarcity lay in enacting
budget cuts in accordance with an overall vision of the district's educational
mission. In October 2009, as he experienced his first fall season of budget deliberations in Beloit, Milt Thompson expressed caution about how the
board was proceeding: "I've looked at the list of cuts, you know, my biggest
concern [is] in a month or so when we sit down and do the strategic plan, will
be not to by default craft the school system, but by design to craft the school
system." Thompson believed that proceeding by default would effectively
reverse the proper steps in the budgeting process, placing decision-makers

in a situation where "we're saying, 'Here's how much money you have, now craft a program as commensurate with the dollars,' instead of, 'Here's the educational program that we want to have, here's the size and scope of it . . . here are the dollars that it takes to create that program.'"[65] Thompson wanted educational goals to determine spending, rather than having spending direct educational goals. John Winklemann voiced confidence that the board would do so, discerning a district "culture that can step back and be able to look in broad aggregate pictures."[66] Yet deliberations about budget cuts exhibited more of Thompson's concern than Winklemann's confidence.

Participants repeatedly worried that budget cuts would overwhelm the district's efforts to deliver its curriculum, thereby increasing class sizes and decreasing course offerings. Michael Ramsdail argued that even in comparatively better economic times, budget cuts had weakened the curriculum: "We all know how painful some of the things that we took out were, learn[ing] how that did change the climate and atmosphere of certain buildings." As an example, Ramsdail observed that the district enrolled "twenty-eight to thirty-some kids in each Spanish class right now in the high school."[67] Other board members and administrators articulated unease that in an era of high-stakes testing, the district would reduce its course offerings to a bare-bones selection of subjects primarily covered in state-mandated tests. Thompson, for instance, foresaw the district heading down a path where it would be forced to cut "enrichment areas that take you beyond the district equivalent of reading, writing, and 'rithmetic that will be gone."[68]

Although he advocated additional cuts, John Winklemann expressed a desire not to "shrink us down to WKCE [i.e., the state test] value."[69] As the board neared the conclusion of its 2009 budget deliberations, Winklemann voiced frustration that test scores figured prominently in public perceptions of the district's worth: "We allow ourselves to be defined by test scores. . . . We've asked across the district for a number of years, give us something else that we can be defined by." John Acomb concurred with this view of the disproportionate influence of test scores at the local, state, and national levels, but he found some consolation in knowing that "we're making progress in our elementary school test scores." Thompson provided the evidence for this conclusion, explaining that "when you look at some of the math achievement in some of our most challenging schools, there's some of the—even on the WKCE—they have some of the highest achievement of high-poverty schools in the state of Wisconsin."[70] Along these lines, budget cuts threatened to halt the progress of a district that had been flagged under state guidelines for failing to meet the adequate yearly progress requirements laid out in NCLB for the two previous academic years.[71]

References to standardized testing constituted one of the infrequent moments when policymakers in Beloit connected their deliberations explicitly to national policy developments. Most of the time, board members and administrators deliberated about the budget in district-specific terms, such as whether the district provided students with enough computer training or employed a sufficient number of math teachers so students could fulfill the district's own graduation requirements. In this case, administrators and board members could not afford to remain ignorant of national developments, since NCLB levied specific sanctions with financial implications against schools and districts that failed to meet adequately yearly progress in successive years.[72] Local officials may have believed that NCLB's testing and standards requirements did not capture the dynamics of educational successes in poor districts—and on this score they gained the company of academic critics of NCLB[73]—but they nevertheless lived in a policy world where districts received powerful lessons about the law. Moreover, high-stakes testing corroborated their economic frame, since testing provided the fungible units of measure and value that permitted state and federal policymakers, parents, and prospective students to distinguish among districts.

The answer to surviving budget cuts in an educationally sound manner lay in doing more with less, however difficult this feat may have seemed. Shannon Scharmer encouraged this approach throughout the deliberations. Emphasizing that community residents found themselves in a similar situation, she asserted that "we're all having to do, be more creative, as our bills go up—as the rest of our incomes are not going up or decreasing. Our taxpayers are doing more with less, and as a school district, I believe, we should be able to do the same."[74] Scharmer's reference to taxpayers cast the issue as a matter of fairness: the school district could not expect different treatment from the community. She also argued that the board could make cuts without affecting instruction; across the meetings, Scharmer insisted that the board could find savings by eliminating unnecessary staff positions and reducing program expenditures.

Central-office and school-level administrators accepted various cuts—for they had no choice—with a mixture of resignation and perseverance. As the board moved through a series of staffing cuts, Assistant Superintendent Steve McNeal acknowledged the "tough hits" that the cuts represented, but he reimagined job duties to manage the reductions in staffing. For instance,

McNeal described the loss of a math coach as "a hard cut for us at this time," especially since the person filling the position had been "a leader of our district in math" and "math teachers are hard to find." However, rather than trying to persuade the board to revisit this decision, McNeal offered that the district could "contract out" to find a person living in the community "at a much reduced cost." McNeal pursued this tack with multiple staff cuts. Losing a technology position also constituted a "tough hit," but McNeal suggested that assistant principals could assume additional responsibilities: "We need to continue to give them added responsibilities so that they can justify that we keep them. . . . As hard as it is, we have to look at all this."[75] Justifying one's keep meant doing more with less; the alternative appeared as termination. McNeal likely did not offer his comments as a threat—indeed, he appeared genuinely concerned about the challenge of meeting the district's mission in a climate of scarcity, citing several "tough hits"—but the threat still registered. District employees who felt overburdened by their new responsibilities could seek jobs elsewhere.

As the references to specific staff positions suggest, board members often considered the district's budget on a line-by-line basis. Citing student-teacher ratios, Scharmer repeatedly argued that modest declines in district enrollments justified fewer teaching positions. At one moment, for example, she demanded to know "how many fewer instructional staff members do we have this year than last year, or how many additional do we have?" Pushing aside distinctions between internally and externally funded staff, she insisted that "I want to know bodies to bodies. I don't care where the money is coming from."[76] She persisted even as her colleagues reminded her that enrollment averages did not signal a reduction in the number of students taking courses in a specific subject area; reductions distributed across the district did not add up to a particular teaching position. Perhaps the most peculiar case of micro-level budgeting came from John Winklemann, who observed during one meeting that "I read an interesting article the other day about how changing your default printer font saves money." Winklemann did not offer this insight as a proposed district policy; he did not insist that all district employees change their computer settings from, say, Arial to a less ink-intensive font like Century Gothic. But he did suggest that "it'd be worth a little poking at that to see."[77] In the absence of any controversial board deliberations over official district fonts, this comment exemplifies the level of detail and care with which board members examined the budget and considered various ways to save money.

Even as board members searched the budget looking for ways to save money, they expressed frustration about their comparative inability to reduce the largest portion of the budget. As administrators, board members, and a few community residents noted, employee salaries and benefits constituted 85 percent of the district budget. Eliminating a few staff positions on the margins—a math coach here and a librarian there—did little to reduce this expense. Moreover, the school board had recently negotiated the contract with the local teachers' union, the Beloit Education Association (BEA), which hampered their ability to ask for pay reductions and/or benefit cuts. Still, with Scharmer leading the charge, board members urged the administration to explore the possibility of renegotiating the teachers' contract. Scharmer held that when the district agreed to the terms of the contract, "we bargained in good faith, believing that our reimbursement from the state would maintain if not go up." Yet, she suggested, the recession had effectively voided the contract, if not legally then ethically: "Everybody's paychecks are smaller than they were a year ago. . . . We need to look deep and find out how we can share the pain."[78] In light of Scharmer's opposition to any tax increase, this call to "share the pain" effected a dissociation between teachers and community residents. In her view, the latter could not afford a single penny more in taxes because the recession had undermined their economic security. Teachers would have suffered as well, since many of them lived in the community and, for nonresidents, the recession did not limit its impact to Beloit. Teachers already would have experienced pain—unless their contracts spared them from the full effects of the recession or board members excluded them from the category of "community resident."

Maintaining conversations with the BEA, Milt Thompson reported that the union would consider revising its contract if the school board used its full taxing authority, since doing so would signal to the union a genuine commitment from the district to establish student interests as the top priority in budget deliberations. Not surprisingly, most board members scoffed at this proposal. Scharmer pushed the administration toward arbitration in any case, but Thompson pushed back: "Throughout my career, I have never seen the arbitrator significantly lower on a negotiated, on a contract that was negotiated. . . . I've been in Wisconsin education for thirty years and I, I'm sorry, I just—whenever it's gone to arbitration, the arbitrator settled close to, if not exactly, what the teacher's union asked for every single time in my memory."[79] Although board members ignored Thompson's pleas about the moral duty to fund education fully, they accepted his counsel on this point; arbitration never arose as a realistic means of reducing expenditures on teachers' salaries and benefits.

For some board members, a lack of movement on this front revealed the inflexibility and selfishness of the teachers' union. From this perspective, union spokespeople cynically deployed arguments about the quality of education, such as objections to increasing class sizes, to sustain their material and symbolic privileges. John Winklemann rebuked them as "willing to feed their people over the cliff as we cut 'em off. . . . They'll come and flood the meeting and inform the public about how big the class sizes are going to grow." Perhaps surprisingly, since he sought to cultivate a good relationship with the BEA, Thompson agreed: "If you talk to them and you say, 'We'll cut fifty positions,' they'll stand on the deck and wave aloha to the fifty people that are going because they already have the constituency. They're more into the veteran teachers."[80] The image of junior teachers walking the plank constituted a severe representation of the perils of a seniority system. Moreover, it intimated a distinction between good and bad teachers. The good teachers entered the profession because they cared about youth. As "team players," in John Acomb's phrasing,[81] they did what was necessary to prevent disruptions to children's education. The bad teachers aligned more closely with the union; they cared more about resources and preserving their piece of the pie than educating children.

Good and bad teachers alike sometimes betrayed an ignorance about their privileged positions. At one meeting, Tia Johnson shared a story of her interactions with a teacher about the relative generosity of the district's health-insurance benefits. In conveying the details of her discussion with a "teacher friend," Johnson explained that her personal finances had suffered as she accumulated thousands of dollars of debt from medical bills. Johnson recalled that the teacher asked if she had insurance; she replied yes, but noted that her benefits were not as generous as those received by Beloit teachers. Johnson wondered, "Do our employees really understand?" Comparing her own situation to teachers' concerns, Johnson critiqued their obliviousness: "We are dipping into our serious, you know, savings that I thought we would never have to. . . . And I've had, I've had teachers complain to me that we're not covering their acupuncture." This anecdote produced knowing laughter and affirming comments from others. Winklemann opined that "they have no clue where people really are." Jim Weise proposed distributing a compensation letter to employees that detailed their benefits. Such a letter could serve as "a real eye opener for people. . . . Sometimes you can be grateful, humbled."[82] This anecdote and the responses it elicited blurred distinctions between good and bad teachers. Whether motivated by greed or ignorance, teachers' demands had drained the district of needed resources and undermined the teachers' supposed commitment to children.

While negative images of teachers circulated as antagonists whom the board periodically battled, a second group of district employees received more sympathetic treatment as the board examined budget items. In spring 2011, Jim Weise approached the board with a proposal to investigate the possibility of outsourcing janitorial services at district schools. Treading lightly, Weise introduced the proposal as "very, very difficult" since it dealt with "very highly valued employees of our district," but he immediately encountered resistance. Ramsdail dismissed the proposal as a nonstarter: "Having come up through the district and being friendly with, with a lot of the staff in that department, I just think that the job is more than just the cleaning. . . . I just have no interest." Although he strongly supported trying to find savings on teachers' pay and benefits, Acomb voiced reluctance when it came to janitors "because of the role with our kids that our custodial folks play and also in part because of the fact that our custodial folks almost without exception live in this community. They are a part of this community." Expressing her opposition, Johnson observed that the janitors "probably have the racial background or make-up that most resembles our community." She added that their work "exceeds just pushing a mop and a bucket if these students have such—developed such bonds that sometimes it is the custodian that is the unnamed mentor to a student. . . . The custodian may be that person that the student will remember."[83] The proposal passed 4–3 over these objections, as Winklemann and Scharmer praised the idea for modeling sound business practices. But this vote likely did not portend the eventual use of outsourcing for janitorial services, since Everson and Henderson cast their votes in the spirit of seeking additional information while expressing an unwillingness to support any policy that displaced the current janitorial staff.

Like teachers, janitors constituted a portion of the 85 percent of the district budget devoted to employee salaries and benefits. So what, then, explains the different treatment by board members of these two groups of employees? The friendships, mentoring relationships, and fond memories that board members associated with janitors also applied to teachers—likely even more so, since teachers interacted with students more frequently and more intensely than did janitors. Johnson's reference to the "racial background" of janitors indicated one possible difference, since African Americans held a higher proportion of custodial jobs than instructor positions. Regardless of whether board members engaged in a racial calculus, this reference constituted a pointed moment in deliberations over the budget where race arose as an explicit concern. Supporting the janitors may have served as a way for board members and administrators—both black and white—to demonstrate their cognizance of and solidarity with the residents of a diverse community and the students in a minority-majority district.

I believe, too, that this differing treatment can be explained by the fact that the janitors did not represent the kind of powerful organized opposition to the board that the teachers represented. The teachers had their own union in the BEA, which constituted a powerful voice in the district that aggressively fought for the interests of its members. The board needed to consult teachers and secure their support to successfully implement a range of district policies. When important issues arose, teachers showed up at board meetings to assert their views. In these ways, teachers represented a regular thorn in the side of the school board. The janitors had no effective voice in board meetings nor did they hold a seat at the table to discuss district issues; they appeared as a more likely object of sympathy.

Communicating with the Community

Beloit school-board members and administrators cared deeply about community members views' on district policy, but their interest went unrequited, since community members rarely attended meetings to voice their preferences. In their absence, meeting participants speculated repeatedly about what community members thought, sharing anecdotes about neighborly and occasionally heated conversations, phone calls, and e-mails. District officials valued communication because it presented an opportunity to learn about public opinion as well as to inform the community about their efforts. Part of the task of informing lay in discovering ways to make meaningful the complex array of numbers, percentages, formulas, rates, trends, and projections that circulated in the deliberations about taxes and budgets.

Board members cited community opinions as powerful evidence to support their positions on raising taxes, cutting budgets, and enacting some combination of the two. Board President Ramsdail encouraged the use of community opinions as a guide for district policy as he held that "we need more input from community members on their position on [the budget]. Are community members at a point where they're saying, 'Ya know, start cutting programs to balance the budget,' or are community members in favor of even more of an increase in taxes to sustain programs that we have right now?"[84] Ramsdail's question reflected a shared sentiment among board members that their roles as elected public officials obligated them to learn about public opinions so they could advance their constituents' interests. They generally saw the role of the representative as serving as the voice of their constituents.[85]

Yet board members and administrators acknowledged that they had heard competing and sometimes contradictory views from the community. Tia Johnson, for instance, reported that while some community members wanted no increase in their taxes, "I've heard from enough constituents that there would be at least an equal number of taxpayers unhappy if we don't increase [the tax levy]."[86] Perhaps frustrated with the lack of a community consensus or the frequency with which interlocutors invoked public opinion, board members sometimes urged their colleagues to practice a different sort of representation by using their best judgment about district finances. At one point, Missy Henderson urged her colleagues to "stop thinking about what other people are thinking." Responding to Scharmer, who had cited calls from community members as a reason not to raise taxes, Henderson retorted that she, too, received calls. But she encouraged other board members to fully embrace their roles as policymakers: "Just think what is gonna be best for the kids. What's going to be best for the city. And don't worry—I mean, we may never be elected again."[87] The representative who worked assiduously to fulfill constituent preferences, Henderson implied, may secure reelection, but the price tag included the passage of potentially bad policy. Henderson countered that the value of good policy warranted the price of a lost election.

For some board members and administrators, repeated references to community views did not necessarily capture public opinion. They pointed instead to the poor showings by community members at meetings. Milt Thompson recounted that only four people attended two meetings held by the district to explain the tax and budgeting process: "Really, there wasn't a lot of interaction; there weren't a lot of questions that were put forward, and yet we did a full forty-five-minute presentation with all the information on the tax levies."[88] At these two meetings, at least, district staff tried to make complex school-funding issues understandable. Ramsdail concluded that the lack of more direct participation by community members, aside from the stories shared by meeting participants, meant that the board could not claim to know what the community wanted. Instead, he wondered if "we're putting lots of words in their mouth." Ramsdail preferred self-representation: "If we had a petition here, or if one hundred or five hundred homeowners came here tonight and said, 'Don't raise my taxes. Keep them flat,' then that's something." Indignant, Shannon Scharmer responded immediately, "The reason you haven't heard from our taxpayers is because they're too busy trying to make ends meet. And, if you want to hear from our taxpayers, look at our foreclosure rate, look at our unemployment rate. We don't have to hear from them, we can see it." In these comments, Scharmer cast participation as a privilege enjoyed by people who could remove themselves from the concerns of daily living and, having met their basic needs, address public affairs.[89]

Despite this exchange, Scharmer and others generally valued communication as a two-way process whereby they learned about the community's views and the community learned about the district's effort to provide children with a sound and cost-effective education. Board members' strong desire to know community views to inform their deliberations signaled the first direction of this process, but district officials also wanted to publicize their hard work in utilizing scarce resources to raise the standing of the school district with the community. Superintendent Thompson wanted community members to know that district officials acted as "good stewards" of the revenues they currently received: "When we do future forums and we present challenges as far as facilities and other things, it will be more to just give people a picture of, 'Here's the way the circumstance really is. There isn't fat, you know, we're building—we're not sitting in Taj Mahal buildings, and here's the way things are.'"[90] On facilities, salaries, and other budget items, district officials spent the taxpayers' money wisely.

Board members and administrators utilized two strategies to promote their fiscal prudence about taxes to the community: distinguishing percentages and dollar amounts and translating dollar amounts into tangible and familiar items. In fall 2010, Jessica Everson unsuccessfully argued for increasing the district's tax levy by the full amount allowable by the state. She believed that her constituents' receptivity to this proposal would depend on the numbers employed to announce the increase: "When you see 22 percent, you would choke." In contrast, if the district foregrounded the dollar amount, she contended, people would support the increase: "If I go and I say, 'We're going to increase the levy; it's gonna cost you less than twelve dollars a month.' . . . The people I have spoken to about this—they support this because they want the best for our schools. But I think we need to be aware that 22.63 percent is a little more painful to look at than a dollar."[91] In a subsequent meeting, Thompson reiterated this point: "When people hear 21 percent, they're thinking of some astronomical figure, and when you look at 21 percent or 14 percent, you look at the actual dollar amount, it helps to take it out of the percentage." Referencing Jim Weise's maxim, Thompson noted that "people don't pay a percentage; people pay dollar amounts."[92] Percentages appeared more fearsome than dollars because percentages, even when stated as "22.63 percent," retained an element of ambiguity about their base calculations. The announcement of a percent increase raised a second question often left unanswered in headlines and quick conversations: a percentage of what? When applied to household budgets, ambiguous percentages threatened to consume huge portions of people's monthly incomes. Moreover, percentages invoked trajectories, especially ominous trajectories of increasing tax rates.

Even when presented as dollar amounts, numbers themselves could not convey the low-tax message the board wished to circulate. To achieve this end, board members and administrators translated dollar amounts into readily identifiable consumer goods. In both 2009 and 2010, the 6.6 percent tax increase approved by the board amounted to an additional three dollars per month in property taxes for the average homeowner in Beloit. Board members likened this increase to "six cans of soda," "three candy bars," "a half a case of Capri Sun," and a meal at McDonald's. The analogy of the McDonald's meal gained the most traction among interlocutors, circulating across their meetings. For instance, Missy Henderson asserted that "it's time for the community to step up and say, 'I'm willing not to go to McDonald's. . . . I'm willing to say that's important that we have good schools.'" While Henderson, Everson, and others deployed the McDonald's analogy to argue for an increase, Scharmer employed the same reference for the opposite end: "It may be only one trip to McDonald's—many families can't go to McDonald's."[93] Scharmer's objection pointed to the relative character of ostensibly small expenses: for a household whose expenses exceeded its income, any additional cost appeared as enormous. However, most meeting participants accepted that a skipped McDonald's meal adequately represented the minimal sacrifice that the district asked of community residents. As Henderson's reference to "stepping up" intimated, sacrifice carried a moral charge. Education constituted a necessary expense, while a McDonald's meal appeared as a luxury. Since no responsible parent would prioritize a luxury over a child's basic needs, this analogy implied that objecting to the school board's tax increase amounted to a self-centered act of gluttony that harmed children in the community.

A System of Scarcity

As Beloit board members deliberated about taxes and budgets, scarcity informed their perceptions and circulated as a prominent theme. Scarcity influenced their judgments of opportunities and costs, challenging the narrow image of the rational actor presumed in the Wisconsin state funding formula. While the formula presumed that local policymakers would leverage local resources to the fullest extent possible to maximize revenue, board members reasoned with a wider sense of community well-being that judged people's economic suffering and their ability to pay. Perhaps Shannon Scharmer hyperbolized when she insisted that Beloit residents could not afford a penny more in taxes, yet her position captured the anguish of a community that suffered through the recession as badly as any community in the state. Even board members supporting tax increases understood that their position called for sacrifice from community members, and they offered their own struggles as an illustration of empathy.

Scarcity augmented relative power differences among constituent groups, fueling resentment and insinuating divisions among community members. Appreciating that salaries and benefits consumed 85 percent of the district budget, board members spied this item as a prime target for cuts. But their desires floundered against the well-organized and powerful teachers' union, which had secured its members' interests through a recently negotiated contract. In their response, frustrated board members and administrators dissociated teachers from the community by questioning the teachers' dedication to their students and accusing teachers of living in blissful comfort while the community suffered. In contrast, a board majority regarded district janitors, who also earned salaries and benefits, with considerable sympathy. Unlike teachers, janitors could exercise little power to assert their interests—their fate rested largely with the board. While this subordinate position may have elicited sympathy, it could not guarantee that the board would continue to support janitors' interests.

As board members experienced the material and perceptual force of scarcity, they needed to consider community members' reactions in learning about board decisions. Representing tax increases and district resources arose as a crucial concern. Any tax increase would materially affect community households, but board members could potentially influence community perceptions through their practices of representation. A seemingly extravagant percentage might appear more reasonable as a dollar figure. Comparing an increase to a readily identifiable consumer good might augment community understanding and acceptance. Comparing an increase to a Mc-Donald's meal carried additional symbolic weight, for doing so contrasted the "luxury" of eating out—even at a fast-food restaurant—with the necessity of education. In these ways, both the board members' deliberations and their efforts to communicate with the community underscored the material and perceptual force of scarcity.

4

EXPERTISE, INTEGRATION, AND
THE PROBLEM OF JUDGMENT

Making decisions on a range of complex and sometimes controversial issues, school boards often must negotiate a tension between utilizing particular types of expertise and engaging the diverse voices of district stakeholders. Decisions about finances, curricula, personnel, and other issues often require careful analysis that implicates technical areas of knowledge, while board members' status as elected officials carries an obligation—and board members in the three districts expressed a desire—to incorporate community perspectives in their decision-making. School boards may face tensions between expertise and engagement acutely, since citizens and policymakers see education as central to individual and national futures. Yet expertise and engagement pull school boards in opposite directions. Expertise implies restricting deliberation and decision-making to "qualified" people, while engagement invites widespread participation.[1] Expertise also draws on a presumably specialized knowledge, while engagement draws on the putative common sense of citizens.[2] Expertise frequently addresses a homogeneous audience of colleagues, while engagement often seeks a heterogeneous audience of everyone potentially implicated in a public issue. Utilizing expertise may encourage board members to erect barriers to circulating knowledge and expanding participation, while facilitating engagement may motivate them to remove such barriers.

Negotiating this tension requires balance—both across these areas as well as within each one. Balance across expertise and engagement entails recognizing how distinctive and shared perspectives may illuminate board decision-making. Relying exclusively on expertise would manifest what Jürgen Habermas and Thomas Goodnight have characterized as the encroachment of technical reason into the public sphere.[3] Although their terminology differs, both theorists critique what they see as the improper use of instrumental reasoning to decide issues that properly invoke a greater public good.

Both Habermas and Goodnight sound alarms about a weakened realm of civil society and a diminished public life in which deliberation proceeds through narrow, unyielding standards and procedures. On the other hand, relying exclusively on engagement would undermine decision-making by obscuring the insights that people may glean through extended analysis of a public problem. Leah Ceccarelli warns of this possibility in her critical articulation of "manufactured" scientific controversies, wherein advocates assert—in the face of clear contrary evidence—that experts disagree about the existence and nature of a technical issue.[4] In these cases, such as the purported scientific debate over climate change, advocates cynically deploy democratic deliberative norms like fairness, open-mindedness, and balance to forestall public action.

Balance within each of these areas entails recognition that both expertise and engagement implicate shared values and invoke particular knowledge and competencies. Achieving this recognition confronts a lingering perception among some experts and laypeople that places "factual" knowledge on one side of a dichotomy and "valued" opinion on the other.[5] Along these lines, economist Paul Wyckoff argues that objective, statistical evidence constitutes the only means of overcoming the rampant partisanship and polarization in the United States that have undermined policymaking. To aid in this effort, Wyckoff formulates a hierarchy of evidence that places case studies and anecdotes, which operate effectively on "an emotional and persuasive level . . . [yet] are riddled with holes from sampling error," on the bottom and large-scale experimental studies at the top.[6] In contrast, critical studies of science and expertise have made plain the value dimensions of technical knowledge.[7] Similarly, we need to recognize engagement as not simply a valued enterprise but as an expression of a distinctive democratic knowledge. Engagement does not represent an empty proceduralism—a step in a process toward reaching a decision undertaken because of a perceived need to meet an expectation—but a means of reaching a better decision.[8] Engagement accesses particular knowledge and competencies. Engagement generates knowledge by eliciting more perspectives that may engender greater understanding of an issue and produce more efficacious solutions.[9] Engagement draws on competencies of perspective-taking that do not exist as inherent properties of processes but arise as skills learned through experience.

During the period of the REDD fieldwork, the Elmbrook school board confronted a tension between expertise and engagement in its deliberations about whether to continue participating in the state's Chapter 220 program. Named for the legislative session in which it was enacted—Chapter 220

of the Laws of 1975—the program seeks to facilitate school integration between the city of Milwaukee and its surrounding suburbs by providing suburban districts with property tax relief for enrolling minority students from
Milwaukee.[10] Required to participate in the Chapter 220 program from the
late 1980s through the mid-1990s, the Elmbrook school district voluntarily
participated thereafter. However, as the fieldwork began, declining resident enrollment, decreased state aid, and declining property tax authority
prompted the school board to reconsider its participation. In a challenging
fiscal climate, Chapter 220 appeared as a tempting target for elimination,
especially since the Chapter 220 families resided outside the district. In fall
2009, the school board voted to open fifteen new seats to Chapter 220 students, but it restricted these seats to siblings of currently enrolled Chapter
220 students. In fall 2010, following an intensive yearlong study of district
enrollment trends, the school board voted to open no new seats to Chapter
220 students.[11] Expressing commitments to currently enrolled Chapter 220
students, board members supported a policy of ending the district's participation in the program through attrition and graduation of current students.

In this chapter, I analyze ten board and committee meetings—four in
the fall of 2009 and six in the fall of 2010—during which board members, administrators, and a few parents deliberated about the advantages
and disadvantages of participating in Chapter 220. Participants appreciated
potential conflicts between what they saw as the benefits of Chapter 220
for all Elmbrook students and the financial costs associated with the program. However, failing to balance these concerns, they permitted expertise
to trump engagement. Working with community members, board members developed highly sophisticated models of the financial implications of
Chapter 220 and other issues affecting the district. These models suggested
an impartial mode of decision-making that assigned weight to—and thus
reconciled—potentially competing values. In controlling for these values,
their models supposedly removed potentially contentious values from their
deliberations. In contrast, the board bluntly and clumsily judged the worth
of Chapter 220 and the integration it fostered, referring to the "social" side
of the debate—in contrast to the finances—as "soft" and anecdotal. Resisting measurement, the programmatic and social benefits of Chapter 220
found voice almost exclusively in the testimony of a few parents of children
from Milwaukee participating in the program. Their testimony appeared as
emotional and personal—value-based but lacking the knowledge produced
by the financial models. Parents could testify only to their children's experiences; they could not articulate the democratic knowledge and competencies

carried in wider practices of perspective-taking that Chapter 220 may have fostered for everyone. In these ways, board members perpetuated a fact-value dichotomy that belied the integrated judgments made through their deliberations about Chapter 220.

I begin this chapter by explicating how school boards challenge distinctions of public and technical roles among interlocutors in deliberation, encouraging scholars to conceptualize public and technical as perspectives rather than people or places. I then discuss briefly the district culture in Elmbrook and the history of the Chapter 220 program. In my analysis of deliberations about Chapter 220, I consider the 2009 and 2010 meetings chronologically, since important differences in the board's treatment of Chapter 220 emerged in these two years. For 2009, I begin by analyzing how board members, administrators, and others treated the development of a new financial forecasting tool that ostensibly revealed—for the very first time—the true financial costs of Chapter 220. While interlocutors could now consider financial items precisely, they struggled to articulate the educational benefits of Chapter 220, leaving most of this task to the parents of Chapter 220 students. In 2010, board members received the report of a study team recommending the effective elimination of Chapter 220. Accepting the larger financial analyses of this team, a majority of board members objected to this particular recommendation by representing Chapter 220 students as adopted children. While defending current students, they sustained a divide between expertise and engagement.

Expertise in Deliberation

In calling for balance between and within expertise and engagement, I recognize that expertise may serve an important function in deliberation, but I maintain that it functions as one perspective among others. Neither irrelevant nor imperialist, expertise calls on interlocutors to make judgments about various claims and evidence advanced by participants in deliberation.[12] Expertise does not merit special treatment, but, like any perspective presented in deliberation, it warrants appropriate treatment that enables judgment through commensurate norms and practices. Conceptualizing expertise as a perspective better accounts for the complex character of school-board deliberations, which address both technical and public issues, than do approaches that locate expertise in particular people or places of deliberation.

In rhetorical and communication scholarship, Thomas Goodnight's 1982 essay on the personal, technical, and public spheres of argument stands as an influential account of the nature of technical and public deliberation and the relationship between the two. Refusing to limit knowledge production to the technical sphere, Goodnight locates knowledge across all three spheres in conceptualizing deliberation as "a form of argumentation through which citizens test and create social knowledge in order to uncover, assess, and re-solve shared problems."[13] By associating knowledge with deliberation gener-ally rather than restricting it to one mode of deliberation, Goodnight implies a balance in each sphere between knowledge production and other qualities of deliberation, which serve as the basis of distinguishing these spheres. He defines spheres as "branches of activity—the grounds upon which argu-ments are built and the authorities to which arguers appeal."[14] This defini-tion highlights the "grounds" and "authorities" of argument. Grounds refer to the implicit and explicit norms and practices that structure arguments. Authorities refer to individuals whom advocates may invoke to substantiate claims and audiences who judge the reasonableness of arguments. Norms and practices provide the value-based complement to knowledge production in the conduct of deliberation. These dimensions converge in the people— advocates, authorizing individuals, and judging audiences—who participate in various modes of deliberation.

In the technical sphere, participants acting as experts deliberate accord-ing to explicitly and implicitly established rules and procedures. For ex-ample, education researchers trained in the social sciences concur that a well-established sample may be used to study a population. In important respects, deliberation in technical fields depends on this background agree-ment—without consensus about what constitutes a representative sample, for instance, education researchers would lose confidence in the findings of many studies. Goodnight writes that in the technical sphere "more lim-ited rules of evidence, presentation, and judgment are stipulated in order to identify arguers of the field and facilitate the pursuit of their interests."[15] These stipulations suggest that the technical sphere invokes a comparatively homogeneous audience. Since its members share background knowledge, a more homogeneous audience permits advocates to utilize more specialized forms of evidence.

Public deliberation proceeds as an encounter among interlocutors who judge proposals and perspectives for what they regard as issues of common concern, thereby promising access (direct or mediated) to everyone who discerns themselves as implicated in debates over public issues. Goodnight explains that deliberation in the public sphere "extend[s] the stakes of argument beyond private needs and the needs of special communities to the interests of the entire community."[16] With extension comes the increased possibility for conflict. Any community—if we understand community in the Deweyan sense of democratic association and not as a grouping of like-minded people—may consist of people with different values and beliefs who draw on different grounds and appeal to different audiences.[17] In this way, public deliberation engages heterogeneous audiences and invokes potentially competing standards for judgment.

While Goodnight views relationships among spheres in fluid terms, his conceptualization of sphere itself situates technical and public deliberation as distinct activities. On fluidity, Goodnight holds that "any particular argumentative artifact *can be taken* to be grounded in any one of the spheres or a combinatory relationship."[18] A specific topic (whether school finances or integration) does not reside inherently in one sphere, nor must particular interlocutors (whether board members or parents) restrict their participation to a specific sphere. Yet Goodnight's definition suggests that these fluidly related spheres maintain some degree of independence, insofar as he defines "sphere" as a "branch of activity," which implies a subdivision or separation among spheres. If all three spheres enable deliberation, then as branches each sphere emphasizes particular qualities or types of deliberation over others. This framework facilitates analysis of some relationships between technical and public deliberation. For instance, academic researchers assembled at a conference may deliberate about the significance of unequal educational opportunities differently than neighbors gathered at a public meeting. However, as I explain below, technical and public roles converge for school-board members.

In the years since the publication of Goodnight's essay, scholars have devoted considerable attention to analyzing interactions between technical and public spheres. While Goodnight expressed concern over the encroachment of technical reasoning in the public sphere, others have examined instances where public pressure has improperly influenced deliberation in technical spheres. Charles Taylor casts this influence in material terms: authoritative public bodies, including policymakers and agency administrators, make funding decisions that shape the outcomes of debates among technical experts.[19] For example, legislators may favor particular forms of student assessment not because these best measure learning, but because they comport with ideological inclinations. Analyzing deliberations preceding the 1986 space shuttle *Challenger* disaster—in which the *Challenger* exploded one minute after liftoff in a nationally televised launch, killing its seven-person crew—Robert Rowland argues that the disaster "should not be blamed primarily on a failure of technical reason or on a usurpation of the proper role of the public sphere by technicians." Instead, Rowland counters, "the *Challenger* accident occurred, because the experts allowed [NASA] managers, who both represented and felt pressure from the public, to make decisions that were outside of their expertise."[20] Rather than basing their decisions on judgments about safety and viability, the managers relied on alternative grounds, namely, maintaining public support for the shuttle program.

A more hopeful possibility may emerge from considering cases where citizens have developed the knowledge and competencies to engage with expert judgment. In this spirit, several public sphere scholars have turned to the efforts of activists challenging existing procedures for developing HIV/AIDS drugs and treatments that defer too strongly to concerns with insular procedures while ignoring or downplaying the exigencies associated with a public health crisis. Dale Brashers and Sally Jackson have examined how in the late 1980s the AIDS Coalition to Unleash Power (ACT UP) engaged with medical researchers to consider alternatives to drug protocols like phased testing, double-blind designs, and restrictive eligibility criteria.[21] ACT UP's participation in the technical sphere of medical research fostered greater balance within this realm. In a complementary study, Valeria Fabj and Matthew Sobnosky explore how AIDS activists have articulated their authority to bridge technical and public spheres.[22] As the cases of the *Challenger* disaster and AIDS activism suggest, public engagement in the technical sphere may weaken or bolster decision-making—but the technical sphere cannot be fortified against public engagement.

These cases suggest, too, the revisable relationship of public and technical, which scholars have cast as "contestation," "fusion," "interdependence," "transcendence," and more.[23] Drawing and redrawing distinctions themselves may constitute a key aspect of deliberation as advocates argue for particular distinctions of public and technical spheres against prevalent and/or competing distinctions. Analyzing a controversy over charges of fraud in breast cancer research, Lisa Keränen explores how different scientists, physicians, patients, policymakers, and others mapped the boundaries of the technical and public spheres differently. These maps carried implications for the composition and conduct of deliberation, serving as "primary argumentative resources through which stakeholders attempt to expand or limit participation of other players or modes of reasoning."[24] Yet "stakeholder" itself constitutes a contested term, and different renderings of public and technical may expand or limit the individuals and groups cast as stakeholders. Further, as Keränen suggests, interlocutors always draw these resources from somewhere (as opposed to beginning with a tabula rasa), and their background and social location informs their maps. Particular maps may appear as more ethical and/or efficacious than others, but none may appear as natural or inevitable.

Recognizing varied relations between technical and public spheres does not fully capture an important aspect of school-board deliberations: the convergence of expertise and engagement in the same person, the school-board member. Just as Goodnight's initial formulation conceived of public and technical as different activities, subsequent reformulations tend to retain distinctions of people and places even as they highlight intersections and overlaps among, say, medical researchers and activists or engineers and managers. In contrast to their federal and state counterparts, school-board members serve as "citizen-policymakers."[25] Board members do not have dedicated staffs who may research various issues and prepare policy briefs and hearing questions. District staff prepare background materials and make recommendations for board members, but they do not work at the behest of board members. Indeed, district staff do not necessarily share the goals and interests of board members. Moreover, board members do not limit themselves to the information provided by staff, nor do they follow staff recommendations unfailingly.[26] Paid a nominal sum for their service, board members often must balance their duties with full-time employment and/or familial responsibilities. While federal and state policymakers meet in a capital, school-board members legislate in their communities. School-board members must make expert and lay judgments on the issues they consider.

For school boards, technical/expertise and public/engagement may refer less to people, places, or activities, and more to different perspectives that board members may adopt in their deliberations. These different perspectives invite board members to consider the issues they address in different ways, to incorporate multiple types of evidence and reasoning, to utilize varying standards for judgment. Shifting to perspective enables a refocus on how expertise and engagement may serve as complementary perspectives facilitating judgment. Along these lines, Zoltan Majdik and William Keith articulate a conception of expertise in democratic deliberation as "an orientation to a particular problem." Drawing on the Aristotelian concept of phronesis, they define expertise as an ability to discover information relevant to a problem and to "engage in an argument that puts the available information and values in dialogue with other values, norms, and information, potentially revising one's judgment."[27] Majdik and Keith appreciate the contributions of expertise while denying its cultural authority as a trump card against other perspectives. Along these lines, Mark Brown explains that laypeople often are defined as lacking relevant knowledge or experience, thereby appearing in contrast to the expert. Yet equating lay with lack ignores a wide range of differences among people in terms of knowledge and experience, and it obscures the transformative power of deliberation, which holds the potential to increase interlocutors' knowledge and understanding of an issue. Resonating with my argument in this section, Brown calls for an "integrat[ion] of lay and expert perspectives in deliberative forums."[28]

Both expertise and engagement may produce evidence and insights for deliberation. However, conceptualizing expertise as a perspective does not relativize expertise. Recognizing that different perspectives may inform deliberation does not mean that all perspectives are equal or that interlocutors cannot evaluate perspectives. Yet evaluation should occur through deliberation, rather than as an authority granted outside of deliberation that dampens engagement. My turn to perspective and call for balance represent an effort to account for tensions between expertise and engagement confronted by school-board members as citizen-policymakers, who, in comparison to state and national legislators, have fewer opportunities to delegate these responsibilities.

Integration, District Culture, and a Difficult History

The members of the Elmbrook school board pride themselves on what they regard as their thorough and productive processes of decision-making, but the district's participation in the Chapter 220 program invokes the messy and controversial history of segregation and failed efforts at integration in the Milwaukee Public Schools and between the city and its suburbs. In an era of educational policy that prizes standards and testing, Elmbrook excels while Milwaukee struggles. Not coincidentally, the districts serve two different student populations. Established in the 1970s, Chapter 220 initially appeared as a voluntary effort to achieve modest integration and greater relations between Milwaukee and neighboring suburbs, but the rise of accountability has facilitated the fall of integration as an educational policy goal. Resisting quantifiable criteria, the issue of integration created challenges for Elmbrook's preferred modes of decision-making. To establish a context for my analysis, in this section I consider the culture of the Elmbrook school district, the history of the Chapter 220 program, and the backgrounds of board members and key administrators.

Success describes the self-image of the Elmbrook school district. Serving the upper-middle-class suburbs west of Milwaukee, the district celebrates its high student test scores and many accolades. Its annual report—a vibrant, glossy document mailed to homes in the district—highlights honors such as the district's two high schools' regular placement in *Newsweek*'s list of the top high schools in the United States and *Forbes* naming the district as one of its "Best Schools for Your Housing Buck."[29] And test scores—always test scores—appear prominently. Students' scores on the Wisconsin Knowledge and Concepts Examination (WKCE)—the standard state measure for evaluating student achievement in reading, language arts, math, science, and social studies—placed the district among the top performers in the region and the state. For the 2009–10 and 2010–11 academic years, roughly 93 percent of all Elmbrook students received "proficient" and "advanced" scores on the WKCE exams. With respect to the higher designation, roughly 65 percent of Elmbrook students received advanced scores on their WKCE exams. In contrast, for the same period, roughly 58 percent of Milwaukee students received proficient and advanced scores, and only 17 percent of Milwaukee students received advanced scores on their exams. Nearly four times as many Elmbrook students than Milwaukee students received advanced scores on their exams. Further, Elmbrook boasted a four-year high-school graduation rate of over 95 percent, whereas Milwaukee reported a 62 percent four-year graduation rate.[30]

While achieving high marks on their standardized tests, Elmbrook students constituted a comparatively homogenous and privileged group. For the 2009–10 and 2010–11 academic years, a large majority of Elmbrook students—roughly 80 percent—were white, while roughly 5 percent of students were black, and 3 percent of students were Hispanic. On the other hand, Milwaukee comprised a majority-minority district of 56 percent black students, 23 percent Hispanic students, and only 15 percent white students.[31] In addition to these racial and ethnic differences, the districts diverged in terms of the socioeconomic status (SES) of the households they served. In its 2009–10 and 2010–11 annual reports, even in the midst of a national recession, Elmbrook prominently listed the average household income of district residents at roughly $94,000 annually, a figure that doubled the state average and nearly tripled the average household income in Milwaukee.[32]

These economic disparities produced disparities in the classroom. During the 2010–11 academic year, only 11 percent of Elmbrook students qualified for free and reduced lunch, while 83 percent of students in Milwaukee qualified for free and reduced lunch.[33] While the district understandably took pride in its academic successes, Elmbrook served a community that could devote significant resources to education both inside and outside the classroom.

The Elmbrook school board displayed a managerial tone in its approach to district policy. The board acted as an operational board, focusing on finances, staffing, and other concerns at the potential expense of its avowed mission of student learning. During the interviews with board members and administrators, which serve as the basis for my next chapter on trust, one board member justified this focus by sharing the adage of a former CFO at her workplace, who said that "mission is important, but without your margin, or your money, you have no mission."[34] This quote, too, intimated the professional background of many Elmbrook board members, who had worked in managerial positions or in medium-sized or larger organizations. Moreover, in both their meetings and in the interviews, board members affirmed the value of specialization. Board members saw themselves—and their colleagues affirmed this perception—as experts in particular areas like finances, human resources, curricula, and more. Board members thus relied on particular colleagues to help frame their deliberations on particular issues. And they exhibited a "hyper-organization" to their approach to issues, dividing their meeting agendas, for instance, into five-minute intervals.

The board drew extensively on quantifiable data and analysis in their decision-making. As one board member explained, "We're working toward making data-based decisions." Several of the board members described themselves as "data-driven." Data appeared as the means to the end of substantiated, efficacious decisions, and it signaled to the community and to wider audiences the seriousness of the board's approach. Data took shape as numbers and figures that board members could enter into spreadsheets and weights they could assign to criteria. From this vantage point, data-free decisions or, more realistically, decisions based on evidence that did not admit itself smoothly to reduction as aggregative, commensurable bits of information may have seemed idiosyncratic, capricious, or tendentious. Yet the school board was not unique in this regard, participating instead in what Carolyn Miller has described as a wider reliance in U.S. public policy on quantification as a prominent mode of decision-making. Miller holds that quantification "legitimizes expert judgment, . . . mak[ing] problems tractable and computable." As evidenced in the contemporary emphasis on standards and testing in educational policy, this approach foregrounds "measurement . . . presum[ing] that values and actions are not at stake."[35] Moreover, privileging particular types of data may frustrate interlocutors' ability to challenge prevailing, albeit often implicit, norms and values.[36] To call attention to this tendency in Elmbrook's deliberations and decision-making is not to question the motives of school-board members. To the contrary, they acted rationally and demonstrated agility in negotiating a policy environment that rewarded and punished districts on the basis of ostensibly commensurate data like test scores and accounting entries.

In 2009 and 2010, Elmbrook attempted to obtain a better understanding of the costs and value of its programming—including Chapter 220—through newly developed and refined decision-making models. In 2009, the district introduced a new enrollment management tool (EMT) utilizing an Excel-based spreadsheet that enabled the board to forecast the financial and enrollment implications of increasing, decreasing, and/or eliminating various programs. Board members treated this tool as a revelation that provided new and more precise information about the consequences of their decision-making. In 2010, the board commissioned an Enrollment Management Study Team (EMST) co-chaired by board president Tom Gehl and community member Shelly Botchek and consisting of seven additional community members, including Jim Hodgson, one of the lead developers of the EMT. Charged with proposing recommendations to alleviate the district's budget gap, the EMST imported a decision-making formula from the business world: Quality Function Deployment (QFD), a "matrix-driven, decision making tool" that scores various criteria and options for arriving at a particular outcome, in this case reducing the district's budget gap.[37] Beginning in January 2010, the EMST met almost weekly to address a budget gap that had arisen from declining residential enrollments and a tightened state budget. The deliberations and final report of the EMST, which the team presented to the board in July 2010, strongly influenced board deliberations. As I elucidate in my analysis, both the EMT and the EMST underscored the data-driven, quantitative perspective that informed board deliberations about the Chapter 220 program.

Created in 1975, the Chapter 220 program arose during a period of local and national turmoil over school desegregation. As the civil rights movement looked northward in the struggle for educational equality, communities sometimes resisted fiercely. In Boston, violence erupted over court-ordered busing. In a 1972 national address, President Nixon called for a congressional moratorium and a constitutional amendment to end the practice.[38] In Milwaukee, white residents directed verbal and physical abuse toward black activists and their white allies seeking to integrate the city's neighborhood schools. To the extent that busing occurred, black students bore the full responsibility for this practice, as the Milwaukee Public Schools implemented a policy of "intact" busing, sending entire classrooms of black students to underutilized schools in white neighborhoods to alleviate overcrowding in the city's black "inner core." Confined to separate classrooms and recesses, these black students could not interact with white students. The school district even bussed black students back to their home schools for lunch periods and returned them to their receiving schools for afternoon classes.[39] In 1976 and again in 1978 (after the U.S. Supreme Court remanded the case), U.S. District Judge John Reynolds ruled in favor of a lawsuit brought by the NAACP that Milwaukee had intentionally segregated its schools and classrooms.[40] As the city awaited these rulings, in 1975, Dennis Conta, a white Democrat from Milwaukee, proposed merging two Milwaukee high-school districts with two neighboring wealthy white districts to promote modest integration. Representative Conta's proposal fell four votes short of passage in the Assembly.[41] In a climate of proposals and counterproposals over desegregation, Democratic and Republican legislators worked together to craft Chapter 220 as a modest, voluntary effort toward integration.

Chapter 220 effectively allows minority students from Milwaukee to attend school in majority-white suburbs, and it permits white suburban students to attend school in Milwaukee.[42] The eligibility criteria specify that minority students from districts where minorities constitute 30 percent or more of the student population may attend school in districts where minorities constitute less than 30 percent of the population. On this same 30 percent basis, nonminority students may attend school in minority districts. Since the program's inception, movement from Milwaukee to the suburbs has been the more popularly traveled route. For the 2009–10 school year, 290 Milwaukee students attended Elmbrook schools through the Chapter 220 program, while only a dozen or so Elmbrook students attended school in Milwaukee.[43] Importantly, the law prescribes that Milwaukee provide transportation for city students attending school in the suburbs. This subsidized transportation is crucial for many of these students, whose families may not own cars or otherwise be able to provide transportation out of the city.

The state has incentivized participation by offering financial aid to participating districts. As the sending district, Milwaukee may count students who leave the district for the suburbs under its total student population, thereby maintaining existing levels of state aid and retaining its taxing authority. Receiving districts like Elmbrook are paid amounts equal to their net cost per pupil multiplied by the number of students attending schools in their districts. For the 2009–10 and 2010–11 academic years, Elmbrook schools enrolled roughly three hundred Chapter 220 students and the district received nearly $3.4 million each year in state aid.[44] State aid effectively reduced property taxes for homeowners in Elmbrook, since the district otherwise would have needed to collect this money through property taxes. However, since this state aid counts under a receiving district's revenue limit, it also reduces the ability of a district to generate revenue by the amount of aid it receives.[45] In effect, by participating in Chapter 220, the Elmbrook school district received a portion of its revenues from the state rather than from local taxpayers, but its overall revenues did not increase. Yet, as board members emphasized in their deliberations, the district still needed to spend money to educate Chapter 220 students.

Starting slowly in its first few years after implementation, participation in the Chapter 220 program increased after a lawsuit by the Milwaukee Public Schools board against its neighboring suburban districts. In the first five years of the program, roughly seven hundred Milwaukee students attended schools in the suburbs each year.[46] Moreover, suburban school boards gauging community sentiment about Chapter 220 discovered strong opposition. In one district, voters in an advisory referendum opposed participation by a three-to-one margin.[47] However, in 1984, alleging that suburban districts hampered efforts at interdistrict integration, the Milwaukee Public Schools board filed suit against several state officials and twenty-three suburban school districts, including Elmbrook. In 1987, the parties reached an agreement that required all of the suburban districts named in the suit to participate in Chapter 220.[48] The original agreement expired in June 1993, but the parties extended the agreement to June 1995. Since 1995, Elmbrook has participated voluntarily in the Chapter 220 program on a year-by-year basis. At the same time, across the region, the number of students that suburban districts have admitted into Chapter 220 has declined significantly from a peak in the mid-1990s. Between 1993–94 and 2007–8, the number of minority students participating in Chapter 220 decreased by 54 percent.[49]

As participation in Chapter 220 declined, suburban districts' interest in a new program arose. Beginning with the 1998–99 academic year, students across the state of Wisconsin could participate in an Open Enrollment program, which permitted students to attend school in any district of their choosing, so long as the receiving district had room and a student's parent or guardian complied with application procedures.[50] Passed in an era of choice and accountability, the Open Enrollment program presumably fostered competition among school districts to improve the quality of their education. Although both programs enabled choices for participants, Chapter 220 emphasized the equity principle of integration while Open Enrollment underscored the market principle of competition. Perhaps unsurprisingly, participants in Open Enrollment were less diverse than their Chapter 220 counterparts. In 2010, although white students constituted only 15 percent of the population in the Milwaukee Public Schools, they accounted for 65 percent of the district's Open Enrollment participants.[51] One commentator characterized the Open Enrollment program as "a new form of white flight."[52]

Less enthusiastic about Chapter 220, suburban districts have seen financial benefits to participating in Open Enrollment. The program pays receiving districts the statewide average cost of educating a student—around $6,500 in 2009–10 and 2010–11—for each Open Enrollment student in their district.[53] Unlike Chapter 220, which provides state aid effectively as tax relief, this money goes directly to the receiving district as new revenue. A *Milwaukee Journal-Sentinel* article noting the shift among suburban districts from Chapter 220 to Open Enrollment quoted Elmbrook Superintendent Matt Gibson, who explained his district's move away from Chapter 220 as "largely financially related."[54] However, unlike Chapter 220, Open Enrollment does not provide transportation for participating students. Instead, participants' families carry the responsibility for transporting their children to the receiving school they wish to attend. Barbara Miner contends that the lack of transportation belies the allegedly "color-blind" character of Open Enrollment. She counters that "in practice it privileged those with more money—an issue closely correlated with race in Milwaukee."[55] The Elmbrook school board considered the issue of transportation in its deliberations over Chapter 220, but, as Gibson's comment suggests, it focused largely on the costs of the program and the potential financial benefits of increasing its population of Open Enrollment students.

During the period of fieldwork, the Elmbrook school board consisted of Tom Gehl (president), Meg Wartman (vice president), Glen Allgaier (treasurer), Bob Ziegler, Jean Lambert, Gary Jones, Dave Marcello (2009–10 academic year), and Kathryn Wilson (2010–11 academic year). All but two of these board members had children who were currently enrolled or had graduated from the district. A retiree, Glen Allgaier provided the most extensive financial analyses of Chapter 220 and other district programs, often offering his own data and assessments alongside the analyses of district staff. Other board members respected Allgaier, but they did not defer to him, instead advancing their own (sometimes contrary) positions on Chapter 220. Of these, Lambert presented the strongest case for discontinuing Elmbrook's participation in Chapter 220, while Ziegler advocated the strongest case for continuing to open new seats in the program. However, clear factions in support of or against Chapter 220 did not emerge over the course of the board's deliberations. On October 26, 2010, with Ziegler voting no, the board voted to open no new seats in the Chapter 220 program.

Superintendent Matt Gibson played a key role in deliberations over Chapter 220. By the end of the fieldwork, Gibson, who retired in June 2012, had served sixteen years as Elmbrook superintendent—a remarkable record of continuity for a position that typically experiences high turnover. Gibson served as superintendent ten years longer than the most senior board member, Tom Gehl, held office. Gibson explicitly cultivated the role of a diplomat, avoiding confrontations and seeking to maintain good relations among board members and between the board and the administration. He expressed views on Chapter 220 and other district issues, but did so in a manner that recognized the views of others, even in disagreement. Gibson also displayed political savvy. When it became clear in fall 2010 that the board would not open up any new seats in Chapter 220, Gibson voiced support for the move despite his long-standing support of the program. Among other administrators, Assistant Superintendent Christine Hedstrom presented staff recommendations regarding the enrollment in Chapter 220, while Assistant Superintendent Keith Brightman outlined the program's financial implications.

A New Tool but No New Resources

At an October 2009 meeting of board members, administrators, and parents of children enrolled in Elmbrook's Chapter 220 program, Superintendent Matt Gibson outlined the issues the district needed to consider in reaching a decision about the number of new Chapter 220 seats to open for the following school year. In a series of meetings that month, the school board needed to negotiate the "educational experience piece" of the program as well as the "financial analysis piece." Gibson explained that these pieces did not fit together neatly into a coherent whole. Instead, decreasing resident enrollments and an increasing budget gap portended difficult choices between the educational value and the financial costs of Chapter 220. Gibson explained that "I find myself wanting to advocate for more Chapter 220 students, because I like what it does for your students [Milwaukee residents] and what it does for the resident students." However, Gibson indicated that resources curbed his desire: "When finances get really tight within the school district, which is occurring, then that [benefit] comes at a greater cost."[56] This dilemma characterized the board's deliberations over Chapter 220 in 2009, but the horns of this dilemma did not receive equal treatment. The district developed a new Enrollment Management Tool (EMT) to guide its judgments about the financial aspects of Chapter 220, but the board struggled with assessing its educational value, leaving most of this work to the testimony of parents of children enrolled in the program.

Board members and administrators associated the EMT with scientific rigor and precision, envisioning a process of testing, refinement, retesting, and confirmation that would produce unassailable results. During an October 13, 2009, school-board meeting, Assistant Superintendent Keith Brightman introduced the EMT to board members, noting that the tool was still in the "beta" phase (i.e., under final development), but that the final version would produce thorough and accurate results. Brightman explained that the development team—which consisted of himself and three community members, one Chartered Financial Analyst (CFA) and two Certified Public Accountants (CPAs)—"has been upgrading and improving the model" since he first mentioned the EMT during a previous board work session. Brightman indicated that the team had planned a "very thorough analysis," and he believed that the EMT would serve as a "valuable tool for decision-making."[57] Brightman's language encouraged the board to see the EMT as moving toward a state of completion, whereby it would present authoritative analyses. The idea of a "beta" version indicated a period of eliminating any "bugs" in the EMT. Once the development team finished its testing, which Brightman asserted would occur in time for the board to determine the number of open seats for Chapter 220, any errors in the EMT would be discovered and eliminated. Brightman and others spoke of the EMT as a researcher might speak of a quantitative instrument; in both cases, the final tool promised its users high degrees of reliability and validity.[58]

Moving beyond the vision of a tool that board members could use for their decision-making, interlocutors anthropomorphized the tool, intimating that the EMT offered its own judgments. During one meeting, Jim Hodgson, a CFA and member of the development team, wavered between attributing judgment to the EMT and the board. He held that "the whole premise of the model is to be able to, um, articulate what is the incremental impact of certain decisions." In this statement, while Hodgson ascribed decision-making to the board, he gave voice to the EMT, which articulated implications.[59] At another moment, he cast the EMT as a decision-maker. He encouraged board members to imagine "scenarios" and suggest them to the EMT: "We probably can just punch it up there just as we sit here."[60] The EMT would articulate how the scenario unfolded. In this way, the EMT mirrored Hodgson's professional role as an investment adviser. Just as Hodgson used his judgment to help clients achieve their financial goals, the EMT could help the district achieve its goals. In both cases, the clients imagined their future, while the adviser showed them the path to reach it. Identifying an attribute that one might look for in a personal financial adviser, Keith Brightman depicted the EMT as "really kind of well-rounded, and it looks at all sorts of programs for us."[61] Acting as one interlocutor among many, the EMT did not trump the school board's decision-making. However, the EMT acted as an especially persuasive interlocutor, emphasizing financial criteria for decision-making and pushing the board in a particular direction.

With the development of the EMT, school-board members brimmed with confidence about the insights and information it provided on Chapter 220. Board president Tom Gehl asserted that "in my four and a half years on the board . . . I'm certain that we've never had more information with which to make this decision." He admitted that the educational benefits of Chapter 220 did not submit to quantification, but "that portion of which can be quantified, I think, it's been done as well as it can be."[62] Likewise, Glen Allgaier, whom other board members perceived as deeply knowledgeable about district finances, maintained that the board had "learned a lot in the past couple of years about the cost of 220 students." In the past, Allgaier believed, Chapter 220 students "were filling empty seats at no cost to the district." The board had begun its investigation of actual costs a year ago: "This year, with a much more sophisticated model, we understand [the cost]."[63] These statements resonated with a spirit of scientific discovery, which also manifests in a long-standing belief among researchers that better information produces better policy.[64]

In the past, when board members made decisions about Chapter 220, they did so in good faith but with bad information. In this manner, they unwittingly worsened the fiscal health of the district. Now, their new interlocutor EMT helped board members better understand the issues they confronted. The EMT brought clarity to the school board's decision-making.

In a period of increasing austerity, any decision about educational programs and services occurred in an "either/or" climate: since the district could not levy additional taxes, funding one program meant withholding or removing funds from another program. Voicing a theme that would grow in urgency over the course of the fieldwork, Meg Wartman held that the district's participation in Chapter 220 meant that "we're going to have to cut things." The board's analyses left no doubt: "There is no ifs, ands, or buts about it that the Chapter 220 program because of financing costs us money."[65] Money materialized the stakes of a decision to continue participating—the board could not pay lip service to the educational value of Chapter 220. If the district really believed in the program, as the saying goes, it had to put its money where its mouth was.

Paying for the program raised a potentially divisive issue, one that invoked the messy racial history of relations between the city and the suburbs: commitments to "resident" students versus commitments to "nonresident" students. Interlocutors did not explicitly cite the demographics of these two groups, but the purposes of Chapter 220 made clear the racial politics of this distinction. The board could either support white suburban children or spend their money on black city children. In this spirit, Glen Allgaier urged his colleagues to consider the implications of funding Chapter 220 on resident students. He asserted that the money spent on the program could have been dedicated to hiring more teachers: "There is less to support that our, that our resident students are getting as a consequence of that." On this basis, he counseled his colleagues "to consciously decide what educational benefits we're willing to concede for our resident students in order to have the benefits of integration." While Allgaier and others raised this issue in 2009, their concerns remained somewhat muted. Yet this putative choice magnified as the board voted to open no new seats in 2010.

The EMT also shed light on the differences between the two nonresident programs in which the district participated: Chapter 220 and Open Enrollment. While Chapter 220 appeared as a financial loser, Open Enrollment emerged as a potential moneymaker. This is because unlike Chapter 220, which offered financial benefits to taxpayers, Open Enrollment generated additional revenues directly for the district. Keith Brightman and other members of the EMT development team reiterated this point during multiple meetings: "Open Enrollment is funded much differently. It's funded as additional revenue. There is no aid adjustment; it's actually additional revenue in the district." The EMT recognized this difference. Directing people to the EMT spreadsheets, Brightman observed that "if we were to look just at this, it would strongly suggest that we should increase Open Enrollment, decrease Chapter 220." However, while the EMT focused on finances, Brightman retorted that "we realize there's more to the program than just the financials."[66] Administrators and board members still wished to balance financial implications against the educational value of Chapter 220. In 2010, however, calls to turn nonresident seats into revenue-producing seats would become louder.

The Soft Side of Chapter 220

Board members and administrators believed that Chapter 220 held value for resident and nonresident students, but they had difficulty assessing this value. Expenditures and revenues lent themselves to easy measurement, arriving as prepackaged, commensurable units that board members could aggregate and analyze. The value of integration seemed more elusive. How many dollars should a board member ascribe to the experience of students from two comparatively homogeneous communities interacting with one another? Did these encounters equal the salary of a teacher? Differences in class size? How much would Elmbrook pay for a more diverse—albeit incrementally so—student population? While board members expressed confidence in their financial analyses, they appeared befuddled with the educational value of Chapter 220. Glen Allgaier conceded that one issue he had "wrestled with is the soft side of 220."[67] Although he had considered "the benefits of the 220 program, it's hard to measure them—the academic, the social."[68] Whereas Allgaier regarded the finances as a reason to reconsider the district's participation in Chapter 220, Bob Ziegler remained steadfast. Yet he conceded this frame for conceptualizing its educational benefits: "Yes, it's soft, Glen, but it's there."[69] Less precise than its financial counterpart, evidence for the educational benefits of Chapter 220 appeared less rigorous and the benefits (in turn) appeared less significant than the costs.

When board members and administrators addressed the benefits of Chapter 220, they typically referenced personal experiences or the experiences of family members. Allgaier himself recounted that he had two foster grandsons who transferred from the Milwaukee Public Schools to another suburban district, "and I saw, and this is anecdotal obviously, but I saw just enormous changes in their lives by being exposed to that environment."[70] As an anecdote, the experience of his foster grandchildren held limited explanatory power. Allgaier saw Chapter 220 as "a very good thing" for Milwaukee children, but he did not extend his observation to the entire student population. He questioned the "added value" for children living in Elmbrook—perhaps because he lacked the direct observation he experienced with his foster grandsons. Speaking to the experiences of Elmbrook students, Tom Gehl concurred that the "benefits to our students, I agree, are softer. They're hard to measure, uh, but I think they're there." Gehl based this observation on the experiences of his own two children, although he declined to share their experiences: "I won't go into that."[71] Unlike Allgaier, Gehl offered a more general claim about the benefits of Chapter 220, but he based this on his children's experience, which others may have regarded as anecdotal. Moreover, his unwillingness to elucidate their experiences may have weakened the force of this evidence for his claim.

Identifying a substantive benefit to Chapter 220, Bob Ziegler emphasized the importance of preparing students for diverse workplaces, which he regarded as the typical experiences of many adults. He held that district students would benefit from developing an "openness to working with people of different backgrounds and cultures," and contrasted this promise with his own experiences growing up in an area where "there were far fewer minorities." Ziegler had since acquired experiences in diverse settings, but he suggested that "quite honestly if I would have been thrown into an environment where I would be working with people of different backgrounds and cultures from my own, it would have been far more difficult for, for me."[72] Referencing the contemporary workplace, Ziegler went further than did his two colleagues in advancing a general claim about the benefits of Chapter 220, but he, too, based this on his own experiences. No board member or administrator offered a systematic assessment of the experiences of students (resident and nonresident) in the district. In the decision-making culture of Elmbrook, which favored clear, systematic, and aggregate evidence, these seemingly disparate accounts provided a comparatively shaky evidentiary basis for the educational benefits of Chapter 220.

Board members and administrators left the primary task of articulating the educational benefits of Chapter 220 to the parents of children participating in the program. Each year, by statute, districts participating in Chapter 220 must hold a planning council meeting of administrators, board members, and parents of participating children. Matt Gibson invited parents to "speak to the benefit of the Chapter 220 program from your experience as a parent and from what your students tell you about it. Speak about the educational pieces and any other pieces you'd like to."[73] Gibson's invitation framed the parents' testimony as personal and expressive. His references to "your experience as a parent" and "your students" confined the parents' perspectives to their families. They could address experiences of people in their homes, but Gibson did not invite them to address a broader parental perspective, or the benefits to the entire student body, or the societal implications of diversity and education. Parents offered a personal contribution to deliberation. Further, even though Gibson invited parents to speak about any "piece" they wished, he indicated that the finances already had been analyzed and the district would not open a large number of new seats. Issuing an open invitation in this context—"any other pieces you'd like to"—appeared less as a means for the district to glean new insights and more as an opportunity for parents to express pent-up concerns. Presumably, parents would feel better after voicing their concerns.

In this context, parents acknowledged their children's good fortune in escaping the Milwaukee Public Schools. Arris Martin recounted how, after she had moved from Racine, Wisconsin, to Milwaukee, she began hearing "horror stories" about the city's public schools. Participating in Chapter 220 enabled her daughter to avoid the "negative aspects of the school classroom." Martin maintained that in Milwaukee teachers needed to "babysit" students—"as opposed to being a teacher, uh, being more of a person who has to essentially child sit and make sure that the students are not acting up."[74] Without disciplinary distractions, teachers and students in Elmbrook concentrated on academics. Sam Jackoyo blamed parents in Milwaukee. In Elmbrook, he observed, "there's just too much parent involvement here . . . [to] let anything go wrong."[75] In comparison, he implied that Milwaukee parents did not exhibit an interest in their children's education—they never volunteered and they skipped open houses. These comments suggested that a transfer to Elmbrook enacted a cultural change as much as an educational one. By enrolling their children in the Chapter 220 program, these parents demonstrated their involvement. Yet other parent testimony intimated the material differences between Elmbrook and Milwaukee. Tamara Ellis explained that her children "benefited from the music programs that they offer here, and, which is something that in MPS and many schools are cutting out music programs. They don't have them anymore."[76] Resources, not good behavior or parental involvement—which themselves may be facilitated by well-paying, steady jobs that provide parents the time and energy to focus on their children's education—explained the differences between the city and the suburbs.

The enrollment of Milwaukee students in Elmbrook schools cast participants as charity cases and the district as a benevolent actor practicing social work to aid the less fortunate. For instance, Tamara Ellis recounted how her youngest daughter struggled when she entered the Elmbrook schools. Instead of ignoring the issue, the district responded by sending Ellis a letter indicating that, if she agreed, her daughter could be removed from her regular courses for special instruction for portions of the school day: "It wasn't something that I was left trying to figure out, you know, with her homework coming home and saying, oh, she's struggling, she's having a hard time, and then I have to deal with the teacher and what's going on, my daughter's not doing well."[77] While Ellis expressed gratitude, her sentiment did not arise from a sense of helplessness that undermined her agency. Rather, Ellis thanked the district for its responsiveness, which meant that she did not need to convince the teacher that her daughter would benefit from individualized instruction, nor did she need to fight for the district to provide this instruction. Her gratitude did not compromise her ability to act as an agent for her daughter. Likewise, the district did not treat Ellis and her daughter as a charity case simply by proactively identifying and responding to a situation warranting individualized instruction. To the contrary, the district earned Ellis's gratitude.

Rather, the framing of this case (and others) as charity and the district's efforts as social work arose from the role played by the parents' testimony in this meeting: they could present illuminating cases and raise possible concerns, but the school board and administration did not treat the parents as equal interlocutors. Tom Gehl thanked every parent after they spoke, but neither he nor any other board member or administrator—save for one instance—engaged the issues raised in the parents' testimony, like, for example, Ellis's reference to the challenge faced by any parent in negotiating school institutions. The district may have responded in this case, but Ellis's experience invited more general reflection about how well the district responded to students' needs. The one exception in Elmbrook occurred when, in response to Sam Jackoyo's observation about varying levels of parental involvement in the city and suburbs, David Marcello asked Jackoyo, "How can we better support, you know, the assistance that we have in place?"[78] This question reinforced the respective roles of the district as provider and the Chapter 220 family as recipient. A similar dynamic informed the district's preference for opening seats for younger students. Glen Allgaier voiced the sentiment of the board when he stated that "the earlier we get them the better . . . because that's when we have the best chance to help the student."[79] While the district tried to "help" city students, it could not guarantee success. City students grew up in an environment rife with alluring distractions and vice.

This environment harmed the people who lived there—sometimes irreparably. If a child spent too much time in the city, their afflictions threatened to assume a permanent character and the chances of remediation faded.

Sometimes, despite the framing of their testimony as personal, parents spoke to the wider benefits of diversity for society. Identifying herself as a "product of 220," Qiana Collins noted that "it's been a fabulous experience for both of my girls." Yet she did not limit these benefits to her children. Collins held that Chapter 220 offered benefits "not just for the minority children that are coming into the district, but also . . . the community that they're touching."[80] The program transformed communities, fostering learning for everyone. Along these lines, Nicole Edwards maintained that children in Elmbrook "who are not exposed to minorities don't reap the benefits of learning new things." Elucidating a "lack of knowledge between people," Edwards mentioned her daughter, who "goes to school and she talks about having hair grease." To this reference to hair-care products, white students queried, "You put Crisco in your hair?" In Edwards's telling, the struggling students in need of individualized instruction were not city children but suburban children—"white, upper mid-, upper middle class"— who knew little about the world outside their daily activities. In these types of statements, Edwards and other parents reversed the relations of charity and social work that ostensibly informed the meeting and the Chapter 220 program. White children learned as much from the program as minority children. And they acquired necessary knowledge that prepared them "to work with people of different backgrounds."[81] Elmbrook readied its students to score well on tests, but by itself the district could not provide resident students with the instruction they needed to succeed after graduation.

While parents expressed their good fortune in placing their children in an attentive and resource-rich environment, board members and administrators reiterated their commitment to currently enrolled Chapter 220 students and, when possible, their siblings. As she initiated the fall 2009 Chapter 220 deliberations during an October 13 meeting, Assistant Superintendent Christine Hedstrom articulated the "values that the board has held with the Chapter 220 program, specifically we've committed to the current Chapter 220 students that if you come to Elmbrook schools, that you will stay in Elmbrook schools through graduation."[82] Tom Gehl emphasized this commitment at this meeting and others, stating that "whatever the board decides two weeks from tonight with respect to the number of 220 students either to admit or not to admit, it does not affect existing 220 students currently enrolled in our district. That's just really critical for all parties to understand."[83]

This statement evidenced the genuine sense of responsibility that the board and administration expressed toward the Chapter 220 students. Had the district not felt a commitment to these students, it would have pushed them out of the district at the earliest opportunity in their transition years from elementary to middle school or from middle to high school, which the statute permits. At the same time, this commitment to graduation stood as a moral obligation, not a legal requirement or a financial calculation. It displayed a sense of judgment not recognized by the EMT.

A desire to open new seats to siblings of currently enrolled students held the same moral standing in the eyes of board members and administrators. Matt Gibson emphasized that the "top administrative priority would be for siblings, so the families could stay together."[84] Even as most board members raised concerns about the cost of the program, they nevertheless agreed with this priority. Meg Wartman reminded colleagues that "putting money into the Chapter 220 program [means] taking it away from something else." Yet she still supported the decision because "it's worth doing it to make sure our siblings are there."[85] Wartman's reference to "our" indicated the feeling of stewardship that board members held for Chapter 220 students. This feeling supported opening up new seats for siblings even as the EMT spreadsheets cautioned against such a move. Undecided about how to proceed, Glen Allgaier acknowledged that "it feels good" to offer seats to siblings.[86] David Marcello asserted that he did not support Chapter 220 over the "long term," since he did not believe that "we're getting as big a bang for the bucks." Marcello preferred more market-based approaches like vouchers or charter schools. Yet he admitted that "I do have a soft spot in my heart for keeping families together."[87] This soft decision to open seats for siblings corresponded to what board members perceived as the soft evidence for the educational benefits of the program. The value of charitable volunteering for the volunteer lay not in financial compensation but in a feeling of doing good deeds.

A New Study, a New Report, No New Seats

In January 2010, an Enrollment Management Study Team (EMST) started meeting in Elmbrook. Co-chaired by the board president and populated by volunteers from the community, the EMST sought to develop proposals for alleviating a budget gap that arose in Elmbrook as a consequence of declining resident enrollments, increasing costs, and state budget cuts. As part of its recommendations, the EMST proposed converting Chapter 220 seats to Open Enrollment, since the latter generated revenue for the district while the former cost money. The EMST report influenced the course of the board's Chapter 220 deliberations, as most of the board quickly adopted the position that the district should offer no new Chapter 220 seats for the following school year. At the same time, most board members strongly objected to the proposal to convert current nonresident students to Open Enrollment, since the absence of subsidized transportation with Open Enrollment threatened the continued participation of current Chapter 220 students. Most board members regarded these students as "our kids."

The EMST purported to act as a more comprehensive version of the EMT, addressing the "soft" side of education while the EMT restricted itself to financial spreadsheets. In this spirit, perhaps, the "S" in its acronym unwittingly included the soft side of educational policy. The claim to comprehensiveness arose from the EMST's use of a decision-making tool imported from the business world: Quality Function Deployment (QFD). QFD purportedly permitted EMST members to identify and weigh various criteria—financial and nonfinancial—and to assess how well particular proposals met these criteria. In its presentations to the school board, which began in July and continued over a series of summer meetings, the EMST identified its three primary criteria as financial results, student learning, and community impact. As they addressed these criteria, members of the EMST admitted that they had difficulty balancing financial and learning goals. Team member Meghan Olsen noted that the EMST weighed both financial results and student learning as a five on a five-point scale of importance. Yet the team struggled to operationalize the latter criterion. Olsen recounted that "we had a lot of discussion about this because we felt like the quality of educational programs and services didn't get enough, wasn't addressed well enough." While the means for assessing financial impacts presented themselves clearly, Olsen countered that "it's hard to address that [educational] criteria. It's very hard to put it all into one subject, into one category. But we gave it the most important weight that we could, which is a five."[88] After a period of extensive deliberation over criteria in the spring of 2010, the team grew comfortable with its decision-making.

For the most part, in both its written report and its presentations to the board, the EMST exhibited a measured approach, weighing and assessing various criteria and proposals. The EMST specified its variables, vetted the 2009 EMT, trained its members in its QFD decision-making tool, and presented detailed tables with specific and aggregate scoring and dollar figures for various options to reduce the budget gap. However, especially in its written report, when addressing the general financial forecast for the district, the EMST exhibited an alarmist tone. Unless the district aligned its expenditures with its revenues, any EMST proposal adopted by the board would provide only a temporary budget balance. Repeatedly, the report referred to rising costs in the district as the "reality" faced by the district—a "profound," "simple reality." It called on "all employees of the district . . . to recognize this reality." This section on costs and revenues, which constituted the longest section in the written report, warned of a "draconian impact" and "potentially draconian measures" if the board did not act forcefully to reduce expenditures—or, at the very least, slow their rate of increase.[89] The EMST identified employee salaries and benefits as the largest culprit by far in this explosion of expenditures, which in the winter and spring of 2011 would become entwined in a divisive statewide fight over union rights for public employees.[90] In the summer and fall of 2010, however, this exigence warranted the school board's rethinking of various programs.

Although the EMST considered its primary criteria with care, its focus on Chapter 220 did not emerge until later in its deliberations, after an initial round of proposals to reduce the budget gap appeared insufficient. Tom Gehl shared with his board colleagues that the EMST's proposal regarding Chapter 220 "was quite literally an eleventh-hour recommendation, and it was predicated on what mechanisms are there within our purview that could get us to close the entire $16 million gap. . . . It was either at the last meeting or the second to last meeting that it was put on the table."[91] While the EMST asserted in its written and oral reports that no long-term solution to the district's impending financial problems could be achieved without reducing expenditures, its turn to Chapter 220 resonated with the sense of alarm that informed its discussion of long-term forecasts. Discerning an exigence, the EMST sought a quick response, and initially believed that Chapter 220 would provide an immediate and easy target, since, unlike potentially contentious proposals like closing an elementary school or implementing four-year-old kindergarten, it did not generate substantial opposition from resident families. Gary Jones recounted how the EMST initially suggested the possibility of conversion to some board members: "When we first talked about [Chapter 220 conversion], it was, do it tomorrow—everybody the same day. Then you found out you couldn't do that."[92] Only after Chapter 220 appeared as a possible target did the EMST discover the statutory constraints on the program, which ensured students a seat until they completed their current level of schooling (i.e., elementary, middle, or high school).

As these recollections suggest, the EMST did not employ its three primary criteria when deliberating about its recommendation for Chapter 220—student learning and community fell by the wayside as financial results became the sole criterion. Tom Gehl recalled that "there was no discussion at the enrollment team as to whether [conversion of Chapter 220] was a good or a bad idea. It was simply a mechanism that allowed full closure of that $16 million gap. . . . I'm not suggesting that to be good or bad, I just want to remind board members where that recommendation came from."[93] Although Gehl expressed reservations about this proposal, other interlocutors envisioned multiple financial benefits from a conversion of Chapter 220 seats to Open Enrollment. Not only did the latter provide revenues inaccessible by the former, but Open Enrollment students ostensibly enabled more cost-efficient instruction. In one meeting, Pat Lacante, one of the developers of the EMT, engaged fellow EMT developer and EMST member Jim Hodgson about the added value of replacing Chapter 220 students—even if they shifted programs—with "true" Open Enrollment students: "If they did really truly become enrollment students, not the 220–Open Enrollment students, there would be a different number." Hodgson agreed that "it would be a bigger savings, potentially." The problem with Chapter 220 students, he explained, is that no matter what program they participated in, "Chapter 220 students actually make a greater use of certain resources than other groups." In business terms, he concluded, "their marginal cost to educate is higher than the average."[94]

In 2010, through the lens of the EMST, the very proactive response and provision of services for which Tamara Ellis offered her gratitude in 2009 became a significant reason for ending the district's participation in Chapter 220. Charity cases and social work may have made volunteers feel good about their deeds, but, according to the EMST, this work represented a luxury that the district could not afford in challenging financial circumstances; diversity did not balance ledgers. Importing a business-based decision-making tool in the district and pressured to close a budget gap, the EMST neglected the educational benefits of Chapter 220.

Our Kids versus Our Kids

Although the school board appreciated the work of the EMST and agreed with many of its recommendations, a majority of board members disagreed with the proposal to convert the seats of current Chapter 220 students to

Open Enrollment. In contrast to the EMST, which assessed these seats in terms of profit maximization, five board members regarded the Chapter 220 students as Elmbrook students, whom they felt an obligation to support through high school graduation. Conversion threatened this relationship, since Open Enrollment did not provide subsidized transportation and a large majority of Chapter 220 students could not transport themselves to Elmbrook. Glen Allgaier and Jean Lambert, along with community residents who spoke at board meetings, objected, insisting that the board's first obligation lay with resident students. They resisted the familial obligations expressed by the majority.

During a special board meeting on July 20, 2010, new board member Katie Wilson expressed in unequivocal terms the feeling of a majority of board members toward Chapter 220: "We've adopted those kids and they're ours, and we need to stick with them." Others echoed this sentiment. Bob Ziegler maintained that "we don't want to treat them as not our students. . . . As Katie said, we've adopted them." Wishing to "add my voice," Gary Jones asserted that "220 students are our students and we ought to keep them as we promised, for years and years."[95] For these board members, distinctions between resident students and Chapter 220 students faded once a child entered an Elmbrook school. Enrollment constituted a threshold, removing a child from the harmful environment of the city and placing the child in the uplifting arms of the district. Once children crossed this threshold, they shed their former identities, changing themselves through their presence in the classroom. Wilson's reference to adoption indicates that the board majority perceived this change in familial terms. They may not have given birth to the Chapter 220 children, but they brought these children into their family. Like siblings, resident students and Chapter 220 students played together. Reiterating that "they are our students," Meg Wartman recounted that the "families have been ingrained in our programs and friends of our children."[96] As parents, the school board could not love its adopted children less intently than its biological children, even if their adjustment into the family presented some challenges. In this way, Chapter 220 students played the role of the poor orphan saved from the ravages of the orphanage by a rich benefactor. A kind and generous soul, the benefactor saw the inner beauty in the orphan and provided a loving and nurturing home for the child's growth.

While families sometimes struggle to sustain loving bonds, the board majority promised that its commitment to its children would stand the test of time. The threat of conversion stemmed from Open Enrollment's failure to transport students to Elmbrook. Surveying Chapter 220 families to see if they could provide their own transportation under an Open Enrollment program, district staff learned that 72 percent of Chapter 220 students would be unable to continue their education in Elmbrook without subsidized transportation. Bob Ziegler reacted by saying that "if the 72 percent number were not so ridiculously high, um, I might be able to stomach eliminating Chapter 220." For Ziegler, the conversion proposal invited a physical response, but the survey results made this proposal indigestible. He retorted that "eliminating [Chapter 220] would disrupt way too many of our students."[97] Even if a conversion reserved seats for current students, it would change the conditions of participation for these students, which amounted to the district breaking its commitment, since many of these students would remain stranded in Milwaukee. Meg Wartman equated conversion with the district "all of a sudden . . . turn[ing] our backs on the students." She viewed this proposal as "going back on an implied promise."[98] Similarly, Tom Gehl believed that conversion "equates to pulling the rug out from underneath their feet."[99] Good parents did not abandon their adoptive children when a family's fortunes changed—the parental bond held strong.

However, as they represented current Chapter 220 students as adopted children, this board majority did not wish to expand their family. Unlike 2009, when the board voted to open up to fifteen new seats for siblings of current students, this majority saw the district's financial forecasts as worrisome enough to justify opening no new seats for siblings. Acknowledging the fiscal "reality" asserted by the EMST, the majority saw a decision to open no new seats as a compromise that maintained a commitment to current students while addressing budget concerns. Expressing his support for "opening no new seats," Tom Gehl characterized this position as a "middle ground."[100] Meg Wartman concurred. She perceived the cost implications of continuing the Chapter 220 program as unsustainable. Moreover, she held that "we don't have a lot of families, then, that I think we're affecting by this decision." Opening no new seats permitted the program to "slowly dwindle off."[101] A commitment to current Chapter 220 students, then, did not entail an ongoing commitment to the program's original purpose of integration. Rather, board members supported current students in personal terms.

These views countered the recommendation of Assistant Superintendent Christine Hedstrom to open up twelve new seats for siblings. Hedstrom stated that "the purpose is to keep families together."[102] She presented this recommendation in keeping with the recent practice of the board, which had initiated a small reduction in the overall percentage of nonresident students in the district but still tried to maintain open seats for siblings. However, in 2010, family acquired a new form in Elmbrook: the familial bonds that mattered most were between the board and current students, not current students and their siblings. The school district family trumped a student's residential family. Restricting enrollment in these terms placed the board in the difficult position sometimes faced by adoptive parents, especially when adoptions proceeded across borders—the board could not adopt every child in Milwaukee. They could only act in what they regarded as a conscientious and fiscally responsible manner. Yet the district still struggled with this "reality." Coming to terms with the board's decision, Superintendent Matt Gibson admitted that "this year I feel a little guilty that I'm not advocating for [Chapter 220] to the extent that I have in the past." However, his interactions with the EMST taught him that "we need to think more financially than we have in the past."[103] Practicing a fiscal sense of responsibility, the district could not adopt more children than it could support.

Only one Chapter 220 parent, Qiana Collins, spoke during the 2010 Chapter 220 planning council meeting, and she, too, addressed the board's decision-making in personal, heartfelt terms. Fearing conversion, Collins expressed relief and gratitude after the board voted against it: "Can I say I was almost brought to tears earlier when I thought about what the impact that it has not only on us and on others." Even with the vote, she still felt some anxiety: "I hope that this can really stand and if nothing else just allow the kids to graduate or the families to decide otherwise. . . . I thank you for the vote."[104] Thankful throughout her participation, Collins effected a deferential posture, acknowledging the difficult decisions faced by the board. Sharing parts of her sympathetic biography as a breast cancer survivor with mounting medical bills, Collins appreciated the good fortune that her daughters experienced as Elmbrook students—others would not be so lucky. She understood the board's decision not to open any new seats, but revealed that "it breaks my heart." She had "always hoped that and thought that—I never thought that I would see this day, truthfully."[105] More sad than angry, Collins did not protest. Her deference underscored the power relations between the school district and Chapter 220 participants—between wealthy adoptive parents, poor children, and the communities the latter leave behind. What could Collins do but plead? Any direct challenge to the board may have threatened her daughters' places in the district. Board members framed their commitment as benevolence. In the setting of a district meeting, Collins had comparatively fewer available resources, if she so desired, to reconfigure this frame.

This middle ground did not satisfy everyone, revealing the tensions that the Chapter 220 program had originally aimed to attenuate. For the two board members and others supporting the conversion of current Chapter 220 seats to Open Enrollment, distinctions between resident and nonresident students remained. As other board members talked about Chapter 220 students in familial terms, these interlocutors effectively equated family with residency, which Chapter 220 students did not possess. Responding to Gehl's assertion that Chapter 220 students "are Elmbrook students," Jean Lambert retorted, "Well, what about the other Elmbrook students that are impacted by that—our resident students? I feel the obligation to our resident students to do what we can to preserve what we have." While Gehl forwarded a unitary category of Elmbrook students, Lambert reasserted a difference. And this difference guided priorities. Glen Allgaier contended that the money spent on Chapter 220 students constituted dollars "that we're not investing in our students." Lambert and Allgaier appreciated the soft educational benefits of Chapter 220, but finite resources required hard decisions. Allgaier emphasized the additional resources consumed by Chapter 220 students: "These students are there creating additional sections required, special-ed resources, ELL [English Language Learners] resources, and so forth."[106] In 2009, when parents of Chapter 220 students addressed the benefits of diversity, they elucidated the productive power of difference: children from different backgrounds could come together in a school setting and learn about their comparative experiences and cultures, collaboratively producing broader outlooks in the process. However, as the fiscal reality identified by the EMST set in for some board members, these differences became a deficit—liabilities from which the district needed to divest.

Beyond balance sheets, some interlocutors represented Chapter 220 students as a threat to the well-being of families living in the Elmbrook school district. For instance, Jim Hodgson typically affected a dispassionate demeanor in his interactions with the board, projecting the persona of a financial adviser presenting different options and scenarios to his clients. However, Hodgson's tone changed when he addressed the stakes of the EMST recommendations. In his view, declining some options would necessarily direct the board to others, which raised ethical issues of responsibility and accountability: "If you decide, for example, to keep 220 because you're feeling obligated to the students of Milwaukee, but you're going to close somebody's school, you need to be able to look them in the eye when you're sitting in the auditorium at that school and say, 'I'm obligated to Milwaukee, I'm closing your school.'" Not many parents of resident students spoke at the board meetings relating to the EMST and Chapter 220, but those who did unanimously supported converting Chapter 220 to Open Enrollment. One parent who spoke immediately after Hodgson challenged the board to "look me in the face and say, 'You know what, those Milwaukee kids are more important than our Brookfield kids.'"[107] In this parent's view, in a context of finite resources, any funding decision effected a judgment of worth. Hodgson and this parent demanded that the board share their judgment directly.

Looking someone in the eye enacts a personal, embodied form of accountability. It serves as an ultimate guarantee of one's sincerity, veracity, and commitment. Language may facilitate deceptions and disavowals, but eye contact establishes a directness that testifies to the truth of an interlocutor's words and one's willingness to stand behind a decision. Eye contact also delivers a message personally. We may look a family member, friend, or neighbor in the eye, but we are less likely to engage a stranger this way, since doing so may provoke a confrontation. From this perspective, Hodgson and the parent's demand amounted to an articulation of betrayal. Supporting current Chapter 220 students meant that board members had to look community members in the eye as advocates of outsiders, city residents who came to Elmbrook and posed a threat to their suburban sanctuary. This support undercut a presumed familiarity and solidarity among board members and Elmbrook residents. The continued presence of the Milwaukee child— the black child—disrupted the white suburban oasis. By consuming a share of finite resources, the black child threatened to lower property values and destroy neighborhoods. The school board aided and abetted this trajectory by siding with Milwaukee students.

Seeking Balance, Enabling Judgment

In their deliberations over Chapter 220, board members struggled to balance expertise and engagement. They oscillated between confidence and befuddlement, precision and vagueness, systematic analyses and disconnected experiences. When discussing the finances of Chapter 220, a sense of expertise prevailed as board members and administrators relied on specialized tools and reports to guide their deliberations. They believed that these guides presented unprecedented knowledge and disclosed an undeniable reality. Yet they did not address the values that informed the spreadsheets, weights, criteria, and recommendations gleaned from these tools. References to "hard data" and financial "realities" denied the value bases of their decisions, effecting a "realist style" common among financial and market discourses that obscures the specificity of these perspectives.[108] In contrast, when addressing the educational benefits of Chapter 220, board members and administrators believed they had no recourse but anecdotes and personal experience, denying these types of evidence the standing to substantiate broader claims about district issues. Moreover, they left most of the task of elucidating educational benefits to parents of Chapter 220 students, who stood in as charity cases illustrating the good work of the district. Chapter 220 parents sometimes asserted wider claims that intimated a balance between expertise and engagement, but the framing of these claims by administrators and board members left these larger issues unexplored.

The uneven treatment of the financial and educational aspects of Chapter 220 produced a circumscribed judgment about the program and associated issues facing the Elmbrook school district. During the deliberations, Tom Gehl held that he saw one of the virtues of the EMST as "demonstrat[ing] pretty clearly that there's different perceptions out there."[109] Perhaps, but the board could have employed other means besides relying on a standardized decision-making matrix to discover different perceptions. Most notably, board members themselves stood as a potential means of accomplishing this end by engaging more fully the perspective-taking potential of deliberation to investigate different views. Board members effectively underestimated their own decision-making capabilities, which may have produced more subtle judgments than the recommendations of the EMST. In drawing these conclusions, I am not questioning the board's motives nor am I arguing that finances are unimportant. To the contrary, board members' references to Chapter 220 students as "our students," their concern for subsidized transportation, their repeated affirmations of commitment, and their empathy all demonstrated their genuine interest in the well-being and success of Chapter 220 students. Further, finances warrant extensive consideration when school boards deliberate about various programs and services. When resources are limited, districts may not provide all the programming they would have offered in more propitious times. Even well-regarded programs may face cuts or elimination if a district cannot find the money to sustain them. However, these decisions constitute value decisions—recognizing this quality of finances changes the framing of these types of issues.

The Elmbrook school board voted to open no new seats in Chapter 220 in 2010 partially because of a fear of its future—a fear that the district would be stretched too far if its leadership did not retreat around a declining number of residential students. Yet this was only one vision of the district's future. During the school board's final fall 2010 meeting about Chapter 220, Katie Wilson reminded her colleagues that "the future of the children in this school district is very much linked to the children in MPS, and that's a question that we need to take up at some point and look for a way to address."[110] No one addressed Wilson's trenchant observation, deferring "some point" for another time. Elmbrook may separate itself from the city as a school district, but its prosperity depends importantly on the economic vitality of the larger metropolitan area. Without cities, suburbs would not exist—even as the latter sometimes wish to disavow the former. This sense of a shared destiny, which Dr. Martin Luther King Jr. articulated in his advocacy of civil rights and social justice, motivated people to develop programs to integrate children's educational experiences—reflecting the belief that people distinguished by race and class could come together.[111] Yet Elmbrook has succeeded in an era that has measured achievement differently, through standards and testing. From the perspective of an accountability regime, expertise trumps engagement.

5

TRUST, RELATIONSHIPS, AND DELIBERATION

Deliberation proceeds through relationships—varied, potentially fulfilling and frustrating human relationships. These relationships take shape through in-person and multimedia forums, simultaneous and asynchronous participation, and neighborhood haunts and global venues. Strangers and intimates may deliberate as contributors to an online discussion thread carried across nations and cultures over several days and weeks, or neighbors may exchange views during a brief get-together at the local coffee shop. In this way, deliberative statements invoke others even when expressed in solitude, such as a comment posted to a blog, which both responds to an original post and anticipates the reading and response of others. The relationality of deliberation arises from its character as a collective weighing of perspectives oriented toward a mutually recognized public problem or issue. Deliberation's advantage over solitary reflection presumably lies in the promise that exchanging reasons among multiple participants will produce sounder decisions, since more people will generate more perspectives on a topic and they will better discern the strengths and weaknesses of proposals than will a solitary individual.[1] Regardless of whether they always realize the epistemic promise of deliberation, school boards, in both controversial and comparatively tranquil episodes, demonstrate its relationality.

The varied relationships that sustain deliberative encounters invite questions about the qualities of productive and unproductive relationships. What circumstances and factors help produce deliberative encounters in which participants believe they have made meaningful contributions to what they regard as a good decision? What circumstances and factors inform fractured deliberative encounters in which participants disavow decisions, express anger and alienation over processes, and become wary of future encounters? For board members and administrators in Beloit, Elmbrook, and West Bend, the answers lie importantly in the concept and practice of trust. When interlocutors craft a trusting relationship, they may address district issues efficaciously in making decisions about policy that may not thrill all stake-holders but nevertheless constitute reasonable decisions that holdouts can understand. When interlocutors do not enact trusting relationships, their deliberations break down, divisions harden, and recriminations abound. In especially troubling cases, the failure to build trusting relationships threat-ens the very possibility of deliberation itself.

Just as soon as trust intimates answers to the question of the quality of deliberative relationships, these answers threaten to disappear in the poly-semy of the term "trust" itself, for trust may refer to attitudes, expectations, practices, people, organizations, institutions, and more.[2] No conception of trust can encompass all of the meanings that circulate in our everyday lan-guage and in scholarly investigations. Different meanings of trust may sig-nal different ideas and events that resist efforts to collapse, synthesize, or create a hierarchy among its various meanings. Considering how trust may inform relationships among participants in deliberation requires a concep-tion that resonates with the dynamic and participatory character of delibera-tion, whereby people's interpretations of their needs, interests, and positions may change through engagement with others. A deliberative conception of trust, as I discuss below, cannot follow the lead of dominant approaches to studying trust and democratic engagement, which rely on survey data to measure levels of trust in society. These surveys, while important for mea-suring attitudes of social and political trust, can only provide snapshots of particular moments in time.

A deliberative conception of trust, too, should illuminate people's partici-pation in activities they view as consequential for themselves and others. In this way, we may distinguish deliberative trust from conceptions that treat trust as a proxy for people's participation in an activity. Political scientist Mark Warren advances a notion of trust as proxy in holding that "when one trusts, one *foregoes* the opportunity to influence decision-making, on the assumption that there are shared or convergent interests between truster and trustee."[3] Warren's position describes situations of large-scale, repre-sentative negotiations and decision-making, where everyone interested in a decision cannot participate in its making. In these situations, negotia-tors need trust because its absence would delegitimize any agreement they reached. Further, Warren's position resonates with interest-based theories of democracy that view negotiation as the primary mode of engagement across differences. However, the idea of foregoing opportunities does not serve school-board members (or, for that matter, citizens in various contexts of deliberative governance) who practice democracy by engaging others.

School-board members do their own deliberating; they do not place their interests in someone else's hands but rather advocate their own positions.

Building on interviews conducted across Beloit, Elmbrook, and West Bend, I develop a deliberative model of trust as a *relational practice*. Mediating theory and practice, this model seeks to explain how interviewees understood trust in their deliberations and to synthesize their responses into a conceptual framework that interviewees themselves did not fully articulate, but one that may offer a more general model of trust in deliberation. From this perspective, trust does not function in deliberation as an all-or-nothing phenomenon that determines a priori the success or failure of deliberation by its presence or absence. Interlocutors may transform relations of trust through their interactions, strengthening or weakening levels of trust in deliberation. As a relationship, deliberative trust functions not as an attribute of one participant or another, but as a quality that may emerge in the interactions of participants—the discursive relationships they mutually construct. Participants still may earn a reputation of trustworthiness, but this label effectively represents a summary of recent interactions.[4] As a practice, trust appears not as a precondition or an outcome of deliberation, but as an activity that unfolds through deliberation. As a relational practice, trust is something that people *do*.

In spring and summer 2011, members of the REDD project conducted thirty-one interviews with all the board members and superintendents in the three districts and with other administrators and a prominent community activist. Coming at the end of two years of fieldwork, and perhaps enabled by this fieldwork, these interviews produced surprisingly frank exchanges. As one interviewee observed, "You haven't come across at all as here to do therapeutic work for us, as here to do anything other than study." We agreed to quote interviewees anonymously in any presentations or publications drawing on the interviews. All interviewees signed a consent letter approved by the Institutional Review Board at the University of Wisconsin–Madison that stipulated the anonymity condition and permitted us to record the interviews, prepare full-length transcripts from the recordings, and use quotations from the interview transcripts. Lasting between one and two hours, the interviews followed a semi-structured, open-ended format. While some of the questions contained slight modifications to account for district-specific issues, the interview protocol addressed three core areas: board dynamics, evidence use, and district culture. In preparing this protocol, we expected the issue of trust to emerge in interviewees' responses to evaluating evidence and their descriptions of decision-making processes.

Interviewees did mention trust in responding to these questions, but they also mentioned trust without prompting throughout the interviews. I was surprised at both the frequency and centrality that interviewees assigned to trust. Virtually all of the interviewees identified trust as central to their deliberation and decision-making. Distinguishing this chapter from the others that draw primarily on board and committee meetings, these interviews offer important insights into interlocutors' perceptions of their interactions.

I begin this chapter by distinguishing conceptions of trust as an attitude, which figure prominently in the scholarship on social capital and civic engagement, from trust as a relationship, which has informed scholarship on organizational trust. I then discuss the resources and contexts for deliberative trust. Drawing on participants' experiences, deliberative trust transforms their experiences through interactions with other interlocutors. Deliberative trust exhibits a temporal orientation that uses the past as a resource and envisions the future as a field for potential applications, thereby exceeding the ephemerality of specific encounters. Next, I explicate three qualities that shape the contexts in which participants may build relationships of deliberative trust: contingency, risk, and reciprocity. Addressing contingent issues, deliberation invites reciprocity, but deliberators need to negotiate perceptions of unequal risk. I then turn to the practice of deliberative trust, synthesizing interviewees' comments on trust into a conceptual framework. Toward this end, I identify four qualities for building trust in deliberation: flexibility, forthrightness, engagement, and heedfulness. These qualities constitute an analytic framework for investigating deliberation as well as a normative framework for bolstering practices of trust in deliberation.

Conceptualizing Trust Dynamically

The REDD interviews offer a glimpse into what one might regard as "trust in action"—how participants in school-board deliberations thought about trust, relied on trust, cultivated trust, and sometimes spurned invitations to build trust as they deliberated district issues. As such, these interviews provide the materials and motivation for an alternative framework for investigating the relationship between trust and democratic engagement. As I explain in this section, some prominent contemporary approaches draw primarily on survey data to diagnose trends in trust and to establish connections between trust and engagement, generally treating the former as a condition for the latter. But these studies tend to neglect *processes* of engagement, perhaps because the survey data that these studies utilize does not illuminate processes. In contrast, the REDD interviews disclose how interlocutors perceived the processes in which they participated, pointing scholarship toward dynamic conceptions of trust.

Turning to comprehensive, longitudinal national and international surveys, scholars analyzing trends in trust have reported resoundingly similar findings: trust is in short supply. In the United States, researchers have cited prominent national surveys like the General Social Survey and the American National Election Studies to explain that trust in society has been declining for more than four decades.[5] When asked whether they could trust "the government in Washington," fewer people have answered affirmatively. In addition to suggesting a lack of trust in governing bodies, respondents' answers also have implicated their interactions with others. Expressing skepticism about interacting with other people, respondents increasingly have doubted that "most people can be trusted," believing instead that "you can't be too careful in dealing with people."[6] Pippa Norris cautions against an oversimplified rendering of trust in the United States as constituting an uninterrupted downward trend. Instead, she notes that reported levels of trust increased briefly in the early 1980s and again in the mid to late 1990s and in the months after the September 11, 2001, terrorist attacks. Nevertheless, Norris agrees that longitudinal measures indicate an overall decline in trust.[7] Scholars studying trust worldwide have reported similar trends in Canada, much of Europe, Japan, Australia, and elsewhere.[8]

Scholars have offered various explanations for this apparent decline in trust. Some point to the performance of government, which in the United States has been implicated in scandals like Watergate and declarations of war but not victory on problems like poverty and terrorism.[9] Others highlight news and entertainment media practices that depict a world of strangers who warrant suspicion, since they may swindle or even physically harm earnest citizens.[10] Still others identify generational changes, explaining that the celebrated "greatest generation" in the United States, which survived the Great Depression and defeated fascists in Europe and Asia, constituted a trusting generation, whereas successive generations have trusted less and less.[11] Emphasizing economics, some scholars maintain that people who feel financially secure report higher levels of trust, but that declining incomes and decreased job security in many Western nations undermine a sense of financial security.[12]

While some scholars interpret declining trust as indicating a healthy skepticism among citizens, others warn of a weakened democracy populated by less engaged citizens.[13] Perhaps no one has done more to circulate this dystopian vision than Robert Putnam, whose studies of trust and social capital have attracted attention from scholars, policymakers, and citizens. In his highly influential book *Bowling Alone* and in related work, Putnam bemoans a loss of community as Americans have engaged less frequently in coordinated group activities. Putnam catalogs declining membership rates in a variety of voluntary associations, including the titular activity of his book. No longer joining bowling leagues, citizens are more likely to bowl alone. Explaining these trends, Putnam turns to generational differences and mass-media consumption: newer generations trust others less readily than their predecessors, and they consume more mass media, especially television. Charging television as his primary culprit, he argues that the more television people watch, the less they trust and engage others.[14] Putnam offers a glimpse into what the United States could lose if people stop trusting one another—inclinations toward volunteering, contributing to charity, joining community organizations, serving on juries, giving blood, paying taxes, and more. These activities thrive when people regard one another as capable agents who have a stake in public affairs. Putnam concludes that "people who trust others are all-round good citizens."[15] They cultivate democratic norms and practices that create opportunities for wider public engagement.

Reports and analyses of declining levels of trust tend to treat trust as a set of attitudes or expectations held by citizens. Whether understood as social trust (i.e., attitudes that citizens hold toward one another) or political trust (i.e., attitudes that citizens hold toward the agents of representative government), trust as an attitude or expectation often serves as an indicator of citizens' confidence in securing particular outcomes from others.[16] In this spirit, Claus Offe likens trust to a "money-saving device" that enables people to forego the "time costs" associated with ensuring an outcome from another person.[17] Shifting from economic to ethical attitudes, Eric Uslaner theorizes trust as a moral framework that functions as "a general outlook on human nature" that "*mostly* does not depend upon personal experiences." Instead, "moralistic trust is a commandment to treat people *as if* they were trustworthy."[18] Offe elucidates the efficiency of a trusting attitude, while Uslaner underscores its moral implications. However, in deliberation, efficient outcomes emerge through people's participation, and morality arises when interaction encourages people to examine their values and beliefs in relation to an other with the promise of increasing understanding of and respect for an other. In both cases, individual attitudes and expectations—even when interlocutors resist change—assume a relational character when justified to others in deliberation.

As the primary policymaking body within local districts, school boards operate within larger webs of relationships that may strengthen or weaken trust. In a well-known study, Anthony Bryk and Barbara Schneider explore relations of trust in the Chicago public schools. Drawing on extensive field-work, Bryk and Schneider develop a model of relational trust as an organizational property of schools and the people who interact therein: students, teachers, administrators, and parents. They see the roles of these different actors as "socially defined in the reciprocal exchanges among participants in a school community."[19] Whether these actors can build trust as they negotiate their relationships affects the functioning of the school and its ability to adapt to changing district policies and initiatives. Bryk and Schneider identify four qualities of trusting relationships: respect, competence, personal regard for others, and integrity.[20] Respect entails recognizing the important roles and mutual dependencies of the various actors in a school setting. Competence refers to an individual's ability to perform a role. Personal regard for others indicates a willingness to act within the school organization with benevolent intentions. Integrity indicates consistency between individuals' stated views and their actions. Offering a general model of relational trust in organizations, Roger Mayer, James Davis, and David Schoorman discern ability, benevolence, and integrity as qualities of trusting relationships.[21] Mayer, Davis, and Schoorman do not mention respect explicitly, but this quality implicitly informs their model. These two models and others present highly resonant models of relational trust in school and nonschool organizations.[22]

In their roles as policymakers, school-board members generally do not interact with the people involved in the district at specific school sites, unless these people show up at board meetings. Still, these models of organizational trust illuminate *non-deliberative* relations of trust operating in school districts that complement the *deliberative* relations of trust built through board meetings. In the REDD interviews, board members and administrators sometimes referenced school and central-office staff who typically did not attend and participate in meetings but nevertheless served as resources for policymakers. Along these lines, Alan Daly and Kara Finnigan highlight the importance of trusting relationships among district leaders in central offices and school sites for policymaking and its implementation.[23] Moreover, these models provide a basis for conceptualizing relations of trust in deliberation, since they exhibit a "broader emphasis on social rather than purely instrumental (resource-based) motives driving trust behavior, including consideration of how actors' self-presentational concerns and identity-related needs influence trust-related cognition and choice."[24] A broader emphasis comports with the REDD interviews, as school-board members and administrators cited a range of factors, including but not limited to resource-based incentives and disincentives, that influenced their deliberations and decision-making. Further, as "multifaceted and multiplex," trusting relationships may exhibit different qualities among the varied actors in a school district.[25] Board members may look for different qualities in their trusting relationships with support staff, teachers, students, and parents than in the relations of trust they build with other board members and top administrators.

A model of deliberative trust shares with these organizational models a view of trust as relational but situates these relationships within the context of the potentially transformative power of deliberation. Deliberation differs from aggregative models of decision-making by foregrounding possibilities where participants may reevaluate and change their interests, preferences, and positions through interacting with others. As Iris Marion Young observes, when applied to democratic practice, deliberative models view decision-making "not [as] merely expressing and registering, but as *transforming* the preferences, interests, beliefs, and judgments of participants."[26] Transformation need not result in board members switching their votes on an issue—although the interviewees generally saw themselves, even when their practices suggested otherwise, as operating without predetermined views on district policies—but may manifest as greater understanding and respect for a different position than one's own as well as reprioritizing issues and recognizing previously neglected issues as worthy of attention.

This transformative power holds several implications for conceptualizing relations of trust. First, just as deliberation constitutes a discursive process, so, too, does deliberative trust unfold through discourse. To be sure, as board members and administrators in Beloit know well, material conditions ineluctably inform deliberative exchanges, but the latter make meaning primarily through the statements and expressions of participants. Second, the relations built through deliberative trust do not fit as clearly with officially delineated roles as other relations in a school-district organization, such as the relationships between teachers and principals or the relationships between central-office staff and the superintendent, where specific job duties often delimit the frequency and quality of these relationships. Third, relatedly, participants in deliberation may find their roles circumscribed by the normative criterion of reason-giving, which presumably drives processes of deliberation. Participants do not always follow this norm—and interviewees expressed frustration with colleagues whom they regarded as stating positions without presenting their reasons—but its prevalence means that participants in deliberation often find themselves in relations with a strong expectation and/or practice of justifying one's views, rather than, say, instructing others to carry out a decision. Fourth, participants in deliberation often encounter one another in situations recognized by participants as requiring problem-solving and assessing multiple potential solutions. While deliberations sometimes may pursue a more exploratory path, school boards and other institutionally situated bodies tend to treat the issues they address as matters needing a decision. This quality heightens the sense of contest characterizing encounters, increases the potential for division, and, in turn, generates opportunities for repairing damaged relationships.

Although independent inquiries into deliberation and trust have generated large, wide-ranging scholarly literatures, there has, to my knowledge, been comparatively little study of their intersection. In a provocative discussion, Matthew Festenstein articulates three ways that deliberation may build trust: enabling participants to present themselves in ways that may overcome negative stereotypes, strengthening goodwill and fidelity among representatives and constituents by foregrounding reason-giving, and fostering respect for diverse viewpoints by situating interlocutors as warranting address.[27] While Festenstein identifies deliberation as a potential source of trust, he stops short of explicating how this process might unfold. Pursuing a rhetorical approach, Gerard Hauser and Chantal Benoit-Barné argue cogently for conceptualizing trust as a rhetorical construct that bolsters the relations of civil society and affords opportunities for deliberation (among other modes of discourse). Raising the question of how to build trust, Hauser and Benoit-Barné answer that "trust emerges from participating in the secondary associations that constitute the web of civil society." They explain that "the rhetorical culture of these associations produces social capital by exposing their members to alternative rhetorics, to the range of difference and the mediating grounds of similarity that make it possible for them to form a civic community based on relations of collaboration."[28] They caution that collaboration does not lead to consensus, but refers instead to working together even amid disagreement. For Hauser and Benoit-Barné, both the source of trust and its function stem from participation in civil society. This duality accords with James Bohman's characterization of trust as a resource that "*increases* through use."[29] As these scholars suggest, the practices that create trust benefit from its operation.

Up to this point, Hauser and Benoit-Barné's discussion of trust resonates with my conception of deliberative trust. We both regard trust as a social phenomenon that people may build by interacting with others. However, we differ in that I conceive of trust as a relational practice and they define trust as "a belief about others on which we form expectations about their behaviors and use these expectations to guide our actions."[30] This definition of trust invokes the attitudes and expectations surveyed in instruments like the General Social Survey and used to assess levels of social capital, which Hauser and Benoit-Barné reference. Addressing guides for action, their discussion of the role of trust in civil society focuses more attention on outcomes, which in turn serve as facilitators of action, rather than processes. Hauser and Benoit-Barné recognize that deliberation may produce trust, but they do not elucidate how trust arises and operates through processes of deliberation themselves.

As a relational practice, deliberative trust remains distinct from conceptions of the character or credibility of an advocate.[31] In the classical tradition, Aristotle discussed the character of a speaker in his treatment of ethos. Aristotle defined ethos as the way that a speaker presents his or her character during a speech and utilizes this represented self for persuasive ends. Indeed, Aristotle saw ethos as "almost, so to speak, the controlling factor in persuasion."[32] Eugene Garver sees ethos as suffusing the whole of Aristotle's rhetoric, which he calls an "art of character," since "*ethos* is necessary for finding and formulating arguments and not just presenting them."[33] In a more circumscribed application, Alan Brinton has described "ethotic argument" as involving a "transfer of 'credibility' from a person to a conclusion."[34] While both intimate discursive practices, neither an expansive nor a limited interpretation of ethos as a speaker's character suggests the relational practice of deliberative trust. This is not because audiences sit passively as they listen to a speaker's arguments—quite the contrary; Aristotle charged audiences with the important task of judgment. But an audience's judgment does not take shape through the mutual consideration of perspectives practiced among participants in deliberation. As related but not necessarily coterminous modes of discourse, speech-making and deliberation situate participants in different discursive relations.

In the board meetings and the REDD interviews, the perceived character of proponents and opponents of policy proposals influenced their reception by others. However, we may gain greater critical purchase by distinguishing perceived qualities associated with a person from perceived qualities of a relationship. In neither the meetings nor the interviews did these perceptions merge. Interlocutors sometimes built trusting relationships in one dimension with people whose character may have seemed questionable in another dimension. Likewise, they sometimes expressed frustration over the difficult relationships they sustained with people whom they perceived as exhibiting ethical character. Perceptions of individual and relational qualities both influence deliberation, which is why we should be careful not to conflate these qualities. When investigating trust, a relational model better comports with the dynamics of deliberation.

Resources and Contexts for Trust

Interlocutors may build trust through deliberation, but they do not build it ex nihilo. Without materials, participants may labor to produce a practice, but trust would arise as an empty set of procedures. To build trust, participants in deliberation draw on their own experiences as an important building material. In this way, interlocutors do not have to create an entirely new and unfamiliar relationship, one that effects a rupture from their everyday experiences and interactions. This requirement would consist less in practicing trust than in taking a leap of faith. As Hauser and Benoit-Barné suggest, trust cannot develop as "a leap of faith with no actual grounding but as a process that relies on the familiar in order to anticipate the unfamiliar."[35] Built through interaction, deliberative trust does not represent a singular relationship ritually reenacted in different circumstances. In this section, I explicate how experience, temporality, and context help create the conditions for deliberative trust.

As a basis for building trust in school-board deliberations, experiences may arise from participants' backgrounds, issue trajectories, and board and administration dynamics. In these cases, experience does not consist simply of activities and events in which people have participated, but the activities and events that people draw on in making meaningful their interactions with others.[36] This process of meaning-making is intersubjective, such that interaction itself constitutes an experience that people may draw upon in building trust. Board members, administrators, and other participants bring their personal experiences to board deliberations. In Elmbrook, for instance, board members often drew on their distinct work experiences to establish areas of mutually recognized expertise that served as a basis for trust. One Elmbrook board member, voicing a sentiment expressed across the interviews with people in this district, maintained that "we're lucky in that between the seven of us, somebody has a large interest in, in different, we've all got interests in different areas." Board members recognized one of their colleagues as the financial point person, another as the curricular point person, another as the legal point person, and so on. Experience did not function in each of these areas as a trump card, determining the quality of an interaction. Rather, individual board members weighed their experiences differently as they interacted with one another.

Issue trajectories constitute an aspect of participants' experiences, as memories of previous deliberations—especially controversial and difficult deliberations—negatively and positively influence efforts to establish trusting relations. In Beloit, for some of the board members interviewed, prior deliberations over the implementation of a human growth and development (HGD) curriculum still stirred traumatic memories. Unable to reach an agreement over the content of an HGD curriculum five years ago, a past board had dropped the subject from the curriculum. As some current board members and community members pushed for the reintroduction of this topic, including discussion of safe-sex practices, other board members resisted—even those who had not served on the board during the past controversy. One board member described prior deliberations over an HGD curriculum as "god-awful. There are, to this day, people in this community who don't speak to each other because of the battle about the human growth and development curriculum that took place five years ago." Deliberations over HGD fractured board and community relations five years ago, and the negative experience among surviving board members and more recently elected board members who witnessed the controversy complicated everyone's efforts to build trusting relations as the board returned to this subject.

The consequences of the HGD controversy illustrate how board and administration dynamics also may constitute part of people's experiences. Refusing to speak to other people represents an extreme case of how negative dynamics may influence ongoing deliberations. Across the three districts during the period of fieldwork, board members and administrators did not refuse to engage one another, but they sometimes approached particular individuals warily or with an inclination to disagree. More positively, interviewees discussed how positive dynamics bolstered relations of trust. Explaining his ability to read people's motivations and veracity, one West Bend board member insisted that "I have a pretty good bullshit detector, you know, so when I know that people are not telling me the truth, I can generally tell it." Referencing an administrator in West Bend, this board member recounted that "I've never had, I've had [this person] at different times, you know, sorta shape the truth. . . . [This person] has always said, 'This is the good, this is the bad, this is how it is.' [This person] has always done that for me. I have been very comfortable with [this person]." A history of ostensibly honest interactions with the administrator influenced this board member's perceptions of their relationship. This history did not free either party from acting forthrightly in their deliberations, but it facilitated an approach to one another that established honesty as a default condition, rather than placing each person on alert for potential misrepresentation and deception.

Across the three districts, some administrators expressed frustration that they needed to negotiate their professional experience during school-board meetings. Instead, they effectively sought to invoke their experience as a trump card, employed less to build relations of trust than to serve as an authoritative argument. One administrator criticized some board members as "two-time-a-month board members who work for the system for ten hours." This administrator drew a contrast with professional experience: "I'm here seventy, eighty hours a week and this is my life, this is my passion, and in one minute, the whole thing can be blown up and taken in a different direction." Another administrator identified as an "expert in this area. . . . This is what I do for a living. This isn't an accident—I kind of get the education gig, I kind of proved that, that's why I'm kind of sitting in this seat today." In the context of extended deliberative encounters, these frustrations likely represented occasions to "vent" about negative experiences in deliberation, since at other moments in the interviews, these administrators (and others) underscored the benefits of building trusting relations with board members.

My references to past, present, and future implicate the temporal orientation of deliberative trust, which draws on a person's past, enables judgments about the future, and proceeds as a practice in the present. In this frame, the past serves deliberative trust as a resource while the future constitutes a field of diverse applications. The temporality of trust operates on two levels: At one level, deliberation is ephemeral, constituted in the viewpoints shared by interlocutors and ending when their discourse ends. To the extent that they build trust, interlocutors do so in achieving the ostensible purposes of their deliberation, which may explicitly address trust but often does so only implicitly as interlocutors pursue other common concerns. At a second level, trust built through deliberation may exceed its moment of enunciation to make meaningful multiple exchanges. As one board member in

West Bend noted when thinking about connections across meetings, "past practice itself is a momentum." Deliberation proceeds over time in a situation and across situations, such that practices undertaken in one situation become resources for another. Working together across multiple meetings also invites participants to imagine their shared future, which suggests the possibility that divergent and concordant visions of the future themselves may influence relations of trust. One frustrated interviewee in Beloit wished that other deliberators would reshape their view of Beloit as a beleaguered community. Possibly exaggerating, this interviewee characterized current self-perceptions of Beloit as the "place where dreams don't come to fruition." This person retorted that "if [we are] going to move forward, [we are] going to have to think positively, how do we do that?" Positive momentum required a positive vision. This interviewee implied that a dystopian vision of the future dampened people's motivation for building trust.

As its significance extends beyond particular encounters, deliberative trust remains context-specific. Its forward-looking orientation may serve as a resource for subsequent encounters, but not as a uniformly applied procedure. Moreover, utilizing this resource depends on the practices established in subsequent encounters. Even if they address the same issue, a familiar group of interlocutors may confront changing contextual forces that strain relations of trust established in a previous encounter. Across the three districts, deliberations about the district budget illustrated how changing contexts may produce strains. Each year, budgeting constitutes one of the most conspicuous and potentially controversial issues addressed by local school boards. In recent years, local school boards in Wisconsin and many other states have felt additional pressures of reduced state aid and limits on their ability to raise taxes at the local level. As one administrator in Elmbrook observed, "The politics in the community and the state have been more toward retrenching, constraining costs, more toward pulling costs out of public education than they have been building models of excellence in public education. I think that's taken its toll." The "toll" taken in the politics of retrenchment had implicated both the quality of the education that students received as well as the working relationships among teachers responsible for educating students and local officials saddled with crafting district policy with fewer and fewer resources. This shifting context increased the possibility for strife even among interlocutors who had previously established trusting relations.

Three qualities shape the contexts in which interlocutors may engage in relational practices of trust: contingency, risk, and reciprocity. The contingent character of this practice arises from the contingencies attending deliberation itself. As scholars have observed, people do not deliberate about issues that present a certain resolution or those that liken engagement to arbitrary involvement.[37] Rather, people deliberate about matters of common concern that invite redress by weighing varying alternatives. Along these lines, some administrators and board members bemoaned what they perceived as a loss of an opportunity to make decisions about educational policy, regarding these decisions as being made for them at the state and federal levels. Citing increasing mandates, one West Bend administrator complained that "we have no local control." This administrator retorted that if the state politicians stood by their promises of limited government, then "this school board would be able to tax whatever they want and teach whatever they want." Other interviewees in West Bend and the other districts agreed with this assessment of circumscription of local governance. Their complaints likely expressed frustration with the changes wrought by the rise of an accountability regime in U.S. education policy and a concurrent foregrounding of common standards and high-stakes testing, tying district funding to student success rates.[38] Yet even in this new era, as this book elucidates, school boards retain responsibility for decisions addressing financial, personnel, and curricular issues, which affect long-term trajectories and day-to-day operations in districts and classrooms. In these contexts, deliberation may produce a shared judgment about how to proceed, or, in the absence of agreement, it may produce better understanding of various alternatives and perspectives. Deliberation cannot eliminate contingency—for this may be an inescapable element of a shared social world—but, to the extent that participants heed deliberation, it may bolster their commitment to a decision, thus enabling people to anticipate the consequences of their actions.

The risk of deliberation is that participants may change their minds on issues that are important to them. This constitutes a "risk" because we presumably care enough about the issues we deliberate to engage in a process of justifying our views to others and trying to persuade others to think differently.[39] Board members demonstrated this caring in the issues that motivated and highlighted their campaigns and the values they brought to public office. For instance, one West Bend board member attributed some of the tensions faced by the board to what he regarded as competing promises made by his colleagues during their campaigns: "[Others] consistently run their campaigns based on money, money, taxes, taxes, money, money, and, so, they've driven the conversation in that direction, just by virtue of their campaigns." This interviewee believed that a narrow campaign focus increased the risk of deliberation for other board members, since they faced a potential voter backlash if they supported programming that required additional funding. This board member believed that he ran a campaign that accounted for the risk of an unexpected decision by foregrounding the tradeoffs of education policy: "I talked about values. I talked about education when I ran for office. I just said, you know, I understand that education costs money." Even so, this board member had to negotiate conflicting values for himself and the community during the GSA controversy and other policy episodes in West Bend. Trust functions in these risky situations to warrant the possibility of changing one's views.

Deliberation occurs in situations that invite but do not guarantee reciprocity. As Amy Gutmann and Dennis Thompson explain, deliberation calls on participants to articulate "justifications for the institutions, laws, and public policies that collectively bind them."[40] What Gutmann and Thompson do not consider is that particular exchanges may not fully realize this principle of reciprocity, since explicit and implicit discursive norms may place uneven burdens on participants to justify their positions.[41] Nor are these disparities limited to particular encounters, since deliberation finds its resources and its inequities in the societies that generate its norms and practices. One Beloit board member broached the connection between deliberative and societal disparities in noting the challenge of conducting financial deliberations in a community where the average resident earns $35,000 annually while a top-level district administrator may earn more than $100,000 annually. This board member explained that "it can be difficult for a community member to understand how we can, how you reduce your budget and still pay these people X amount of dollars, right?" The hypothetical resident cited in this comment discerned a lack of reciprocity in interlocutors' justificatory burdens. Compared to the struggling community member, the well-paid administrator may have more readily perceived an increase in the district's tax levy as a modest sum. A comparative lack of reciprocity effectively unbalances the risk of engagement, whereby some participants and perspectives may appear beyond critique while others become objects of sustained criticism.

This imbalance creates an apparent paradox between the need for trust and the situations in which trust may appear. As Patti Lenard explains, "Extending trust expresses a willingness to put oneself in a position of vulnerability"; however, "when one comes to feel vulnerable more globally, extending trust (and thereby exacerbating one's vulnerable condition) becomes more difficult and less likely."[42] People who experience discrimination, suffer threats of violence, and struggle economically encounter more risk in their everyday lives than others who hold more privileged positions. On the basis of income alone, the average Beloit resident may experience more financial risk than the administrative leadership. If we treat Lenard's point about making oneself vulnerable as one person extending trust to an other—which does not account for power and sustains a static view of trust, risk, and reciprocity—this paradox may appear irresolvable. Demanding that people who already risk too much make themselves vulnerable as a precondition of deliberation makes its promises appear as naïve and politically quietistic. This would have required policymakers in Beloit to insist that community residents forswear any sense of economic anxiety as a precondition of speaking at board meetings about budgets and taxes. Instead, if we consider Lenard's trenchant observation in the potentially dynamic contexts of deliberation, we may consider perceptions of trust, risk, and reciprocity as mutually modifiable: one term does not appear as the condition for the others, but each term may enable the others. Differences in socioeconomic status (as well as race, sex, sexual orientation, and more) do not determine people's positions, but perceptions of significant differences may require extra effort by interlocutors to establish reciprocity. By moving scholarship away from prescriptions that assume that everyone approaches deliberation from the same position, we instead may recognize that practicing trust in deliberation may make risk more reciprocal.

Practicing Trust in Deliberation

In answering questions, the REDD interviewees discussed a series of practices that they regarded as capable of building trust in deliberation. Their answers have served as the inspiration for my conception of trust as a relational practice and the materials for its explication. Interviewees mentioned specific practices like keeping an open mind about issues and listening to others. Developing a conceptual framework that interviewees themselves did not articulate, I have synthesized their answers as four qualities of building trust in deliberation: flexibility, forthrightness, engagement, and heedfulness. These qualities constitute an analytic framework for investigating deliberation as well as a normative framework for bolstering practices of trust in deliberation. As such, these qualities maintain a relatively autonomous but mutually reinforcing relationship. Their relative autonomy suggests that practicing even one quality may bolster trust, but that the appearance of more than one quality may carry a cumulative force. At the same time, their relative autonomy intimates a negative relationship. An adamant refusal to practice one of these qualities—such as an unwillingness to engage others, which interviewees sometimes attributed to stubborn interlocutors—may frustrate efforts to build trust in other ways. As an analytic framework, these qualities indicate different moments in a deliberative encounter, from a participant's approach to a shared judgment. As a normative framework, these qualities may be practiced at various moments in deliberation, such that an effort to engage the perspective of a seemingly rigid interlocutor, for example, may encourage that person to adopt a flexible approach to deliberation.

Drawing on interviews to explicate a deliberative conception of trust may raise a reporting issue insofar as interviewees may self-interestedly associate themselves with positive actions while attributing negative actions to others. In important respects, the perspectival character of deliberation makes this issue unavoidable. The processes of meaning-making that characterize deliberations over district policy encompass both the policies crafted as well as participants' self-understanding of their roles in these processes. Referencing particular practices, a conception of deliberative trust includes participants' perceptions of these practices. However, the inescapability of perspective does not mean that scholars cannot engage in comparative evaluations or that interlocutors cannot change their practices. To the contrary, the qualities of deliberative trust that I have identified still carry normative force even if interviewees' reports of their deliberation may diverge in some degree from a critical assessment of their practices as well as the perceptions of other interlocutors. This normative force lies in participants' recognition of particular practices as conducive of deliberative trust. To the extent that participants seek to operate as efficacious deliberators, which facilitates board members' abilities to craft policy, the perceptions of others may act as regulatory guides on individual action. A desire for recognition as someone who builds trusting relations provides the aspiration for interviewees to adopt the practices they associate with deliberative trust.

Addressing a variety of aspects of deliberation, a flexible approach among interlocutors may bolster their relations and enable them to build trust. By remaining flexible in the positions they advocate, participants in deliberation recognize other positions as potentially reasoned and justifiable. One school board member in West Bend highlighted this point as crucial for promoting efficacious deliberation and decision-making: "Spend your time asking questions, exploring options, do the research on the outside and keep an open mind as long as you can—until you have to make that decision. I'm not saying you have to delay that decision, but keep an open mind during the process of evaluation." For this board member, an open mind signaled a recognition of the contingency of deliberation, which sometimes proceeded in unexpected directions, "because you never know when you're going to get a piece of information that may change your course." An open mind enabled the agility necessary to address the unexpected: "If you lock yourself into a certain point of view without much study . . . it may be difficult to retract from that spot—even though you know it's the right thing to do, but you may not have the personal, uh, horsepower to do that. So don't jump to a decision too early." This board member's reference to "a piece of information" also illustrates that flexibility entails an openness to supporting and contrary evidence, articulating one's own evidence, and acknowledging the evidence presented by others.

Flexibility may direct interlocutors to the diverse values that may inform a deliberative encounter and facilitate their appreciation of how these values may conflict. Citing the GSA controversy and other issues, another West Bend school-board member resisted what he perceived as an effort by other board members to impose their values on the district: "I have values, too, but, and you have values, but my job is not to make you believe my values, it's to respect your values and hopefully you respect my values." This board member cast efforts to impose values on the district as akin to a failed conversion: "Some of these people think by not, by denying clubs like this or, you know, all of a sudden everybody is going to be not-gay. . . . Oh my god. That's, don't, don't force your ideals on me. I have my own and I'm happy with them." The GSA controversy also exemplified an awareness among most board members of the constraints that may affect judgment—including established laws and policies, time pressures, and resource limits.

Flexibility affirms the relationality of deliberation, sustaining reciprocity and sharing risk. A flexible interlocutor acknowledges the participation of others—this person "hears" others. Moreover, flexibility suggests that one's own views may be formed or re-formed in collaboration with an other. One Beloit board member stressed a key aspect of decision-making as "listening to other people's opinions before I made a vote because I didn't want to go into it and not hear anything other people said." This board member credited interacting with others for producing better decisions: "Because either I would be aware of something else, or I'd learn something from it, or, you know, it could have changed my mind." This statement affirms the transformative power of deliberation. In this spirit, another Beloit board member located the key to decision-making in "asking the right question." Discovering this question required "sorting through our own biases as well that we bring to the table, our own agenda that we bring to the table or our own, you know, how are they playing off each other today." Flexibility facilitated learning about oneself and others.

In contrast, the inflexible interlocutor appears to get along just fine without others. Participation in deliberation holds no transformative power over this person's views. Belief comes from outside—whether talking points, religious faith, hubris, or something else—and stays outside. In an admission of inflexibility, one Beloit board member struggled when asked to name a situation where someone else's argument changed their position: "I'm usually the one that makes people change their minds. I'm trying to think. Hmm. Honestly, I can't think of an experience like that, but I am honest in saying that there have been situations where I have changed other people's minds." This board member conceded that this situation probably had happened but could not recall a specific example. While this admission represents an unusual case, it illustrates the rejection of relationality perpetrated by inflexibility. Without naming this board member, an administrator in Beloit addressed the baneful consequences of this approach. At the level of board dynamics, inflexibility stalled decision-making: "It's not fun when you're dealing with people who are ideological, you know, and hold to positions no matter what. . . . When you're dealing with people where that's the, that's where they come down, there is no, you know, there's no place. You can't win them." Insofar as inflexibility produced wider divisions, it threatened the larger community: "You destroy a community eventually, with that kind of thinking." Inflexibility undermines the relationality of trust by making the other unnecessary. Whereas flexibility sees the deliberative encounter as productive and potentially transformative, inflexibility prejudges the encounter and outcome, rendering participation as perfunctory.

Even though interlocutors may appreciate when others demonstrate flexibility in deliberation, practicing flexibility oneself may present a challenge, as the Beloit board member's admission illustrates. Commitment to a position may lead to defensiveness when confronted with opposing viewpoints and information that challenges a worldview. Interlocutors may attribute negative motives to the dissenting other, regard contrary information as flawed or biased, or retreat to a protective liberalism that disavows participation in the deliberative life of a democracy. This dynamic arose in the

West Bend interviews, where board members professed flexibility in their own practices while charging others with inflexibility and bearing charges of inflexibility from others. For instance, in one interview, a board member disavowed operating with a narrow "political or social agenda" that predetermined his decisions on district policy. Yet in describing this person, another board member quipped, "[This person]'s never wrong. Just ask him, and he'll tell you he's never wrong." These conflicting perceptions do not require us to determine which person is correct, but they illustrate the tension between voicing support for a practice and practicing a practice.

Conceptualizing trust as a practice may prevent scholars from treating flexibility and inflexibility as mutually exclusive conditions. Processes of deliberation may exhibit both flexibility and inflexibility, suggesting their malleability over the course of an encounter and among various aspects of deliberation. Inflexibility at one moment in deliberation may become flexibility at another moment. Even as some board members in West Bend expressed difficulties in practicing flexibility, they had changed some of their positions and observed others doing the same. One board member recalled how his own views had shifted from a campaign platform of fiscal restraint to his view as a board member that the district needed to invest "in this community to grow the education system, to make this a stronger community." Rather than tossing him out of office, the community reelected him with "more votes than any school board member in the last ten years has got." Participants may exhibit inflexibility toward one aspect of deliberation— whether positions, evidence, values, or constraints—while being flexible toward another. One Beloit board member alluded to the fluidity of this process when explaining that newly elected board members underestimate how "their values get pushed. Um, you know, I don't think people go into this process thinking, 'This is going to push. How do I really feel about this?'" Flexibility and inflexibility do not appear as fixed qualities that prompt openness or defensiveness, but as changing qualities shaped by the encounter itself.

Associating trust and forthrightness attends to the pragmatic orientation of deliberation. If participants in deliberation cannot operate with a sense that others mean what they say, then deliberation loses its coherence. An administrator in West Bend feared that divisions on the board had moved the district precariously close to this state: "There's so little trust there if, if they're not all in the room together they're automatically going to ask questions." This administrator suggested that sparring board members doubted that others would conduct meetings honestly or report the deliberations of a subcommittee accurately to the full board. Expecting interlocutors to mean what they say resonates with our everyday usage of trust in other non-deliberative contexts; we do not trust people whom we believe may deceive us or hide things from us.

Interviewees regularly cited secrecy about information and hidden agendas as practices that frustrated efforts to build trust. While generally affirming the conduct of the administration, one board member in Beloit expressed some wariness about the seeming lack of clarity in the targets for reductions in ongoing budget deliberations: "I feel really frustrated and upset and worried that I don't know the exact number, and I'm bothered that I also don't know why I don't know the exact number. It creates a sense of distrust, and I don't like to have to go in questioning." The question of "why" raised the issue of forthrightness: "Am I getting all of the facts? . . . Is the administration just trying to bamboozle us with their fuzzy math and whatnot?" Another board member tied a decision to run for school board with a perception that the board at that time had been driven by personal agendas: "I kind of saw and heard things that the board was doing, more like personal agendas, things of that nature, and that really bothered me." This interviewee believed that the dynamics had changed with the current board. Most of the board tried to find the best collective answer to the issues they addressed, but a few board members still employed unspoken agendas as guides for their behavior: "It was better than what I thought it was going to be from that respect, but I still see the agendas, and it drives me nuts." Perceptions of withheld information and concealed agendas created gaps between people's statements and interpretations of their meaning.

When practiced, forthrightness may help to direct contingency and warrant risk. Even if we conceptualize forthrightness in terms of an ideal speech situation—which, as I discuss below, suggests an undesirable standard—its practice would not eliminate contingency from deliberation. Rather, forthright practices may enable interlocutors to address the contingencies associated with topics, values, evidence, and other aspects of deliberation, facilitating publicly justified agreement and disagreement. Expressing a view shared among board members, one interviewee in Beloit favorably compared the forthrightness of the current administration with the previous one. Previously, "there was a belief that became almost universal among the board members that, you know, [an administrator] was manipulating data and information in order to fool us into thinking that we were doing better than we really were." This belief created a sense of unmanageable contingency. Not only did board members need to address issues that availed themselves to various answers, but they also needed to check the information they used to address these issues. Board members could not focus their attention on the uncertainties of district issues and policy. However, the current administration answered doubts about information: "[A current administrator is] Mr. Transparent. And that [sense of manipulation] just went away."

In encounters in which interlocutors act forthrightly, the attendant risk of deliberation may seem warranted. Without its practice, deliberation may appear as a potentially dangerous encounter where a participant makes themself vulnerable without a sense of reciprocity from the other and without a mutual commitment to the potentially transformative power of deliberation. One West Bend board member located part of his frustration with some of his colleagues in what he perceived as their unwillingness to be transparent about the reasons they held their views. He maintained that "the transparency that I feel is a problem of board members' behavior, not of the process." This interviewee felt that the board meetings offered opportunities for members to share their views, but some members refused to do so: "That should be, 'Here are the reasons why I support this. This is what I see. This is why I'm . . .' Tell [us your reasons]. I try to be more transparent about how I feel about things, but I don't see all my peers always doing that." Refusing to articulate reasons in deliberation rejects reciprocity with interlocutors who participate in a process of reason-giving. The latter make themselves vulnerable by exposing their reasoning to criticism by others. The board member who simply states a position undertakes comparatively little risk in school-board deliberations. In the absence of reciprocity, if the risk of deliberation appears too great, vulnerability appears as pointless self-sacrifice.

Even as we recognize a connection between building trust and forthrightness, scholars should resist overly restrictive readings of its operation, since requiring too much from participants would dampen the dynamic—and sometimes confrontational—power of deliberation itself. In this spirit, Elizabeth Markovits warns of placing too great an emphasis on sincerity in models of deliberation, which may produce overidealized images that espouse norms of civility that restrict interaction to ostensibly disinterested modes of communication. Calling these images norms of "hyper-sensitivity," Markovits maintains that they may propagate a "gentlemen's club" model of deliberation in which "self-confidence, certainty, and a seemingly dispassionate tone demonstrate the speaker's commitment to the discussion."[43] In this spirit, one administrator in Beloit spoke of conscious efforts to resist a notion that administrators should remain objective when interacting with board members. This administrator asserted that "because I'm honest enough, [board members] know where I stand on most issues, you know. But I will remind them." This interviewee ascribed a lack of commitment to objectivity: "Most people are only objective about things they don't care about. And if you can be objective about everything as [an administrator], you shouldn't have the job, because then you really don't care about much." Similarly, a Beloit board member operating with a style characterized by others as confrontational associated this approach with forthrightness: "If I say something, I'd better be willing to stand behind it." As Markovits reminds scholars and as these comments indicate, a complex range of human motivations may serve deliberation, including earnestness but also passion, indignation, and pride.

Practicing forthrightness does not demand that interlocutors dissociate efforts to reach understanding from goals of persuading one another. Treating persuasion as antithetical to forthrightness commits the error of hyper-sensitivity that Markovits counsels against. Among theorists of deliberation, Jürgen Habermas (in)famously pursues this path. He instructively calls attention to the ways that interlocutors operate with assumptions about the statements and motives of others in their everyday communication practices. Habermas holds that "agreement in the communicative practice of everyday life rests simultaneously on intersubjectively shared propositional knowledge, on normative accord, and on mutual trust."[44] Unless they have reasons to believe otherwise, Habermas maintains, interlocutors tend to make positive attributions about these aspects of their communication with an other. When disagreements arise that challenge these attributions, interlocutors may engage in various forms of argumentation to resolve their disagreements. The problem is that Habermas conceptualizes this argumentation in overly narrow terms. In his view, communicative action, as the *original mode* of language use," operates with "an orientation toward reaching understanding."[45] Habermas regards strategic uses of language as "parasitic" and outside the proper boundaries of deliberation.

Dissociating understanding and persuasion may hamper relations of trust by failing to account for the dynamics of deliberation. By treating communicative action and persuasion as qualitatively distinct forms of interaction, Habermas makes reason—not people—the agent in deliberation. He identifies the driving force in these interactions as "the force of the better argument."[46] But arguments do not present themselves, people do. Because trust draws on experience, abstracting people from this process offers participants no basis for building relations of trust. Moreover, this restricted sense of forthrightness calls attention to the gendered and classist character of a "gentlemen's club" model of deliberation—manifest as a bourgeois public sphere—since the view of reason as self-evident reflects a culturally specific mode of interaction. Perhaps unsurprisingly, then, Habermas equates strategy with deception, asserting that a speaker can pursue these aims "only when he deceives his partner concerning the fact that he is acting strategically."[47] An interlocutor's honesty about persuasive intent presumably would undermine the chances of persuasive success.

Yet interviewees critiqued this distinction and its supposed consequences. They insisted that understanding and persuasion both would be served by making plain one's persuasive goals and reasons. In an illustrative case, one board member in Beloit critiqued colleagues whom he/she perceived as cynically referencing economic struggles in the community in order to block tax increases. This interviewee held that "I think inquiry is productive always, right? What I find to be unproductive is people's motivation for their inquiry, right, where it's not to understand the other, or not to understand the opposing view, right?" In distinguishing some motives from understanding, this interviewee's statement may seem to confirm Habermas's conception. However, later in the interview, this board member suggested a contrary relationship between persuasion and transparency. This board member voiced frustration with colleagues who disingenuously claimed, "'I'm here because I care about the disenfranchised,' you know." This board member wanted to "cut through that bullshit. You're not, you know. You're here because this is your ax to grind, and you're not going to support this because you don't value it." Rather than undermining it, transparency facilitated persuasion: "You know, if you could put that right on the table, and then have that be the end of the discussion, you know, that's far more valuable than sitting there and lying and blowing smoke up people's asses and trying to disguise what your true values are." Moreover, as a reference to "true values" suggests, making plain one's persuasive goals also promoted understanding.

From one perspective, flexibility and forthrightness may seem to pull deliberators in opposite directions by intimating alternative—and potentially contrasting—practices. This tension appears in the comments of various board members and administrators. On the one hand, they endorsed practices that avoided "lock[ing] yourself into a certain point of view," "hold[ing] to positions no matter what," or "not hear[ing] anything other people said." These comments appear to suggest that flexibility entails a disavowal of advocacy, thereby leaving interlocutors open to the persuasion of others. On the other hand, forthrightness seems to reinforce the connection between interlocutors and their positions. In this spirit, board members' comments invoked practices that entailed stating, "Here are the reasons why I support this." In acting forthrightly, board members indicated that they were "willing to stand behind a view," and they hoped that others would "put that right on the table." In important respects, deliberators cannot avoid this tension, which informs deliberation as a process of weighing different perspectives. As participants in this process, interlocutors need to articulate and evaluate all perspectives, including their own. Advocacy does not forestall self-evaluation; rather, advocacy ensures that one's own perspective will receive a fair hearing along with other perspectives weighed in deliberation. Interlocutors need to balance a commitment to their perspectives in deliberation with a commitment to situating their perspectives alongside others, which facilitates a shared judgment.

As a process of justifying values, interests, identities, and goals, deliberation offers board members and administrators the opportunity to engage one another's perspectives. To the extent that they pursue these opportunities, deliberators may learn about different perspectives, including understanding why people hold their beliefs, how these beliefs may be different from and similar to one's own, how people may take a different route to a shared judgment, and how similar starting points may lead to different interpretations and judgments. A Beloit board member explained that the learning potential of engagement appeared especially handy during deliberations over district finances: "It's valuable listening to the other people's, other board members' questions and the questions that I may come up with. I think we're all learning . . . because school finances are incredibly messy." This board member intimated that no single person—not even the most experienced board member—could address the issue as thoroughly as the group. Learning about others also may enable participants to learn about themselves, understanding better how one's views may be situated among different perspectives and how others understand one's views. Another Beloit school-board member broached this point when discussing their preparation for the financial deliberations: "I made sure not to ask people [about the issue] that I knew would give me the answer that I wanted." Seeking unexpected and even undesired answers enables examination of one's views.

Engagement may generate a sense of familiarity that facilitates relations of trust by making seemingly mysterious and potentially dangerous differences appear knowable—even if in disagreement. A few interviewees in West Bend had identified a greater sense of familiarity as a remedy for the divisions that had emerged among the board and between the board and the administration. One board member maintained that "I think we need to get to a point where we sit down and we talk to each other about why, in all honesty, why I don't like somebody or I don't trust them, and how can we fix that." Another board member recalled how he had been able to bridge differences with a board colleague by learning more about the person. Reaching out did not come easily: "It takes an effort on the board member's part to reach out to the person on the other side and sit down and say, 'We can go talk so that you can learn about me and I can learn about you.'" Still, this effort produced results, which the board member saw in his own relationship with another colleague: "Once that happens, then you can respect their opinion, you don't have to agree with it, but you can respect where they're coming from, and understand where they're coming from." Engagement draws on the experiences that people bring to deliberation and modifies these experiences with the participation of an other. Reaching out to an interlocutor may transfigure experiences positively.

Engagement functions ethically by treating people as capable agents who may participate fully in a collaborative process of reaching a shared judgment. By engaging, participants in deliberation regard one another as worthy of attention, warranting the time and energy of inquiry because they may learn valuable lessons from one another. Alluding to an issue addressed by scholars examining deliberation in diverse contexts, an administrator in Elmbrook located the value of engagement in bringing together people who otherwise may not interact. This administrator observed that "very seldom do people get together with people that they don't have—that they have differences with." For children and adults alike, public schools presented a rare opportunity to learn about difference: "The public school forces people to have to get together and form community in order to move anything forward." This administrator cast their role as "help[ing] people understand one another. Put[ting] them together in places that they have to be aware of themselves, be aware of other people, be aware of what the issue is, and then try to drive that to closure." This statement underscores the ethics of learning about one another. In learning about others, people may build relationships where none exist. They may heal fractured communities and divided societies.

As this administrator's references to "awareness" suggest, realizing the ethical value of engagement requires more than permitting someone to speak, not interrupting someone, or forswearing the use of ad hominem attacks. Simply waiting one's turn or adhering to an official code of conduct may help people tolerate different perspectives, but these behaviors do not recognize other perspectives as legitimate or instructive. As one board member in Beloit maintained, engagement employs conflict productively. This board member saw "conflict as a positive, in that it generates discussion and, um, thought-provoking, for me, often thought-changing, vote-changing discussion." While casting conflict as thought-provoking also intimated the cognitive capacity of engagement, this board member underscored its ethics in treating others as warranting attention and justification: "The willingness to hear what someone else is saying. . . . [The motivation] to explain to you why I feel the way that I do, and having the respect of everybody else to listen." Engagement does not proceed by adhering to established rules and procedures, but by interacting with an other as a mutually capable, contributing agent. In this way, engagement may fight the alienation that people feel when devalued by others and the attendant problems that alienation produces for building trust.

Board members and administrators also discerned the ethics of engagement in their shared judgment that deliberations worked best when participants did not personalize their disagreements. To be sure, they did not always follow this practice, but many interviewees strongly recommended it. For instance, one often-contentious board member in West Bend held that productive deliberation happens when interlocutors "keep it professional, keep it on the issues, and don't make it personal." Character attacks denigrated the agency of others and stalled decision-making. In contrast, "when people truly listen to each other, consider their points of view, challenge their biases and assumptions, and do what is right always for the community and always have that central in their minds, that's how you get the best outcomes." Even as his statement distills qualities of engagement, this interviewee alludes to the difficulty of its practice, since doing "what is right" for a community may engender contesting interpretations. Yet interlocutors could work toward productive disagreement with practice. As another West Bend board member maintained, "You've got to disagree with the idea and not inflame the person in the process, and that's a learned skill." In this spirit, one Beloit board member conceded that upon first joining the board, "I don't think I understood the dynamics that I was bringing to the board and how disruptive it may have felt to others. I don't know if I was as respectful of their vantage points." This reflection substantiates the point that trust need not appear fully formed for deliberation to proceed.

Engaging the perspectives of others enables participants to address the power relationships that may frustrate efforts to build trust. Perspectives connect the experiences that people bring to deliberation with their experience of deliberation; differences among participants' perspectives may mark their different experiences of power. Conceptualizing the relationship between these experiences presents a challenge for a deliberative account of trust, since people's experiences outside of deliberation may make them more or less comfortable in using deliberation as a means of building trust. A first step in addressing this challenge requires a renunciation of an intellectual commitment to what Nancy Fraser has critiqued as "status bracketing": the belief that different social experiences have no bearing on the conduct of deliberation and thus may be bracketed in favor of more pressing issues. Referencing the bourgeois public sphere, Fraser notes that calls to bracket status effectively smuggled in culturally specific participatory norms and practices that "functioned informally to marginalize women and members of the plebeian classes and to prevent them from participating as peers."[48] These norms derived their force from their seemingly neutral character.

One interviewee had effectively practiced status-bracketing in mentoring young administrators. This interviewee counseled these mentees that their performance and not their background mattered for professional advancement. When asked by young women about whether a "glass ceiling" would impede their career aspirations, this person responded that "the gender issue is bullshit. Seriously, I've said that." However, statements by some board members advocating traditional gender roles and questioning the value of advanced degrees had shaken the confidence of administrators and some board members in this district that everyone experienced equal treatment. These interviewees conceded that prejudicial beliefs about gender and class influenced people's interactions. Similarly, a board member in another district admitted to one REDD interviewer—a mother, no less—that "I think women should be home taking care of their kids. They shouldn't be in the workforce." These sentiments warrant censure. Board members and administrators who think differently need to work to create an environment where interlocutors will not suffer marginalization because of their identities and background. By explicitly addressing differences among interlocutors, Fraser argues, participants committed to more just deliberations may have greater success in discrediting regressive views about the role of women in society and other disempowering beliefs.

A second step entails appreciating how perspectives may elucidate relations of power in non-reductive ways. As Iris Marion Young explains, perspectives introduce difference into deliberation without assuming that all members of social groups think alike, thus affirming participants' agency without abstracting their experiences. According to Young, the concept of perspective facilitates recognition that "agents who are 'close' in a social field have a similar point of view on the field and the occurrences within it, while those who are socially distant are more likely to see things differently."[49] Because they do not function deterministically, social perspectives comport with the flexibility that participants may utilize to build trust. Young explains that "social perspective consists in a set of questions, kinds of experience, and assumptions with which reasoning begins, rather than the conclusions drawn."[50] Engaging perspectives invites others to articulate the experiences they bring to deliberation, how these experiences make them more or less inclined to trust, and what they need and desire in deliberation to build trust.

While interviewees generally recognized how differences could inform their deliberations, they sometimes struggled to treat difference nonreductively. In West Bend, besides perceptions of gender roles influencing some deliberators' behavior, interviewees reported anxieties about class and education, in which the latter stood as a proxy for the former. Rather than seeing the graduate degrees of some of the administrators as resources that brought additional perspectives to bear on district issues, some board members dismissed these degrees as elitist markers that excused a smugness among some administrators. One board member held that the administration had developed a habit of "presenting the case and expecting there to be no argument with it." This board member expressed some anxiety about matching the professional background of administrators: "It often is hard to argue points with someone who holds a PhD, and, you know, you may have philosophical differences but it's hard to bring those up in terms of equal points." Other interviewees reiterated this sentiment, including one who charged the administration with dismissing differences in opinion by disqualifying others: "There's a refusal to accept that somebody may have gained an understanding of a particular technical aspect of it because, you know, I'm not a PhD in education." Several interviewees offered "background-based" explanations to account for divisions among board members and between board members and the administration. Seeking to redress this perception, one administrator maintained that "if we have a business professional on our board, they are treated differently from people who are blue-collar." This administrator confessed that "we've been subtly disrespecting our board because of their, whatever their background is." Although uncorroborated by others, if true this claim intimates additional disempowering beliefs. Moreover, this unsettling potential dynamic—trading class bias for gender bias—points to the need to treat perspective not as an apparent answer that closes off deliberation but as a question that opens up deliberation.

Interviewees sometimes identified publicity itself as an obstacle to engagement, specifically, the presence of larger audiences at meetings and the broadcast of board meetings on local television. Along these lines, one Elmbrook board member held that "committee forums or meetings that are frankly not real well-attended provide us the best opportunity to lay our hearts on the table and our brains on the table and share in a way that gets us to really good conclusions." This board member explained that better-attended meetings tended to attract community members interested only in specific issues and uninformed about or unwilling to consider these issues within the wider context of district policies. As a consequence, board members seemed less willing to offer exploratory, tentative positions for fear of being taken out of context. This interviewee worried about the possibility of someone "that has to leave to pick up their kid, take the note about what I said and then it goes and has its life of its own, or it starts a rumor mill that becomes really difficult to manage, and gets people all upset over nothing." In contrast, this board member valued less publicized meetings to interact with colleagues because these meetings provided an opportunity to "banter about and not feel a sense of responsibility for the things we say that could be misconstrued."

Television, too, seemed to influence the willingness of some board members to engage one another. One West Bend board member discerned a shift in the board's practices in committee meetings and televised board meetings. This interviewee claimed that when he first joined the board, his colleagues did most of their work in committee meetings, using the televised meetings, which he called a "dog-and-pony show," for motions and votes. More recently, however, board members seemed to wait "until they were in front of the camera in the open board meeting and bring a question out." This interviewee's comments cast this supposed shift as an increased interest in grandstanding, where board members appear more interested in voicing positions that pleased perceived constituencies rather than engaging their colleagues. Without attributing negative motives to colleagues, other interviewees also called attention to the potentially dampening influence of television cameras. For instance, an Elmbrook board member stated that "we can take some of the discussion and move it into a more relaxed format off-camera, which makes a difference to some people—um, not me—but you can talk more openly, more freely, in a more relaxed manner." With the exception of closed sessions, these off-camera meetings remained public, but board members' comments suggested that they associated television cameras with larger, less-informed audiences. Concerns about meeting attendance and television broadcasts underscored the risks of deliberation. Presumably, deliberations witnessed by larger audiences—whether physically present or watching at home—carried greater risks because changing one's mind or voicing unpopular views would potentially raise the ire of more people. Interviewees sometimes expressed a desire to reduce the risk of their deliberation by minimizing its publicity. While we may appreciate this desire, we may also note its futility, since interlocutors cannot escape the publicity of deliberation—save for intimates involved in "private" deliberations, which does not describe the work of school boards.

When interlocutors believe that their deliberation matters to other participants, when they believe that others will heed its collective judgment, they may be more willing to practice trust. When people perceive that deliberation does not matter—either because their interlocutors have initiated deliberation simply to provide political cover for a decision that already has been made or because interlocutors will conduct their future actions without any reference to relevant deliberations—they may substitute feelings of cynicism and alienation for practices of trust. One Elmbrook board member expressed concern that the district had developed a reputation for soliciting recommendations from community groups and subsequently ignoring them, which may have appeared especially salient in light of the duties that the school board assigned to the Enrollment Management Study Team during the Chapter 220 deliberations. The board member held that "I am pretty convinced that that's a bad way of doing business. If you ask a committee, a respected group of people from the community, to work on a problem and they give you an answer, you better be prepared to take it seriously." While other board members challenged the claim that these community recommendations had been ignored, this statement points to the possibility that participants may grow more frustrated and less inclined to participate actively in deliberations in the future if they feel that their contributions have carried no influence.

In a more extreme case, some West Bend board members charged the administration with colluding with other board members to manipulate meetings to produce contrived deliberation. One board member insisted that issues had "been decided already before [they] got to the board level, and you were there just to agree with it. And if you disagreed, you raised the ire of whoever was opposed, whoever is on the other side. So, I felt like the process was pretty much, pretty much a foregone conclusion." Regard-less of the veracity of these charges, their circulation creates obstacles to building trust. Perceiving that an encounter has been rigged situates the supposed guilty parties as having violated the very conditions for engag-ing in deliberation. Removing the contingency that contextualizes delibera-tion, an allegedly rigged encounter also makes risk unreciprocated. At best, under such conditions, the risking interlocutor may waste time engaging in reason-giving with an other who already has or soon will disregard any rea-sons presented through deliberation. More troubling, a risking interlocutor may unwittingly help to legitimate positions that he or she finds objection-able. Further, accepting the consequentiality of deliberation when others do not may bring symbolic and material harm to the risking interlocutor.

This is why participants may practice trust when they signal to one an-other that they will heed their interactions when undertaking subsequent activities relevant to their deliberation. Participants may heed others by ar-ticulating a willingness to account for their perspectives. Both *articulating* and *accounting for* constitute important aspects of heedfulness. Board mem-bers addressed these qualities in terms of their relations with both their colleagues and community members. Among board members, heedfulness concerned the practices they exercised as well as the decisions they made in their meetings. Between board members and community members, heed-fulness served as a measure of conduct that board members, in their delib-eration and decision-making, could signal to community members. Board members' campaign pledges and their ongoing relations with constituents carried a reasonable expectation that they would align their conduct as poli-cymakers with stated perspectives and positions. This expectation included situations where board members' positions changed through engagement with their colleagues, in which case board members could convey these changes and their reasoning to constituents.

Board members and administrators across the districts captured the quality of heedfulness (among other connotations) in their periodic refer-ences to "boardsmanship," which invoked a set of ethical practices that in-cluded working for the good of the district and valuing the contributions of others in a collaborative decision-making process. One Beloit board member addressed the difficulty of ending deliberation on issues while ensuring that all board members felt they had an opportunity to contribute meaningfully: "That's, I think, part of the boardsmanship, to figure out how you're gonna do that, because you're gonna have to live with each other every Tuesday night and, ah, you gotta be able to do that." Turning to the community, one

West Bend board member underscored the importance of making plain one's values, principles, and goals when running for office and then keeping these commitments after obtaining office: "If they're supporting you, they should have an expectation of you, um, doing what you're saying you're going to do." This interviewee recognized the need to remain open to contrary evidence and to changing one's views, but he effectively held that board members should treat their campaign pledges as presumptions while assigning a burden of proof to arguments for change.

Articulating indicates that signals about heedfulness should happen during deliberation itself, which is potentially tricky because deliberation often refers to specific decisions about things that will occur after deliberation has concluded. In their study of trust in schools, Bryk and Schneider associate trust with competence. They note that "gross incompetence . . . is corrosive to trust relations," in that teachers, principals, and parents alike recognize when someone cannot carry out a task supported by others, such as changing classroom instruction, maintaining building safety, or getting students to school on time.[51] Although they address speaking and listening as conducive to trust, Bryk and Schneider develop an organizational theory of trust, in which competence (defined as the ability to execute a decision) serves as an appropriate quality. But scholars of deliberation cannot turn to a post hoc measure to evaluate deliberation, since doing so would undermine justifications for studying trust in deliberation. Moreover, for scholars and advocates alike, decisions receive attention during and after deliberation, and so we lose sight of an important aspect of trust-building if we do not consider how people may commit themselves to actions through deliberation. In the Beloit case, waiting to call a vote until participants mostly feel satisfied with their deliberation offers an example of how board members may articulate heedfulness during their meetings. In the West Bend case, if deliberation scholars assessed heedfulness by considering when implemented policies conform to campaign promises, then we would inappropriately adopt a post hoc measure. Instead, if scholars focus on deliberations leading to a vote and the justifications that boards members offer for their votes, we may consider how deliberators articulate heedfulness.

Accounting for suggests that the commitments made in deliberation need not entail agreement about specific outcomes or subsequent actions, since participants may reach judgment in cases of agreement and disagreement. Interviewees appreciated the difficulty of demonstrating heedfulness amid disagreement. Offering an observation echoed by others, one West Bend board member chided community members who complained that "if

I wasn't doing what you wanted me to do, you're not listening to me. . . . It's not that we're not listening, it's that we're not doing what you think we should do, and that's described as not listening." This board member interpreted "not listening" as a "code word" employed whenever a segment of the community disagreed with a district proposal they perceived as threatening to their interests: "The moment you start to push forward, and you start to advance proposals, you'll get this 'transparency' and 'not listening.'" Even as this complaint voiced frustration, it expressed the need to account for the diverse interests in local communities.

Heedfulness in the absence of a specific agreement entails articulating the influence of engagement on one's thought and actions. Along these lines, one Elmbrook administrator praised the school board for its "strong desire to be stakeholder-sensitive." Sometimes this desire for sensitivity slowed down decision-making, but the administrator explained that "even if one person comments at the podium or comments in an e-mail opposed to some issue, I think we have a culture in which we take that seriously, and we'll go back and kind of revisit that." Even after decisions had been made, one Beloit interviewee suggested that the board could signal heedfulness by continuing to engage the community. This interviewee maintained that board members had built a working relationship that enabled them to move forward after divisive issues like deliberations over the tax levy, but "where the repair needs to be done is with the community." Yet board members believed that the community needed to act, too. One West Bend board member estimated tartly that "there are about fifty members of the community who actually engage with the school board, and that means that there's about 115,000 that don't." While this comment may have underestimated community participation, it affirmed the relationality of deliberative trust.

Tending to Trust

Considering trust as a deliberative practice draws critical attention to the human relationships that sustain deliberation itself. Whereas social and political trust function as orientations that individuals may extend to institutions or a generalized other, deliberative trust does not take shape in isolation. Nor does deliberation. Inviting reciprocity, deliberation involves participants in a mutual process of attending to reasons and perspectives that may transform people's views. While some people may express greater tolerance than others for the risks entailed in this process, all participants may sense a potential threat to their commitments, values, and beliefs in the prospect of changing their minds in particular contexts. Seeking ways to encourage deliberative risk-taking, scholars sometimes may be tempted to think that if they can just establish the proper forums, rules, and procedures, people will pursue this path over other putatively arbitrary and coercive methods of decision-making. For instance, seeking to establish rules for reasonable deliberation in diverse societies, John Rawls calls on interlocutors to abide by a "duty of civility," which, on matters of basic justice, calls on people to explain to one another "how the principles and policies they advocate and vote for can be supported by the political values of public reason."[52] Developing an a priori, top-down model, Rawls hopes to set the conditions for ethical and efficacious deliberation.

Yet this approach discounts the constitutive power of human relationships—the power that Hannah Arendt celebrates when people come together. Rejecting views of power as a possession, Arendt counters that "power springs up between [people] when they act together and vanishes the moment they disperse."[53] Power discloses the limits of individual effort and the creative potential of coordinated action. In contrast, an a priori, procedural approach situates human interaction on a prefabricated social field. Privileging rules and social structures over human relationships neglects how experience and context inform deliberative practice. Moreover, by assuming people's willingness to deliberate, a rule-based approach skirts a tricky question about how negative experiences and perceptions of others may make people reluctant to undergo the risks of deliberation. Seeing deliberation as enacted through human relationships affords recognition of its volitional character—people cannot be made to deliberate, they must choose it. A steadfast refusal to participate will counteract carefully designed procedures, inclusive norms, and more.

Short of covering one's mouth, eyes, and ears during meetings or refusing to attend meetings altogether, school-board members cannot refrain completely from deliberation.[54] Even the more reticent board members in the three districts made their views known and judged the competing arguments of their more vocal colleagues. A deliberative conception of trust suggests that board members and other policymakers may build trust through their interactions gradually, haltingly, and nonlinearly. As they do, interlocutors may bolster their practices of deliberation. As the interviewees suggest, this process is full of potential frustrations and pitfalls. However, conceptualizing trust as something that must be built—rather than assumed or imposed—signals hope because this means that trust need not exist as a precondition of deliberating across differences. People need not wait for trust to deliberate. Instead, deliberation itself may serve as a means by which we come to trust others, and our trust may become stronger with practice.

CONCLUSION:
RECONNECTING DEMOCRACY AND EDUCATION

Appreciating the mutually informative relationship of democracy and education, John Dewey did not believe that they always acted in harmony. In perhaps his best-known assessment of the condition of democratic publics, *The Public and Its Problems*, Dewey held that education had failed to develop in citizens the skills they needed to navigate a complex society and address the ever-expanding consequences of human action. Struggling to make meaningful and learn from their experiences, citizens felt but did not understand their implication in public affairs: "Many consequences are felt rather than perceived; they are suffered, but they cannot be said to be known."[1] Amid this social alienation, which demanded a coherent and integrative public response, knowledge stood "divided against itself."[2] As disciplines looked inward, oppositions between pure and applied inquiry sharpened, reducing application to a set of techniques utilized by a profit-seeking mercantile class while forsaking the notion of knowledge in the service of a greater public good. To redress this situation, Dewey called for the development of a practice of critical social inquiry and the wide dissemination of its findings. He discerned a crucial role for an art of communication to "break through the crust of conventionalized and routine consciousness" to refashion a public in eclipse as a Great Community.[3]

A Great Community represented for Dewey a reinvigorated and reengaged public that would attend to shared concerns and problems, exploring their varied aspects and articulating satisfactory responses. A Great Community would constitute a "society in which the ever-expanding and intricately ramifying consequences of associated activities shall be known in the full sense of that word," as the convergence of understanding and communication.[4] Dewey envisioned a Great Community as a network of locally based publics that would come together to generate action while interacting with and learning from dispersed publics. In this vision, Dewey championed the local as a stabilizing, community building force even as he remained wary of its limitations. Functioning well, local engagements could ground public affairs, making abstract forces tangible and manageable and thereby providing citizens a point of entry for directing their environments. Further, local encounters promised efficacy because they presented regular and familiar opportunities for engagement; citizens could practice participating in public, and they could come to know the people with whom they interacted. And yet, Dewey did not neglect the potentially narrowing and exclusive aspects of localities. Localism could breed provincialism and prejudice, imposing a stifling conformity of opinion and threatening people who seemed different. Dewey hoped that the networked aspects of a Great Community would resist these pressures: "Mobility may in the end supply the means by which the spoils of remote and indirect interaction and interdependence flow back into local life." The result would be dynamic, productive publics that "will be alive and flexible as well as stable, responsive to the complex and world-wide scene in which [they are] enmeshed."[5]

A Great Community provides a potentially illuminating perspective for considering the role of school boards in an accountability regime and beyond. The networked nature of a Great Community resonates with the networked character of the public sphere in which diverse actors craft education policy. While Dewey articulates an ideal vision, contemporary deliberations over education policy often operate far from an ideal, as my discussion of the rise of an accountability regime and my analyses of Beloit, Elmbrook, and West Bend suggest. Nevertheless, by valuing vibrant communicative practices within and across sites, a Great Community may serve as a heuristic for an engaged public sphere. From the perspective of a Great Community, education policy should not be formulated through an isolated approach that seeks to situate authority with one source, as in the top-down approach of No Child Left Behind. Rather, insofar as competing needs and interests produce struggles over symbolic and material resources, the decentered character of the network itself may facilitate better deliberation about balancing the tensions that arise. A Great Community sketches out a place for school boards, as local policymaking bodies in education policy, offering clues about the value of board participation as well as the constraints and opportunities for participation. A Great Community raises a serious challenge to the contemporary era: whereas an accountability regime orients itself to the market, a Great Community reconnects education with democracy.

In this conclusion, I draw inspiration from the vision of a Great Community to consider a role for engaged local deliberations about education policy as well as to call for reframing policy deliberations at all levels to foreground the democratic worth of education. First, acknowledging the limits of local participation, I argue for its value for both individuals as well as publics. Enacting a vision of democracy as a mode of associated living, local participation cultivates subjectivities, empowers individuals and communities, offers important perspectives on policies, and contextualizes policymaking and implementation. Second, I argue for a reorientation of education policy toward the individual and collective practices of democratic communities. Asking democratically oriented questions, school-board deliberations may explore the roles that schools may serve in bolstering the reciprocal relations of individual and community.

Recognizing the Value of Local Deliberation

The pervasiveness of school boards across the cities and towns of the United States has not ensured their popularity. To the contrary, at various moments in U.S. history, reformers have decried school boards as regressive institutions. Progressive Era reformers dedicated part of their efforts to removing authority from what they regarded as politicized local boards.[6] Yet these reforms did not alleviate dissatisfaction with school boards. For example, one recent commentator has rebuked schools boards as "a flawed exercise in democracy."[7] In the eyes of their critics, school boards perpetuate ineptitude, dysfunction, and even intolerance. Populated by laypeople, these critics contend, school boards make bad decisions about education because their members lack any training; perpetuate petty grievances that stand in the way of good decision-making; and listen only to evidence and people with whom they already agree. School boards are far from perfect, but, as I argue in this section, the value of a substantive local contribution to education policy remains. Importantly, as a Great Community intimates, we need not limit a view of local contributions to the current practices of school boards.

To value local participation is not to assert that local deliberations inherently exhibit virtuous qualities and produce enlightened outcomes. On the theme of ideology, as deliberations in West Bend over the Gay-Straight Alliance (GSA) indicated, the limits of the local may manifest in narrow-mindedness and provincialism. Ideology may operate ominously at the local level as a force that perpetuates fear of the other as an enemy within and insists on conformist thinking as a condition of membership. Scarcity may dampen participation at the local level, promote the pursuit of self-interest, and augment unequal relations of power. In Beloit, board members dealing with scarcity confronted a series of invidious choices between addressing the needs of students and recognizing the hardships faced by community members. Even as expertise may bolster educational decision-making, deliberations in Elmbrook about Chapter 220 revealed some of the limits of local expertise in narrowing the board's perspective and frustrating the board's ability to perceive developments that their methods did not capture neatly. Chapter 220 parents' testimony provided an alternative, but these parents did not hold the decision-making authority to check the hegemony of financial expertise. Just as trust may bolster relationships at the local level, if invoked as a substitute for critical judgment, trust also may enable ill-considered and imprudent decision-making. Without judgment, trust at the local level may shore up existing patterns of authority and thereby excuse incompetence by restricting participation to specific allies.

The case for local participation rests with the relationship we imagine between democracy and education. If democracy constitutes "a mode of associated living," as Dewey suggests in *Democracy and Education*, then enabling ordinary folks—or at least members of their communities—to have some say about institutionalized instruction in the practices of associated living fulfills an implicit promise of justice.[8] Dictating to people the terms by which they may make meaningful their relationships with one another, which education ostensibly develops, contravenes the practice of democracy. Limiting local participation in education policy limits the vision of democracy that education may serve. Some commentators, including Dewey's well-known antagonist Walter Lippmann, have argued for this view. Lippmann believed that overly ambitious ideas about democracy stood in the way of effective action. He retorted that the public could participate in governance only in times of crisis—and then only indirectly by supporting the proper leaders. Lippmann held that "the ideal of public opinion is to align men during the crisis of a problem in such a way as to favor the action of those individuals who may be able to compose the crisis." This task required a minimal program of education that consisted of impressing in citizens "clear signs" that they could use to "discern those individuals."[9] In contrast, "living" democracy requires action from citizens themselves, not as something separate from their everyday activities but as part of these activities. And this action, in turn, develops as a kind of continuing education that exceeds static signs or, in the language of an accountability regime, standards. Local participation in the formulation of education policy enacts both democracy and education as processes of meaning-making. Policies partially made by members of a community help construct ways of living in a community.

The distinctive constitutive force that education carries for individual and collective subjectivities also justifies local participation.[10] The power of education exceeds the boundaries implied by its content. In West Bend, for example, high school students learned about traditional and nontraditional types of families in their social studies courses. This curricular material may have generated awareness for students—especially students who lived in homes with married heterosexual parents—that the type of family structure they experienced personally did not represent everyone's experiences. In the process, this curricular material invited a judgment about the moral worth of diverse families and people. As an extra-curricular club, the Gay-Straight Alliance advocated for the position that heterosexual and homosexual families and people warranted respect. The members of the GSA developed subjectivities that bridged the curricular and extra-curricular by welcoming their peers into an inclusive and affirming student body. To the extent that they supported the GSA by refusing to engage in or stay silent when witnessing bullying, nonmember students also could develop subjectivities as people who welcomed and valued diversity.

Beyond individual judgments, curricular and non-curricular forces informed the collective subjectivity of high school students and community members in West Bend. The official recognition of a GSA—even as controversy attended this recognition—implicated everyone, including the GSA's most vociferous opponents, as members of a welcoming and affirming community. Opposition to the GSA did not vitiate this outcome, as difference informs the formation of collective subjectivities. Shared meanings must be made, which entails a process that draws from diverse values and beliefs. Local participation does not guarantee a particular outcome, but the stakes of education policy justify local participation. In West Bend, exemplifying the spirit of mobility of a Great Community, GSA advocates successfully leveraged forces from outside the community (i.e., federal law) to craft a shared local subjectivity. In doing so, they fulfilled the promise of democratic association to facilitate wider and fuller connections that enable people to realize their potential.

Vibrant images of democracy and processes of subject formation indicate that local participation embodies personal and community empowerment. Empowerment draws attention to the specific opportunities (or lack thereof) for local communities to create and sustain associations as well as form their subjectivities. Empowerment also relies on sufficient resources for action, which, in an accountability regime, are distributed unequally. In Beloit, for example, as they weighed budget cuts and tax increases, board members referenced personal experience with lost jobs, frozen wages, and declining income, revealing that they shared the economic struggles of their neighbors. As a consequence of economic woes, both individuals and the community as a whole felt their agency circumscribed. No one could address all of their needs. For board members, this meant that they could not sustain a sufficiently supported learning environment for students while remaining sensitive to the struggles of community members. Yet even in this situation, they resisted the incentives of the state funding formula to consider only one criterion—financial returns—in making their decisions. As local policymakers, they considered a wider and more complex range of factors in deciding where to set the tax levy. They demonstrated their savvy to an accountability regime that designates Beloit as an economic loser. In this case, empowerment would have been bolstered by greater movement of resources across policy networks.

School-board deliberations constitute a pervasive form of local participation in a networked public sphere, but these deliberations do not represent an especially valued form of participation by other actors in an education policy network. Revaluing local participation may offer benefits to policymakers at state and national sites in the network. Local participation can offer important perspectives on state and national policies, including the ways that school districts take up these policies. For instance, open enrollment policies, like other contemporary education policies that foreground choice and competition, seek to unsettle and reinvigorate existing educational practices by compelling local schools to compete for students in the same way that commercial enterprises compete for customers. Neglecting the unequal distribution of resources, these policies presume that competition spurs improvement, thereby benefiting everyone. However, deliberations in Elmbrook over Chapter 220 reveal another way in which Open Enrollment resonates with a market logic by inducing school districts to compete for higher-paying customers. In the school board's decision-making, when they admitted Chapter 220 students, the district lost revenue. In contrast, when they admitted Open Enrollment students, the district gained revenue. This system of incentives disqualified efforts to improve education by recruiting and maintaining a diverse student body; through a market lens, diversity became a form of charity. As they made these financial decisions, Elmbrook board members appreciated the negative implications for minority students in Milwaukee and, to a lesser degree, the losses that resident students would experience as they learned with a less diverse student body.

Revaluing local participation may create forums for addressing these issues. Regardless of state legislators' intentions, the effect of the different financial structures for Chapter 220 and Open Enrollment has been to move suburban Milwaukee districts from the former to the latter—and this largely has proceeded without any public discussion. As the Elmbrook school board deliberated about its participation in Chapter 220, a report sponsored by the Harvard School of Public Health circulated in state and national media identifying schools in the Milwaukee metropolitan area as some of the most segregated among the hundred largest metropolitan areas in the United States. On race, metropolitan Milwaukee sat only behind metropolitan Chicago in terms of having the most segregated schools.[11] With the exception of Katie Wilson, who reminded her colleagues about the intertwined futures of Elmbrook and Milwaukee children, no board member or administrator in Elmbrook adopted a regional perspective.[12] The incentives of school financing did not reward such thinking. Yet local districts offered potentially valuable perspectives in understanding larger regional trends about segregation—budgetary considerations moved them away from diversity. Connecting disparate discussions across districts, which would require state legislators to seek out the perspectives of board members, would elucidate the social implications of ostensibly discrete financial decisions.

Revaluing local perspectives could help to contextualize policy developments proceeding concurrently and over time across districts within a region, state, or the United States. In an accountability regime, standards and testing have arisen as a mutually reinforcing pair of policy tools to compel states and localities to improve public education. As he advocated for NCLB, President George W. Bush exhorted that leaders "set the highest of high standards" for student learning and that schools employ tests as accountability measures to "determine whether or not children are learning."[13] Similarly, as he has urged state education officials to compete in a "Race to the Top," President Barack Obama explained that federal officials would consider "whether states are designing and enforcing higher and clearer standards and assessments" to enable student success through graduation and beyond.[14] These calls for higher standards intimate that state and local officials—either because of a lack of motivation, competence, or both—have been satisfied with lower standards and require some system of monitoring to ensure that standards rise. Standards also imply a move toward standardization—toward establishing a uniform threshold for success, criteria for assessment, content for instruction. From this approach, standards offer the same opportunities and hold the same expectations for students in Beloit, Elmbrook, and West Bend.

Engaging the spirit of these calls, local perspectives can illuminate structural impediments requiring removal as well as the resources necessary to achieve success. Bush and Obama's calls rightly assert that equality should inform the education of children in diverse districts. Policymakers should not limit the options available to students in Beloit and Elmbrook because of the working-class and upper-middle-class characters of their respective communities. More specifically, children in Beloit should be taught with the same expectations that they can engage sophisticated material as children in Elmbrook; they should be regarded as equally capable of attending and succeeding in college and beyond. Yet these calls, as abstract pronouncements, do little to address the specific contexts that make children in Elmbrook more likely to attend and succeed in college. Abstract calls may reinforce wider public perceptions that people in poorer communities lack the ambition and determination of their wealthier peers. Local perspectives may illuminate the ways that local policymakers cannot pursue pedagogically ameliorative practices because they lack the resources to do so. When connected across localities, local perspectives may reveal how current educational structures like financial incentives and funding formulas may not overcome resource disparities.

Against abstract policy programs, local perspectives remind us that education policy happens in particular places and amid specific histories. As NCLB placed great weight on standards and testing, the legislation foregrounded "scientifically based research" as the means for determining which programs may foster positive results.[15] Promising efficacy, scientifically based research in this usage connotes rigor. Yet it also insinuates a distinction from supposedly tendentious, political approaches that serve adults more than children. Science also conveys the image of the laboratory as a place of knowledge creation from which findings may be disseminated in the field. In the lab, successful experiments verify pedagogy; the laws of nature encompass the classroom.[16] To the extent that this image holds, practitioners may apply the same pedagogical instrument without regard to district variation. However, as my case studies suggest, variations among districts matter. Even as both districts desired success, Beloit and Elmbrook needed to tailor their curriculum and instruction to their different student populations. Board members, administrators, and teachers in Beloit could not rely on students' families to offer the material classroom support that educators and officials may have taken for granted in Elmbrook. Specifics of place include such elements as the development and zoning of Elmbrook as a prosperous suburb versus the status of Beloit as a small city. These differences invoke alternative histories: Elmbrook has fulfilled the history of the suburb as an oasis that primarily serves white, economically prosperous families as "a refuge for the problems of race, crime, and poverty."[17] By contrast, Beloit has struggled with the consequences of a declining industrial base that cannot provide high-school graduates a stable income and lifestyle.

As Dewey's vision of a Great Community suggests, local participation should entail engagement with other sites in a networked policy sphere rather than in isolation. Just as state and federal policymakers should seek out local perspectives, so, too, should school board members interact with state and federal policymakers as well as with policymakers from other locales. Bringing together multiple local, state, and federal perspectives may bolster deliberation about education policy by increasing awareness, understanding, and commitment among actors in the network. Policymakers may better understand the capabilities and resources of actors across the network when they articulate expectations and demands. Circulation across the network of successful and failed experiences in one locale may offer lessons for future reform efforts. Vibrant interaction may serve justice by enabling different actors in a network to work together to share resources equitably, to counteract prejudice, to inspire students to realize their dreams and strengthen their communities, and more.

The GSA controversy in West Bend constitutes a compelling example of the power of network interaction. Had the high school students in West Bend not retained attorneys, and had their attorneys not filed suit in federal court, the GSA likely would not have gained recognition as a school-sponsored club. Further, the GSA attorneys sought redress under the federal Equal Access Act, which Congress had originally passed to protect religious speech, demonstrating the ways in which actors may appropriate resources in a network for different purposes. Moreover, even as GSA advocates appealed to federal law, the energy for change resided within their local community. Community members themselves—the students and their attorneys, families, and supporters in West Bend—sought recognition for diverse students as valuable, capable members of their schools. Community members themselves sought to refashion collective subjectivity in West Bend from one that marginalized people through narrow prohibitions to a subjectivity that welcomed diversity and appreciated different ways of being. Not everyone welcomed this change, but local communities do not speak with one voice. In this case, claims to social justice prevailed over claims to individual conviction.

This case demonstrates, too, that interaction involves school boards and their local communities negotiating tensions of representation. Board members opposing the GSA saw themselves representing the values of what they regarded as a socially conservative community. GSA advocates acknowledged this culture, but they could have pointed to the presence of dozens of GSA supporters, who had attended the board meetings in far greater numbers than opponents, to argue that a majority of the community supported the GSA. Alternatively, board members supporting and opposing the GSA also cited their personal beliefs as reasons for their decisions; Dave Weigand referenced his religious beliefs as a reason for his opposition, while Rick Parks shared his personal experiences with the students in the GSA as a reason for his support. These different bases for decision-making—community opinion and personal judgment—reveal the implication of school-board deliberations in historical debates over the role of the representative as a delegate or trustee.[18] In these debates, the delegate tries as best as one can to learn about and advocate for constituents' views, whereas the trustee employs his or her best judgment (regardless of whether this judgment matches community sentiment) in making decisions. Even if school-board members try to balance these pressures by listening to community members and considering their own educational philosophies in decision-making, questions of proportion and influence remain. What, if any, degree of community consensus warrants assent? How, if at all, may a school-board member distinguish reasonable and unreasonable community opinion? On what bases—including policy preferences, core convictions, a commitment to rights, and more—may a school-board member articulate an independent view?

Although these questions do not elicit conclusive answers, school-board members may consider them while remaining cognizant of advancing democracy. As "a mode of associated living," democracy takes shape in relations of individuals and communities.[19] Democracy offers individuals a responsible role in directing the activities of their communities and in sharing the benefits of their communities. Reciprocally, democracy liberates individual potentiality. In this spirit, Dewey writes that "communal life is moral, that is emotionally, intellectually, consciously sustained."[20] School-board members may regard action that weakens this mutually beneficial relationship of individual and community—exclusion, marginalization, coercion, prejudice, to name a few—as undemocratic. More positively, school-board members may seek a balance of community opinion and personal judgment that bolsters individuals' abilities to contribute meaningfully to their communities and communities' capacities to foster individual growth.

Reclaiming a Democratic Public for Public Education

In the contemporary context, envisioning school boards as local democratic bodies would entail a revision of a prominent feature—perhaps *the* prominent feature—of an accountability regime, namely, its market orientation. Education theorist Gert Biesta explains that, in the abstract, accountability is a polysemous term that need not militate against democracy. In a different climate, accountability could realize democratic connotations of "answering to" and "taking responsibility," as in governing institutions answering to the demos and elected officials taking responsibility for the successes and failures of their policies. But, Biesta notes, a different sense of accountability has taken hold in the contemporary era, a financial-managerial sense of accountability as referring "narrowly to the duty to present auditable accounts." He maintains that the discourse of "accountability operates precisely on the basis of a 'quick switch' between the two meanings": drawing on the democratic resonance of accountability, an accountability regime focuses instead on balance sheets, aligning dollars with standards and test scores.[21] In this way, an accountability regime likens public education to a marketplace in which schools and districts compete for consumers, while state and federal policymakers demand regular audits to provide consumers with information for their purchasing decisions.

A marketplace recasts the modes of associated living that education may inculcate and embody. Dissociating the reciprocal relationship of individual and community that informs democratic modes of association, a market approach positions not only schools as competitors, but students and their families as well. Rather than signaling personal development and meaningful community engagement, students' success appears in relative terms as besting their peers. The rankings of an education marketplace celebrate top-performing schools and districts while disparaging ostensibly low-performing others. Stewart Ranson writes that an education marketplace fosters a "possessive individualism" that situates one student's development "at the expense of someone else's. It is to make every interaction and relationship a 'zero-sum' game."[22] A market approach exacerbates educational inequalities, incentivizing families and districts with access to superior resources to maintain their distinct advantages. An education market "confirms and reinforces the pre-existing social class order of wealth and privilege." Moreover, an educational market offers families limited opportunities to critique existing structures—individual choice in the form of market exit appears as the primary means of consumer feedback. Ranson holds that an education market substitutes "the power of resources in exchange for the power of better reasons in public discourse."[23] An education market dispenses with deliberation.

In the past few decades, prominent calls for education reform have associated markets not only with the means but also the ends of reform. In the 1980s, when the members of the National Commission on Excellence in Education sounded alarms about a nation at risk, they did so in the name of global competitiveness. In the past, they argued, the bountiful resources of an expansive country and the indomitable spirit of its people assured national prosperity. But now Americans lived in "one global village. We live among determined, well-educated, and strongly motivated competitors. We compete with them for international standing and markets." Competition arose from Asia, where nations challenged the United States on ostensibly American products such as cars, and from Europe and other parts of the globe. The committee exhorted that "knowledge, learning, information, and skilled intelligence are the new raw materials of international commerce."[24] Just as the nation had previously mined its natural resources, so, too, could reform enable effective utilization of its intellectual resources. Competition compelled reform.

Presidents also have highlighted market motives for reform. As he urged Americans to leave no child behind, President George W. Bush linked accountability to federal expenditures, "making sure our money is spent well. A priority has got to be diligence when it comes to taxpayers' money."[25] Further, he associated successful reform with sound business leadership: "When you find a good principal, the CEO of a school, you'll find a school that achieves what we all want: every child learning." Like the business counterpart, the school CEO combined a clear vision with high expectations from subordinates. A captain of the education industry, the school CEO distinguished talk from action, "refus[ing] to accept excuses" when standards were not met.[26] Maintaining a commitment to standards and testing, President Barack Obama invoked the competitive metaphor of a race as he urged states to best one another in developing educational innovations. Observing that "American prosperity has long rested on how well we educate our children," President Obama discerned intensified competition in the contemporary global era: "Countries that out-educate us today will out-compete us tomorrow." Obama proclaimed that "the currency of today's economy is knowledge."[27] Facilitating exchange, knowledge could be accumulated, invested, and spent. As currency, knowledge did not support equality, as nations could "out-educate" one another. Since, as any investor knows, it takes money to make money, knowledge as currency provided greater benefits for countries that already possessed greater resources. Casting this competition in the context of a global economy, Obama inferred that all Americans could benefit. But the operation of currency abroad functioned similarly at home, rewarding Americans who possessed the funds for investment.

Drawing education into the field of economic competition relies on its presumptive power to produce financial gains. For instance, as adult community members in Beloit knew, their children could not enter the potentially lucrative fields of law, medicine, or finance (among others) without completing high school and postsecondary education. Yet an instrumental association of education with economic advancement oversimplifies the challenges facing members of low-income communities. Individual advancement often depends on already obtained collective material and symbolic resources held by a student's family and community, such as those present in communities like Elmbrook. Education alone—in the absence of employment, community stability, and more—typically cannot overcome relative deprivation. Further, a narrowly instrumental association of education and economic success may endorse limited, technocratic reforms that highlight ostensibly vocational instruction over seemingly superfluous activities. However, as Martha Nussbaum notes, a citizen cannot learn the skills of democratic association through exclusively technical instruction. Important democratic skills elude a technocratic education, as citizens should develop the capacities to ask questions of themselves and their traditions, to imagine the situations of people different from themselves, to see connections with diverse others.[28]

An education marketplace cannot develop the competencies of democratic citizenship because an education marketplace operates without a notion of a public good. This has long been a lacuna in market-based proposals for education reform. In his 1962 book *Capitalism and Freedom*, Milton Friedman acknowledged the value of education for democracy, but Friedman rejected what he regarded as an unjust government monopoly on primary and secondary education. Friedman sought to separate the financing of a basic education, which he accepted as a government responsibility, from the provision of education. To facilitate this separation, he introduced the idea of education vouchers to a wider reading public. Vouchers would redress the fundamental problem with public education, which "conflicts with the preservation of freedom itself." Compulsory delivery systems for educational products circumscribed individual autonomy and threatened to blur the line between providing basic knowledge and "indoctrination inhibiting freedom of thought and belief." Vouchers bolstered individual freedom by aligning the provision of education with the market value of consumer choice: "Parents could express their views about schools directly by withdrawing their children from one school and sending them to another, to a much greater extent than is now possible."[29] In Friedman's view, economic efficiency and individual liberty merged: by meeting consumer demand, an education marketplace empowered citizens.

Yet Friedman could not imagine any other alternative because he would not recognize the power of the public, which arises when people come together to coordinate their activities. As he began his book, Friedman made plain his view that references to a public constituted a fiction, asserting that "a free man" rightly discerned the constitution of a country "as a collection of individuals who compose it, not something over and above them." A free man, he continued, "recognizes no national goal except as it is the consensus of the goals that the citizens severally serve. He recognizes no national purpose except as it is the consensus of the purposes for which the citizens severally strive."[30] The public consisted of an aggregation of "I"s—each of whom did their own thing—rather than a jointly crafted "we" that could work together to address commonly recognized problems. Indeed, his formulation ruled out common recognition—any effort to move citizens in this direction represented a move toward tyranny. Friedman celebrated the heroic individual while denying the possibility of community.

A robust vision of democracy—one that values democracy as more than a set of mechanisms for aggregating individual preferences—requires recognition of both I and we. Both personal fulfillment and community affiliation create meaning in citizens' lives, as they develop a sense of themselves and their capabilities in relation to others. Indeed, the very term "citizen" connotes membership and belonging. Individuals alone do not make meaningful their experiences but draw on social resources in understanding and directing their experiences. Since we cannot escape the social aspect of living a meaningful life, denying this aspect only distorts our sense of who we are and how we relate to one another. Friedman construed relations through the terms of a contract, but people's lives and associations exhibit far greater variety and richness than this one-dimensional rendering. Human relationships inspire us, uplift us, empower us. Far from delimiting agency, associations augment agency by expanding meaning and purpose in our environments and providing greater resources for action.

While powerful, productive human relationships do not take shape innately as functions of a biological organism. We must learn to interact with one another in ways that foster individual development and strengthen community. In this spirit, John Dewey distinguishes between the bare fact of human association and the consciously cultivated bonds of democratic community: "Wherever there is conjoint activity whose consequences are appreciated as good by all singular persons who take part in it, and where the realization of the good is such as to effect an energetic desire and effort to sustain it in being just because it is a good shared by all, there is in so far a community."[31] Learning to develop these bonds does not proceed through indoctrination but by providing an institutional educational setting (as well as cultivating non-institutional settings) in which students themselves may make meaningful and learn to direct their experiences. Democratic education bolsters individual agency as it promotes students' connections with others. As students learn with one another, their educational experiences resonate with their experiences as members of democratic communities.

School boards alone cannot transform the orientation of an accountability regime, but school-board members can start to ask one another different questions than those prescribed by an accountability regime. They may resist a myopic focus on balance sheets filled with columns of dollar amounts and test scores. They may assess the democratic state of their communities—the ways in which people feel empowered and disempowered—and consider how their district schools may reconnect individuals to their community. School-board members may foreground meaning-making as a primary educational activity, committing themselves to processes that enable students to ascribe meaning to their environments so that they may act in their communities. Insofar as board members promote policies and programs that develop schools as vibrant actors in their local communities, they may contribute to the realization of a Great Community.

NOTES

INTRODUCTION

1. Dewey, "Creative Democracy," 226, and *Democracy*, 76.
2. Dewey, *Democracy*, 19.
3. Dewey, *Public*, 15.
4. Ibid., 207.
5. Ibid., 213.
6. Shawn Batt notes that education "not only represents a substantive policy area about which controversy continually erupts, but it also represents a constitutive force in the creation and maintenance of culture." Batt, "Keeping Company," 86.
7. Dewey, *Democracy*, 2, 4.
8. Tracy, *Challenges*, 196.
9. Ibid., 6.
10. Howell, "Introduction," 5.
11. Ibid., 8–9; Jacobsen and Saultz, "Who Should Control Education?"
12. On vernacular rhetoric, see Hauser, *Vernacular Voices*; Howard, "Vernacular Mode."
13. Stone, *Policy Paradox*, 10.
14. Ibid., 249–50.
15. Fischer, *Reframing*, 11, 13.
16. Zarefsky, *President Johnson's War*, 2.
17. Ibid., 5.
18. I develop this argument in detail in Asen, "Reflections."
19. On polysemy in rhetorical studies, see Ceccarelli, "Polysemy."
20. Murphy, "Mikhail Bakhtin," 260.
21. Burkhalter, Gastil, and Kelshaw, "Conceptual Definition," 401.
22. Barker, McAfee, and McIvor, "Introduction," 2–3.
23. Young, *Inclusion and Democracy*, 136–37.
24. Citing changing perceptions about the public standing of domestic violence, Nancy Fraser writes that "what will count as a matter of common concern will be decided precisely through discursive contestation." Fraser, "Rethinking," 129.
25. Keith, *Democracy*, 169.
26. Ivie, "Rhetorical Deliberation," 278–79. Ivie contrasts "a rhetorical conception of deliberation" with "the modernist ideal of dispassionate and disembodied dialogue [that] would achieve the illusion of objectivity and universal reason only by bracketing or masking relations of power" (278).
27. Willard, "Valuing Dissensus," 145.
28. Smith, "Scientifically Based Research." See also Honig and Coburn, "Evidence-Based Decision Making"; Slavin, "Evidence-Based Education"; Wiseman, "Uses of Evidence."
29. *No Child Left Behind Act*, 1552.
30. Tseng, "Uses of Research," 3.

31. REDD team members included myself, co-leader Deb Gurke (an officer at the Wisconsin Association of School Boards), Pamela Conners, Ryan Solomon, Elsa Gumm, and Michelle Murray Yang. Conners, Solomon, Gumm, and Murray Yang were all PhD students in rhetoric at the University of Wisconsin–Madison during the period of fieldwork for the REDD project.

32. I obtained these statistics from the Wisconsin Information Network for Successful Schools, *WINSS*.

33. Among the publications resulting from our collaboration, see Asen, Gurke, Conners, Solomon, and Gumm, "Research Evidence," and "Research Says."

34. The REDD team members agreed that we would collaborate on the specific question of research use, while the materials we gathered would serve as a common resource available for further individual and/or collaborative inquiry. From the beginning, I planned to reach beyond the question of research use to consider school boards as local sites of democratic engagement and policymaking. As I developed a plan for this book, I decided to focus on cases and themes that we did not address in our REDD team publications and presentations.

35. On discovery and interpretation as alternative paths to ethical knowledge, see Walzer, *Interpretation*. In his discussion, Walzer foregrounds the interpretive role of the social critic.

36. Pezzullo, "Resisting," 350.

37. On the politics of rhetorical canons, see Bizzell and Jarratt, "Rhetorical Traditions"; Meyer, "Women Speak(ing)."

38. Pezzullo, "Resisting," 350.

39. Hauser, "Attending the Vernacular," 164.

40. Middleton, Senda-Cook, and Endres, "Rhetorical Field Methods," 390.

41. Conquergood, "Ethnography," 81.

42. On conceptual criticism, see Jasinski, "Status of Theory."

43. Hess, "Critical-Rhetorical Ethnography," 132.

CHAPTER I

1. See Brouwer and Asen, "Introduction," 6–8; Friedland, Hove, and Rojas, "Networked."

2. Hauser, *Vernacular Voices*, 71–72.

3. Warner, *Publics*, 75.

4. Jürgen Habermas maintains a distinction between legislative bodies and lay publics, charging the former with addressing public problems and the latter with discovering and identifying public problems. Habermas, *Between Facts and Norms*, 307. As I indicate above, I see both as agents in a networked public sphere. For another view of the critical value of including state institutions in a conception of the public sphere, see Schudson, "Public Sphere."

5. Kaestle, *Pillars*, 21.

6. Ibid., 112.

7. Reese, *America's Public Schools*, 58, 60.

8. Tyack, *Seeking Common Ground*, 144–46.

9. See DeBray, *Politics*; McGuinn, *No Child*; Ravitch, *Death and Life*.

10. Tyack, *Seeking Common Ground*, 153–54.

11. Ravitch, "Why Public Schools," 24.

12. *Civil Rights Act of 1964*, 252. Gareth Davies notes that Title VI proved to be a more powerful tool for fighting discrimination than federal policymakers themselves

had anticipated. Davies, *See Government Grow*, 120–22. For an overview of federal education policy in the 1960s, see Graham, *Uncertain Triumph*.

13. Carroll, "Constitution," 658; Perry, "Justice Hugo Black," 62–64.

14. *Everson v. Board of Education*.

15. In his memoirs, President Johnson recalled that "we sought a way to make this 'child benefit' theory apply to this case." Johnson, *Vantage Point*, 210. For a detailed discussion of the passage of ESEA, see Jeffrey, *Education*, 59–95.

16. McGuinn, *No Child*, 31.

17. Johnson, *Public Papers*, 1:26.

18. For a discussion of the ways in which this confidence in innovation informed liberal public policy in the 1960s, see Murphy, "Language."

19. Johnson, *Public Papers*, 1:26.

20. Ibid., 1:25.

21. Ibid., 1:27–28.

22. Ibid., 1:26.

23. Ibid. The ranking Republican on the Education and Labor Committee, Senator Robert Taft announced in the mid-1940s that he had reconsidered his views and favored federal aid for education. Although the legislation stalled in the House, Taft guided a bill through the Senate in 1948 that provided federal funds to the nation's schools, marking "the first time in sixty years that the Senate had approved general federal aid to education." Ravitch, *Troubled Crusade*, 28.

24. Johnson, *Public Papers*, 1:28. In congressional testimony, Benjamin Willis, superintendent of the Chicago Public Schools, presented a more detailed version of this rationale. In part, he testified that "we cannot continue to meet [our student's needs] without the assistance of financial resources which are more broadly based than the tax on local property which now constitutes our primary source of support for schools. There must be a sharing of income from taxes from other sources and other levels of government." U.S. Senate Subcommittee on Education, *Elementary*, 1205.

25. Graham, *Schooling America*, 159. Thomas Toch notes that *A Nation at Risk* generated so much interest that "within ten months of its release 150,000 copies had been distributed by the Department of Education, another 70,000 had been purchased through the Government Printing Office, and several million additional copies and extended excerpts were estimated to be in circulation through reprints in the general and professional press." Toch, *In the Name of Excellence*, 15.

26. National Commission on Excellence in Education, *Nation at Risk*, 5.

27. McIntush, "Defining Education."

28. George Bush, *Public Papers*, 2:1275. As Ann Staton and Jennifer Peeples note, Bush's reference to "radical reforms" demonstrated the urgency of his approach, as he alternatively referred to his education agenda as part of a "revolution" and "crusade." Staton and Peeples, "Education Reform," 312–14. See also McIntush, "Political Truancy."

29. For an overview of standard-based reforms in the 1990s, see Jennings, *Why National Standards*.

30. Riley, "Reflections," 380.

31. For detailed descriptions of the No Child Left Behind Act, see Hayes, *No Child*; Riddle and Skinner, *Elementary*.

32. For a discussion of the legislative maneuvering surrounding NCLB, see McGuinn, *No Child*, 165–77.

33. George W. Bush, *Public Papers*, 1:12.

34. Ibid., 1:13.

35. Ibid., 1:112.

36. Ibid., 1:17.

37. Ibid., 1:12.

38. Ibid., 1:17.

39. Ibid., 1:12.

40. Ibid., 1:18.

41. Ibid., 1:12.

42. Ibid., 1:18.

43. Ibid., 1:112.

44. Ibid., 1:13.

45. *Oxford English Dictionary*, 2nd ed. (online), s.v. "control."

46. Briffault, "Local School," 24.

47. Ibid., 29–30.

48. Wisconsin Constitution, Art. X, Sec. 1 and 3.

49. Briffault, "Local School," 40.

50. Walsh, "Erasing Race."

51. Sedler, "Profound Impact"; Chemerinsky, "Segregation."

52. Briffault, "Local School," 49.

53. Tracy, *Challenges*, 7.

54. Hess, *School Boards*, 33.

55. Hochschild, "School Boards," 326.

56. Hess, *School Boards*, 33.

57. Hochschild, "School Boards," 326.

58. On the election of school boards, see Hess, *School Boards*, 32. On the appointment and election of superintendents, see Education Commission of the States, "K–12 Governance," and "Local Superintendents." Elected superintendents reside largely in Alabama, Florida, and Mississippi, which all have some combination of appointed and elected superintendents.

59. See Iannaccone and Lutz, *Politics, Power, and Policy.*

60. I am grateful to Deb Gurke for calling my attention to this saying.

61. Romano, "Gibson Recalls." Hess notes that the nationwide average length of service for a superintendent in a particular district is 5.48 years. Hess, *School Boards*, 22.

62. Land, "Local School Boards," 253.

63. See Delagardelle, "Lighthouse Inquiry."

64. Mountford, "Historical and Current Tensions," 98.

65. Steinberger, "Superintendent–School Board Relations," 10, 14.

66. National Center for Education Statistics, *Digest.*

67. Kava and Merrifield, "State Aid," 3.

68. Berkman and Plutzer, *Ten Thousand Democracies*, 19–21.

69. National Center for Education Statistics, *Digest.*

70. DeBray, *Politics*, 108–10.

71. McGuinn, *No Child*, 185.

72. National Center for Education Statistics, *Digest.*

73. Cornman, Young, and Herrell, *Revenues and Expenditures*, 5.

74. Tracy, *Challenges*, 10.

75. U.S. Census Bureau, "Local Governments."

76. Hess, *School Boards*, 28.

77. Tracy, *Challenges*, 3–4.

78. Ibid., 203, 205.

79. Ibid., 196.

80. Fraser, "Rethinking," 134.

81. Tracy, *Challenges*, 11.
82. Asen, Gurke, Conners, Solomon, and Gumm, "Research Evidence," 37.

CHAPTER 2

1. "In a Decisive Victory," 10; Washington County Clerk, "Election Summary."
2. Kristula-Green, "How Badly"; Terkel, "Glenn Grothman, Wisconsin Pol."
3. "America's 100."
4. Hanna, "Library Fight."
5. Zarefsky, "Strategic Maneuvering," 323. For excellent syntheses of the uses of ideology in rhetorical scholarship, see Crowley, "Reflections"; Cyphert, "Ideology"; Cloud and Gunn, "W(h)ither Ideology?"
6. As Thomas Goodnight maintains, controversy may "push the limits of the available means of communication." Goodnight, "Controversy," 2.
7. Eagleton, *Ideology*, 28–30.
8. Mouffe, *Democratic Paradox*, 105. See also Mouffe, *Agonistics*, 8.
9. Pace and Schoob, "West Bend High School," 1.
10. Tell, "Augustinian Political Theory," 229.
11. Audi, *Religious Commitment*, 86.
12. Rorty, "Religion," 142.
13. Ibid., 145–46.
14. Rawls, *Political Liberalism*, 224.
15. Ibid., 217.
16. Ibid., li–lii. See also Rawls, "Idea of Public Reason."
17. Habermas, *Structural Transformation*.
18. Habermas, *Between Naturalism and Religion*, 130. See also Habermas, Brieskorn, Reder, Ricken, and Schmidt, *Awareness*; Butler, Habermas, Taylor, and West, *Power of Religion*.
19. Habermas, *Between Naturalism and Religion*, 132.
20. Ibid., 142.
21. Troup, "Civic Engagement," 244.
22. Steiner, "Reconceptualizing."
23. Medhurst, "Mitt Romney," 214.
24. Calhoun, "Secularism," 86.
25. Lafont, "Deliberative Obligations," 135. See also Lafont, "Habermas's Conception."
26. Baumeister, "Use of 'Public Reason,'" 228.
27. Ibid., 231.
28. Ibid., 233–34.
29. See Asen, "Ideology."
30. Brouwer, "Communication," 200.
31. Ibid., 197.
32. Rawls, *Political Liberalism*, 220.
33. Felski, *Beyond Feminist Aesthetics*, 168.
34. See Asen, "Seeking the 'Counter.'"
35. Hessel, "West Bend."
36. Muckelbauer, "School Levy Increase Rejected."
37. West Bend School Board, "Annual Meeting," 8.
38. U.S. Census Bureau, "Wisconsin Population"; U.S. Census Bureau, "Washington County."

39. West Bend School Board, "Annual Meeting," 18.

40. Quoted in Muckelbauer, "School Board Starts Cutting."

41. Quoted in Rank, "Pencils Sharp."

42. Muckelbauer, "School Board OKs."

43. West Bend School Board, "October Board Meeting," 20.

44. Robinson, "Lessons."

45. Marquardt, letter to the editor, October 31.

46. Kubisiak, "Incumbents."

47. Marquardt, "Announcement."

48. Weigand, "Have You Been Disappointed."

49. Robinson, "It's for the Children."

50. Marquardt, *Common Sense.*

51. Peterson, "Peeking Behind."

52. Schneiberg, letter to the editor.

53. Kubisiak, "School Board."

54. Marquardt, "Results Are In!"

55. Badzinski and Kubisiak, "After the Election."

56. Eagle Forum of Washington County, "West Bend."

57. Peterson, "Common Sense."

58. Marquardt, letter to the editor, February 2.

59. West Bend School Board, "November Board Meeting," 38.

60. Ibid., 6.

61. Ibid., 55.

62. Weigand, "Navigating Charter School."

63. Kubisiak, "Ethics Complaints."

64. Kubisiak, "Charter School Facing Obstacles," and "Charter School Proposal."

65. Williams, letter to the editor, January 28.

66. Ibid., March 31.

67. Rawls, *Political Liberalism,* 223–24, 231–40.

68. West Bend School District, "Board Policy 370: Extracurricular." I have quoted from the version included with the GSA application. In March 2012, the West Bend school board revised the beginning of Board Policy 370 to delete the nondiscrimination sentence and to require parental approval for participation in co-curricular activities. References to nondiscrimination remain in "Board Policy 370, Exhibit B," which was revised most recently on March 25, 2011.

69. West Bend School Board, "Committee," 11, 14.

70. Zarling, memorandum.

71. West Bend School Board, "Committee," 1–2.

72. West Bend School District, "Board Policy 370, Exhibit C."

73. West Bend School Board, "Committee," 22.

74. Ibid., 20.

75. Glauber, "State Voters."

76. West Bend School Board, "Committee," 8–9.

77. West Bend School Board, "June Board Meeting," 10–11.

78. Kubisiak, "Day of Silence."

79. West Bend School Board, "June Board Meeting," 10–11.

80. *Pupil Nondiscrimination Act.*

81. *Equal Access Act of 1984,* 1302.

82. As Todd DeMitchell and Richard Fossey explain, "By passing the EAA, Congress inadvertently gave gay and lesbian students a statutory right to form their own student groups and meet on school premises during non-instructional

time." DeMitchell and Fossey, "Student Speech," 93. See also McCarthy, "Religious Influences."

83. Vorwald, "Rights Conflict"; Zeidel, "Forecasting Disruption." On the Lubbock, Texas, case where the court decided against the GSA, see Orman, "Being Gay."

84. DeMitchell and Fossey, "Student Speech," 122. See also Pratt, "Protecting the Marketplace."

85. West Bend School Board, "Committee," 13.

86. West Bend School Board, "May Board Meeting," 2.

87. Ibid., 19.

88. West Bend School Board, "June Board Meeting," 2.

89. Ibid., 7.

90. Observing that Marquardt "took the time to carefully research the Equal Access Act," *Daily News* columnist Mark Peterson praised Marquardt for "plac[ing] his public duty above his personal moral preferences." Peterson, "Right Thing."

91. West Bend School Board, "June Board Meeting," 12–13.

92. Ibid., 18.

93. Ibid., 19.

94. West Bend School Board, "Committee," 26.

95. West Bend School Board, "May Board Meeting," 2.

96. West Bend School Board, "June Board Meeting," 14.

97. Ibid., 7–8.

98. West Bend School Board, "May Board Meeting," 6–7.

99. West Bend School Board, "Committee," 23.

100. Ibid., 23–24.

101. Ibid., 24.

102. West Bend School Board, "May Board Meeting," 23.

103. Ibid., 18.

104. On the increasingly prescriptive trajectory of federal education policy, see McGuinn, *No Child*; Ravitch, *Death and Life*.

105. On the distinction between institutional and vernacular discourses, see Howard, "Vernacular Mode."

106. Habermas writes that "the publics of parliamentary bodies are structured predominantly as a *context of justification*. These bodies rely not only on the administration's preparatory work and further processing but also on the *context of discovery* provided by a procedurally unregulated public sphere that is borne by the general public of citizens." Habermas, *Between Facts and Norms*, 307. For a more fluid discussion of this relationship, see Asen and Brouwer, "Introduction," 13–17.

107. Fraser, "Rethinking," 123.

108. West Bend School Board, "Committee," 28.

109. West Bend School Board, "June Board Meeting," 18.

110. Ibid., 3.

111. West Bend School Board, "May Board Meeting," 22.

112. West Bend School Board, "June Board Meeting," 4.

113. West Bend School Board, "May Board Meeting," 8.

114. West Bend School Board, "June Board Meeting," 4.

115. Ibid., 4.

116. West Bend School Board, "May Board Meeting," 9. In referencing "sexual behaviors," Maziarka may have created some ambiguity in asserting what she regarded as the nature of the GSA. In a May letter to the editor published in the *Daily News*, she left no doubt, flatly rebuking the GSA as a "sex club": "Sex clubs should not be invited, introduced or supported by West Bend's taxpayer money." Maziarka, letter to the editor.

117. West Bend School Board, "June Board Meeting," 15.

118. Ibid., 3.

119. West Bend School Board, "May Board Meeting," 7.

120. Ibid.

121. West Bend School Board, "Committee," 17.

122. For discussions of bullying, heteronormativity, and high school culture, see Pascoe, *Dude*; Payne and Smith, "LGBTQ Kids."

123. Brouwer, "ACT-ing UP," 88.

124. West Bend School Board, "May Board Meeting," 20–21.

125. Nancy Fraser defines weak publics as "publics whose deliberative practice consists exclusively in opinion formation and does not also encompass decision making." Fraser defines strong publics as "publics whose discourse encompasses both opinion formation and decision making." Fraser, "Rethinking," 134.

126. Habermas, *Communicative Action*, 1:25.

CHAPTER 3

1. Kava and Merrifield, "State Aid."

2. See Koski and Reich, "When 'Adequate' Isn't"; Rebell, "Fiscal Equity"; Reynolds, "Skybox Schools"; Ryan, *Five Miles Away*.

3. Macedo, "Property-Owning Plutocracy," 46, 50. See also Macedo, "School Reform."

4. Reed, "Not in My Schoolyard." See also McDermott, *Controlling Public*, 20–25.

5. Coleman et al., *Equality*; Kozol, *Savage Inequalities*.

6. See, e.g., Reich, "Great Recession"; Krugman, *End This Depression Now!*

7. "Jobless Rate Up."

8. Wisconsin Department of Workforce Development, "Local Area Unemployment."

9. U.S. Census Bureau, *2007–2011 American Community*.

10. Wisconsin Department of Public Instruction, "Enrollment"; Gavan, "4 of 5 Beloit Pupils."

11. Rawls, *Political Liberalism*, lix.

12. The scholarly literatures on campaign finance and economic inequality are voluminous. For a discussion of campaign finance, especially the 2010 *Citizens United v. Federal Election Commission* ruling, see, e.g., Greene, "Arguing with Money"; Heresco, "Citizens Divided." On the increasing economic inequality in the United States, see, e.g., Chetty, Hendren, Kline, and Saez, "Land of Opportunity?"; DeNavas-Walt, Proctor, and Smith, *Income*.

13. Rawls, *Political Liberalism*, lix.

14. Hicks, "Promise(s)," 231.

15. Ibid., 234. Gutmann and Thompson write that the basic opportunity principle "obligates government to ensure that all citizens may secure the resources they need to live a decent life and enjoy other (non-basic) opportunities in our society." Gutmann and Thompson, *Democracy and Disagreement*, 217.

16. Cohen, "Deliberation," 77.

17. Campbell, "Agency," 3. See also Lyon, *Deliberative Acts*, 57.

18. I characterize this dynamic as a distinction between direct and indirect exclusions. See Asen, "Imagining," 345. See also Palczewski, "Argument"; Benhabib, *Situating the Self*; Young, *Inclusion and Democracy*.

19. Benhabib, "Toward a Deliberative Model," 71.

20. Estlund, "Beyond Fairness."

21. Burkhalter, Gastil, and Kelshaw, "Conceptual Definition," 401.
22. *Oxford English Dictionary*, 2nd ed. (online), s.v. "weigh."
23. Kock and Villadsen, "Introduction," 4.
24. See Asen, "Discourse Theory."
25. Aristotle, *Nicomachean Ethics*, Bk. VI, Sec. 9.
26. Kava and Merrifield, "State Aid," 3.
27. Ryan, *Five Miles Away*, 127, 137.
28. DeNardis, "Equity to Adequacy," 5.
29. Ryan, *Five Miles Away*, 135.
30. Walsh, "Erasing Race."
31. Ryan, *Five Miles Away*, 139.
32. Koski and Reich, "When 'Adequate' Isn't," 557.
33. Wisconsin Constitution, Art. X, Sec. 3.
34. Sutton, *"San Antonio,"* 1977–85.
35. Hoxby, "Finance Equalizations."
36. Maher, Skidmore, and Statz, "State Policy," 628. My understanding of Wisconsin school financing relies extensively on Maher, Skidmore, and Statz's excellent analysis.
37. Ibid., 630–36.
38. Ibid., 643.
39. Wisconsin Department of Public Instruction, "School District Tax."
40. Wisconsin Department of Public Instruction, "2010–2011 Comparative Revenue."
41. Ibid.
42. Baker, "Emerging Shape"; Duncombe and Yinger, "How Much More"; Reschovsky and Imazeki, "Achieving Educational Adequacy," and "Let No Child."
43. Wisconsin Department of Public Instruction, "Enrollment."
44. For an engaging discussion of these issues, see Rothstein, *Class and Schools*.
45. Dickinson, "Beloit School Board"; Weaver, "School District OKs."
46. Beloit School Board, "October 29 Special," 15.
47. Beloit School Board, "October 27 Special," 20.
48. Beloit School Board, "October 20 Special," 17.
49. Ibid., 13, 14.
50. Beloit School Board, "October 19 Special," 52–53.
51. Beloit School Board, "October 27 Budget," 13, 15.
52. Ibid., 6.
53. Ibid., 11.
54. Beloit School Board, "July 6 Special," 92.
55. Beloit School Board, "October 22 Special," 31–32.
56. Beloit School Board, "February 16 Budget," 33–34.
57. Wundrow, "New Corporate Campus."
58. Rhodebeck, "Kerry Shows Off."
59. Beloit School Board, "October 29 Special," 16.
60. Beloit School Board, "October 27 Budget," 3.
61. Beloit School Board, "February 16 Budget," 9.
62. Ibid., 12.
63. Beloit School Board, "October 19 Special," 30–31.
64. Ibid., 23.
65. Beloit School Board, "October 20 Special," 7.
66. Ibid., 4.
67. Beloit School Board, "October 22 Special," 32–33.

68. Beloit School Board, "October 20 Special," 8.

69. Beloit School Board, "October 22 Special," 49.

70. Beloit School Board, "October 29 Special," 25, 27.

71. Wolf, "Beloit Schools."

72. For detailed descriptions of the No Child Left Behind Act, see Hayes, *No Child*; Riddle and Skinner, *Elementary*.

73. See, e.g., Moses and Nanna, "Testing Culture"; Ravitch, *Death and Life*; Ryan, "Perverse Incentives."

74. Beloit School Board, "October 26 Regular," 27.

75. Beloit School Board, "March 11 Special," 56–57.

76. Beloit School Board, "October 19 Special," 14–15.

77. Beloit School Board, "Meeting of the Finance," 13.

78. Beloit School Board, "October 27 Special," 5, 9.

79. Ibid., 10.

80. Beloit School Board, "October 22 Special," 34–35.

81. Beloit School Board, "October 27 Special," 8.

82. Beloit School Board, "Meeting of the Finance," 11.

83. Beloit School Board, "March 11 Special," 43–45, 47–48.

84. Beloit School Board, "February 16 Budget," 31–32.

85. See Pitkin, *Representation*.

86. Beloit School Board, "October 19 Special," 64.

87. Ibid., 35.

88. Beloit School Board, "October 26 Regular," 2.

89. Ibid., 50–51. In *The Human Condition*, Hannah Arendt uses this distinction to differentiate between the household as a realm of necessity and the polis as a space of freedom. Arendt, *Human Condition*, 28–37.

90. Beloit School Board, "October 12 Special, 60.

91. Beloit School Board, "October 19 Special," 20.

92. Beloit School Board, "October 26 Regular," 6–7.

93. Beloit School Board, "October 29 Special," 15, 23–24.

CHAPTER 4

1. Even as he sees public officials' reliance on experts as rational, Charles Willard holds that employing such expertise in decision-making "has the effect of foreclosing debate." Willard, "Authority," 11. See also Willard, *Liberalism*, 134–40.

2. In contrast to the promise of equality offered in democratic deliberation as a mode of engagement, as John Lyne and Henry Howe observe, "expertise presumes a functional inequality of knowledge among different groups." Lyne and Howe, "Rhetoric," 135.

3. Habermas, *Communicative Action*, 2:391–96; Goodnight, "Personal," 223–25.

4. Ceccarelli, "Manufactured," 196, 212.

5. As Christopher Eisenhart notes, scholars reproducing this dichotomy see "expertise [as] often defined in terms of generating facts; advocacy is defined in terms of debating values." Eisenhart, "Humanist," 151.

6. Wyckoff, *Policy*, 19.

7. Philosopher Philip Kitcher urges greater sensitivity to the values that undergird technical judgment. He sees the decisions made in technical sites like laboratories as "eminently reasonable" but incapable of being reduced to "formalisms often taken as constitutive of rationality." Kitcher, *Science*, 36. See also Douglas, *Science*, 87–114.

8. Michael Sandel maintains that deliberating about the common good "requires a knowledge of public affairs and also a sense of belonging, a concern for the whole, a moral bond with the community whose fate is at stake." Sandel, *Democracy's Discontent*, 4.

9. Benhabib, "Toward a Deliberative Model," 71.

10. See Kava, "School Integration"; Public Policy Forum, "Interdistrict."

11. Hamari, "District."

12. On the interaction of research-based and other types of evidence in deliberation, see Asen, Gurke, Conners, Solomon, and Gumm, "Research Evidence."

13. Goodnight, "Personal," 214.

14. Ibid., 216.

15. Ibid., 220.

16. Ibid., 219–20.

17. Dewey, *Public*, 148–56.

18. Goodnight, "Personal," 220.

19. Taylor, "On the Public Closure."

20. Rowland, "Relationship," 141. For a similar assessment of the limits of public judgment, see Schiappa, "Defining Marriage."

21. Brashers and Jackson, "Politically-Savvy."

22. Fabj and Sobnosky, "AIDS Activism," 164.

23. On contestation, see Ceccarelli, "Let Us." On "fusion," see Biesecker, "Recalculating." On "interdependence," see Boyd, "Public and Technical." On "transcendence," see Benoit-Barné, "Socio-technical."

24. Keränen, "Mapping Misconduct," 111. Johanna Hartelius holds that a rhetorical approach to expertise elucidates one of its functions as "invit[ing] the audience to acquiesce or get involved." Hartelius, *Rhetoric of Expertise*, 23.

25. Asen, Gurke, Conners, Solomon, and Gumm, "Research Evidence," 37.

26. Their reliance on staff expertise represents what Mark Warren has described in terms of an efficient allocation of expert and deliberative resources. Board members arrange their agendas to "allocate their deliberative resources to the issues and spheres they find relatively important," while leaving background preparation and some technical judgments to staff. Warren, "Deliberative Democracy," 58.

27. Majdik and Keith, "Expertise," 382, 378. In a response to a sole-authored article by Majdik, John Lynch cautions against creating dichotomies of information and meaning whereby "'information' exists as a stable set of facts about which people produce 'meanings' in the process of deliberation." Lynch, "Information," 370. See Majdik, "Judging."

28. Brown, *Science*, 234. See also Fischer, *Democracy*, 155–61.

29. Elmbrook School District, "Annual Report, 2010–11," and "Annual Report, 2011–12."

30. Wisconsin Information Network for Successful Schools, *WINSS*.

31. Ibid.

32. Elmbrook School District, "Annual Report, 2010–11," and "Annual Report, 2011–12"; "Wisconsin's Median Income."

33. Wisconsin Department of Public Instruction, "Enrollment."

34. As I explain in the next chapter on trust, I promised interviewees anonymity in any presentations or publications resulting from the REDD project.

35. Miller, "Presumptions," 196–97.

36. Wallinger, "Regulatory Rhetoric," 79.

37. Elmbrook Enrollment Management Study Team, "Report," 4.

38. Nixon, *Public Papers*, 426.

39. Dougherty, *More Than One Struggle*, 94.

40. Ibid., 152–53, 163–64.

41. Miner, *Lessons*; Kritek, "Voluntary Desegregation," 83.

42. The law defines minority as a student who is "Black or African American, Hispanic, American Indian, an Alaskan native, or a person of Asian or Pacific Island origin." Kava, "School Integration," 2.

43. Elmbrook School District, "Chapter 220," 2.

44. Kava, "School Integration," 6.

45. Ibid., 2.

46. Bonds, Farmer-Hinton, and Epps, "African Americans," 61.

47. Stolee, "Milwaukee Desegregation," 258.

48. Public Policy Forum, "Interdistrict," 1–2; Witte and Thorn, "Who Chooses," 192.

49. Bonds, Farmer-Hinton, and Epps, "African Americans," 60.

50. Kava, "Open Enrollment"; Dickman, Kurhajetz, and Van Dunk, "Choosing Integration."

51. Miner, *Lessons*, 227.

52. Borsuk, "MPS."

53. Kava, "Open Enrollment," 8.

54. Hetzner, "Some Places."

55. Miner, *Lessons*, 226.

56. Elmbrook School Board, "October 19 Chapter 220," 1–3.

57. Elmbrook School Board, "October 13 School," 3.

58. On these qualities of communication scholarship, see Krippendorf, "Reliability" and "Validity."

59. Elmbrook School Board, "Finance and Operations," 4.

60. Ibid., 5.

61. Elmbrook School Board, "October 19 Chapter 220," 20.

62. Elmbrook School Board, "October 13 School," 14.

63. Elmbrook School Board, "October 27 School," 5.

64. Fischer, *Reframing*, 5–11.

65. Elmbrook School Board, "October 19 Chapter 220," 45.

66. Ibid., 21.

67. Elmbrook School Board, "October 13 School," 14.

68. Elmbrook School Board, "October 27 School," 4.

69. Ibid., 11.

70. Elmbrook School Board, "October 13 School," 14.

71. Elmbrook School Board, "October 27 School," 13.

72. Ibid., 10.

73. Elmbrook School Board, "October 19 Chapter 220," 3.

74. Ibid., 4.

75. Ibid., 16.

76. Ibid., 6.

77. Ibid., 16.

78. Ibid., 18.

79. Ibid., 40.

80. Ibid., 34.

81. Ibid., 11.

82. Elmbrook School Board, "October 13 School," 1.

83. Ibid., 5.

84. Elmbrook School Board, "October 19 Chapter 220," 30.

85. Ibid., 45–46.
86. Elmbrook School Board, "October 27 School," 7.
87. Ibid., 9–10.
88. Elmbrook School Board, "July 13 School," 13.
89. Elmbrook Enrollment Management Study Team, "Report," 5–6.
90. Miner, *Lessons*, 250–65.
91. Elmbrook School Board, "October 12 School," 6.
92. Elmbrook School Board, "July 13 School," 27.
93. Elmbrook School Board, "October 12 School," 6.
94. Elmbrook School Board, "July 20 Special," 7–8.
95. Ibid., 2, 5, 15. Katie Wilson won an election to replace David Marcello, who resigned from the board to run for mayor of Brookfield, Wisconsin, a race he subsequently lost.
96. Elmbrook School Board, "October 12 School," 10.
97. Elmbrook School Board, "August 11 School," 6.
98. Elmbrook School Board, "October 26 Chapter 220," 18.
99. Elmbrook School Board, "October 26 School," 5.
100. Elmbrook School Board, "October 26 Chapter 220," 15.
101. Elmbrook School Board, "October 12 School," 7, and "October 26 Chapter 220," 17.
102. Elmbrook School Board, "October 12 School," 2.
103. Elmbrook School Board, "October 26 School," 7.
104. Elmbrook School Board, "October 26 Chapter 220," 22.
105. Ibid., 19.
106. Elmbrook School Board, "August 11 School," 7, 9.
107. Ibid., 55–56.
108. James Aune explains that "realism is the default rhetoric for defenders of the free market." Aune, *Selling*, 40. See also Hariman, *Political Style*.
109. Elmbrook School Board, "July 20 Special," 23.
110. Elmbrook School Board, "October 26 School," 5.
111. In his "Letter from Birmingham Jail," King wrote that "injustice anywhere is a threat to justice everywhere. We are caught in an inescapable network of mutuality, tied in a single garment of destiny." King, "Letter," 239. In his acceptance speech for the 1964 Nobel Peace Prize, King maintained that "both rich and poor are tied in a single garment of destiny." King, "Quest," 341.

CHAPTER 5

1. Benhabib, "Toward a Deliberative Model"; Hicks, "Promise(s)."
2. Observing that scholars "elucidate quite different visions" of trust, Russell Hardin concludes that the term conveys multiple and sometimes conflicting meanings. Hardin, *Trust and Trustworthiness*, 54.
3. Warren, "Introduction," 4.
4. I am grateful to Stephen Weatherford for this insight.
5. See Putnam, "Tuning In," and *Bowling Alone*. For a selection of different perspectives in this literature, see Hardin, *Trust*; Misztal, *Trust*; Uslaner, "Producing"; Zmerli and Newton, "Social Trust"; Wuthnow, "Role of Trust."
6. American National Election Studies, *ANES Guide;* Davis and Smith, *General Social Surveys*.
7. Norris, *Democratic Deficits*, 64–66.

8. Catterberg and Moreno, "Individual Bases"; Mackie, "Patterns"; Mishler and Rose, "Five Years"; Newton, "Trust."

9. See, e.g., Behn, "Government Performance."

10. Joseph Cappella and Kathleen Hall Jamieson have argued that contemporary journalistic practices enable a "contagious cynicism" that contributes to public distrust of governing and media institutions alike. See Cappella and Jamieson, *Spiral*.

11. Putnam identifies differences in trust among generations as a key factor in its overall decline. See Putnam, *Bowling Alone*, 137–44.

12. See, e.g., Patterson, "Liberty."

13. Hetherington, *Why Trust Matters*; Inglehart, "Postmodernism."

14. Putnam, *Bowling Alone*, 231. Some scholars, including Eric Uslaner, have challenged this explanation. See Uslaner, "Social Capital."

15. Putnam, *Bowling Alone*, 137.

16. See Luhmann, *Trust and Power*, 10, 25; Misztal, *Trust*, 121–39.

17. Offe, "How Can We," 52–54.

18. Uslaner, *Moral Foundations*, 17, 18.

19. Bryk and Schneider, *Trust in Schools*, 22.

20. Ibid., 22–26.

21. Mayer, Davis, and Schoorman, "Integrative Model." See also Schoorman, Mayer, and Davis, "Integrative Model."

22. Enumerating similar qualities, Patrick Forsyth, Curt Adams, and Wayne Hoy develop a model of "collective trust" for school organizations. They write that "collective trust is socially constructed out of talk and nonverbal interactions among group members." Forsyth, Adams, and Hoy, *Collective Trust*, 24. For conceptions of trust from organizational scholars, see Pirson and Malhotra, "Foundations"; Sheppard and Sherman, "Grammars."

23. Daly and Finnigan, "Exploring the Space."

24. Kramer, "Trust and Distrust," 574.

25. Lewicki, McAllister, and Bies, "Trust and Distrust," 442.

26. Young, *Inclusion and Democracy*, 26.

27. Festenstein, *Negotiating Diversity*, 143.

28. Hauser and Benoit-Barné, "Reflections," 272.

29. Bohman, *Public Deliberation*, 169.

30. Hauser and Benoit-Barné, "Reflections," 268.

31. Following James Jasinski, I see credibility—when applied to an advocate as opposed to, say, evidence—as synonymous with character. Jasinski identifies "source credibility" as a twentieth-century displacement of the classical notion of ethos. James Jasinski, *Sourcebook*, 230. For an alternative view of rhetoric, trust, and character, see Allen, *Talking to Strangers*.

32. Aristotle, *On Rhetoric*, 1356a.

33. Garver, *Aristotle's*, 191.

34. Brinton, "Ethotic Argument," 252.

35. Hauser and Benoit-Barné, "Reflections," 270.

36. Some scholars, such as Francis Fukuyama, associate the experiential basis of trust with shared experiences, values, and beliefs. Fukuyama argues that "trust is the expectation that arises within a community of regular, honest, and cooperative behavior, based on commonly shared norms, on the part of other members of that community." Francis Fukuyama, *Trust*, 26. However, as Festenstein (*Negotiating Diversity*, 145–46) observes, Fukuyama ascribes unanimity and transparency to a culture and its members. Presumably, members of a culture share not only norms but also an understanding of the meaning and consequence of these norms for deliberation and other

modes of interaction. Yet culture may serve as a site of contestation, whereby members of a society advocate alternative and often-competing interpretations of their values, histories, and identities.

37. See, e.g., Farrell, *Norms*; Ivie, "Democratic Deliberation."

38. See Kuehl, "Rhetorical Presidency"; McGuinn, *No Child*.

39. I amplify this point in my discussion of the risks of public engagement. Asen, "Discourse Theory," 200–201.

40. Gutmann and Thompson, *Why Deliberative Democracy?* 133.

41. See Brouwer, "Communication."

42. Lenard, "Rebuilding Trust," 81.

43. Markovits, "Trouble," 258. See also Markovits, *Politics of Sincerity*.

44. Habermas, *Moral Consciousness*, 136.

45. Habermas, *Communicative Action*, 1:288.

46. Ibid., 25.

47. Ibid., 294.

48. Fraser, "Rethinking," 119.

49. Young, *Inclusion and Democracy*, 136.

50. Ibid., 137.

51. Bryk and Schneider, *Trust in Schools*, 25.

52. Rawls, *Political Liberalism*, 217.

53. Arendt, *Human Condition*, 200. Leo Penta maintains that Arendt's conception of power comports with her relational view of subjectivity: "There is for Arendt no political self prior to the power relationship with others, or, from the point of view of the community, no we of action prior to the power relationship of the self and the others." Penta, "Hannah Arendt," 218.

54. The empirical question of the extent to which ordinary people avoid deliberation about public affairs has drawn varied answers. See Eliasoph, *Avoiding Politics*; Jacobs, Cook, and Delli Carpini, *Talking Together*; Mutz, *Hearing*.

CONCLUSION

1. Dewey, *Public*, 131.

2. Ibid., 175.

3. Ibid., 183.

4. Ibid., 184.

5. Ibid., 216.

6. Reese, *America's Public Schools*.

7. Maeroff, *School Boards*.

8. Dewey, *Democracy*, 87.

9. Lippmann, *Phantom*, 58.

10. On the socializing force of education, see Smith-Sanders and Harter, "Democracy," 110–11.

11. McArdle, Osypuk, and Acevedo-García, "Segregation," 8.

12. Elmbrook School Board, "October 26 School," 5.

13. George W. Bush, *Public Papers*, 1:17.

14. Obama, *Public Papers*, 2:1168.

15. Smith, "Scientifically Based Research."

16. For critiques of the experimental approach of NCLB, see, e.g., Giangreco and Taylor, "Scientifically Based Research"; Hess, "When Education Research Matters"; Howe, "Question."

17. Jackson, *Crabgrass Frontier*, 219.

18. See Tracy, *Challenges*, 55–57, 192. For a discussion of historical debates of representation, see Pitkin, *Representation*, 144–67.

19. Dewey, *Democracy*, 87.

20. Dewey, *Public*, 151.

21. Biesta, "Education," 235.

22. Ranson, "Markets," 334.

23. Ibid., 337, 339.

24. National Commission on Excellence in Education, *Nation at Risk*, 6–7.

25. George W. Bush, *Public Papers*, 1:113.

26. Ibid., 1:17.

27. Obama, *Public Papers*, 2:1632.

28. Nussbaum, "Education," 388–91.

29. Friedman, *Capitalism and Freedom*, 90–91.

30. Ibid., 1–2.

31. Dewey, *Public*, 149.

BIBLIOGRAPHY

Allen, Danielle S. *Talking to Strangers: Anxieties of Citizenship since "Brown v. Board of Education."* Chicago: University of Chicago Press, 2004.

American National Election Studies. *The ANES Guide to Public Opinion and Political Behavior.* 2010. http://www.electionstudies.org/nesguide/toptable/tab5a_1.htm.

"America's 100 Most Conservative-Friendly Counties." *Daily Caller,* March 16, 2010. http://dailycaller.com/2010/03/16/americas-100-most-conservative-friendly -counties-numbers-80-61/.

Arendt, Hannah. *The Human Condition.* Chicago: University of Chicago Press, 1958.

Aristotle. *Nicomachean Ethics.* Translated by W. D. Ross. Oxford: Clarendon Press, 1908.

———. *On Rhetoric.* Translated by George A. Kennedy. New York: Oxford University Press, 1991.

Asen, Robert. "A Discourse Theory of Citizenship." *Quarterly Journal of Speech* 90, no. 2 (2004): 189–211.

———. "Ideology, Materiality, and Counterpublicity: William E. Simon and the Rise of a Conservative Counterintelligentsia." *Quarterly Journal of Speech* 95, no. 3 (2009): 263–88.

———. "Imagining in the Public Sphere." *Philosophy and Rhetoric* 35, no. 4 (2002): 345–67.

———. "Reflections on the Role of Rhetoric in Public Policy." *Rhetoric and Public Affairs* 13, no. 1 (2010): 121–43.

———. "Seeking the 'Counter' in Counterpublics." *Communication Theory* 10, no. 4 (2000): 424–46.

Asen, Robert, and Daniel C. Brouwer. "Introduction: Reconfigurations of the Public Sphere." In *Counterpublics and the State,* edited by Robert Asen and Daniel C. Brouwer, 1–32. Albany: State University of New York Press, 2001.

Asen, Robert, Deb Gurke, Pamela Conners, Ryan Solomon, and Elsa Gumm. "Research Evidence and School-Board Deliberations: Lessons from Three Wisconsin School Districts." *Educational Policy* 27, no. 1 (2013): 33–63.

———. "'The Research Says': Definitions and Uses of a Key Policy Term in Federal Law and Local School Board Deliberations." *Argumentation and Advocacy* 47, no. 4 (2011): 195–213.

Audi, Robert. *Religious Commitment and Secular Reason.* New York: Cambridge University Press, 2000.

Aune, James Arnt. *Selling the Free Market: The Rhetoric of Economic Correctness.* New York: Guilford Press, 2001.

Badzinski, Jill, and Kristen Kubisiak. "After the Election: What Now?" *Daily News,* April 8, 2010.

Baker, Bruce B. "The Emerging Shape of Educational Adequacy: From Theoretical Assumptions to Empirical Evidence." *Journal of Education Finance* 30, no. 3 (2005): 259–87.

Barker, Derek W. M., Noëlle McAfee, and David W. McIvor. "Introduction: Democratiz-
     ing Deliberation." In *Democratizing Deliberation: A Political Theory Anthology*,
     edited by Derek W. M. Barker, Noëlle McAfee, and David W. McIvor, 1–17. Day-
     ton, Ohio: Kettering Foundation Press, 2012.
Batt, Shawn. "Keeping Company in Controversy: Education Reform, Spheres of Ar-
     gument, and Ethical Criticism." *Argumentation and Advocacy* 40, no. 2 (2003):
     85–104.
Baumeister, Andrea. "The Use of 'Public Reason' by Religious and Secular Citizens:
     Limitations of Habermas' Conception of the Role of Religion in the Public
     Realm." *Constellations* 18, no. 2 (2011): 222–43.
Behn, Robert D. "Government Performance and the Conundrum of Public Trust."
     In *Market-Based Governance: Supply Side, Demand Side, Upside, and Downside*,
     edited by John D. Donahue and Joseph S. Nye Jr., 323–48. Washington, D.C.:
     Brookings Institution Press, 2002.
Beloit School Board. "February 16 Budget Listening Session." February 16, 2010. [Per-
     sonal transcript.]
———. "July 6 Special Board Meeting." July 6, 2010. [Personal transcript.]
———. "March 11 Special Board Meeting." March 11, 2011. [Personal transcript.]
———. "Meeting of the Finance, Transportation, and Property Committee." April 13,
     2010. [Personal transcript.]
———. "October 12 Special Board Meeting." October 12, 2010. [Personal transcript.]
———. "October 19 Special Board Meeting." October 19, 2010. [Personal transcript.]
———. "October 20 Special Board Meeting." October 20, 2009. [Personal transcript.]
———. "October 22 Special Board Meeting." October 22, 2009. [Personal transcript.]
———. "October 26 Regular School Board Meeting." October 26, 2010. [Personal tran-
     script.]
———. "October 27 Budget Hearing." October 27, 2009. [Personal transcript.]
———. "October 27 Special Board Meeting." October 27, 2009. [Personal transcript.]
———. "October 29 Special Board Meeting." October 29, 2009. [Personal transcript.]
Benhabib, Seyla. *Situating the Self: Gender, Community, and Postmodernism in Contem-
     porary Ethics*. New York: Routledge, 1992.
———. "Toward a Deliberative Model of Democratic Legitimacy." In *Democracy and
     Difference: Contesting the Boundaries of the Political*, edited by Seyla Benhabib,
     67–94. Princeton: Princeton University Press, 1996.
Benoit-Barné, Chantal. "Socio-technical Deliberation about Free and Open Source
     Software: Accounting for the Status of Artifacts in Public Life." *Quarterly Jour-
     nal of Speech* 93, no. 2 (2007): 211–35.
Berkman, Michael B., and Eric Plutzer. *Ten Thousand Democracies: Politics and Public
     Opinion in America's School Districts*. Washington, D.C.: Georgetown University
     Press, 2005.
Biesecker, Barbara. "Recalculating the Relationship of the Public and Technical
     Spheres." In *Spheres of Argument: Proceedings of the Sixth SCA/AFA Conference
     on Argumentation*, edited by Bruce E. Gronbeck, 66–70. Annandale, Va.: Speech
     Communication Association, 1989.
Biesta, Gert J. J. "Education, Accountability, and the Ethical Demand: Can the Demo-
     cratic Potential of Accountability Be Regained?" *Educational Theory* 54, no. 3
     (2004): 233–50.
Bizzell, Patricia, and Susan Jarratt. "Rhetorical Traditions, Pluralized Canons, Rele-
     vant History, and Other Disputed Terms: A Report from the History of Rhetoric
     Discussion Groups at the ARS Conference." *Rhetoric Society Quarterly* 34, no. 3
     (2004): 19–25.

Bohman, James. *Public Deliberation: Pluralism, Complexity, and Democracy.* Cambridge: Massachusetts Institute of Technology Press, 1996.

Bonds, Michael, Raquel L. Farmer-Hinton, and Edgar G. Epps. "African Americans' Continuing Struggle for Quality Education in Milwaukee, Wisconsin." *Journal of Negro Education* 78, no. 1 (2009): 55–69.

Borsuk, Alan J. "MPS Watches Students Hop the Border: Exodus Adds Challenges for State's Largest School District." *Milwaukee Journal Sentinel*, February 5, 2011.

Boyd, Josh. "Public and Technical Interdependence: Regulatory Controversy, Out-Law Discourse, and the Messy Case of Olestra." *Argumentation and Advocacy* 39, no. 2 (2002): 91–109.

Brashers, Dale E., and Sally Jackson. "'Politically-Savvy Sick People': Public Penetration of the Technical Sphere." In *Argument in Controversy: Proceedings of the Seventh SCA/AFA Conference on Argumentation*, edited by Donn W. Parson, 284–88. Annandale, Va.: Speech Communication Association, 1991.

Briffault, Richard. "The Local School District in American Law." In *Besieged: School Boards and the Future of Education Politics*, edited by William G. Howell, 24–55. Washington, D.C.: Brookings Institution Press, 2005.

Brinton, Alan. "Ethotic Argument." *History of Philosophy Quarterly* 3, no. 3 (1986): 245–58.

Brouwer, Daniel C. "ACT-ing UP in Congressional Hearings." In *Counterpublics and the State*, edited by Robert Asen and Daniel C. Brouwer, 87–109. Albany: State University of New York Press, 2001.

———. "Communication as Counterpublic." In *Communication as . . . : Perspectives on Theory*, edited by Gregory J. Shepherd, Jeffrey St. John, and Ted Striphas, 195–208. Thousand Oaks, Calif.: Sage, 2006.

Brouwer, Daniel C., and Robert Asen. "Introduction: Public Modalities, or the Metaphors We Theorize By." In *Public Modalities: Rhetoric, Culture, Media, and the Shape of Public Life*, edited by Daniel C. Brouwer and Robert Asen, 1–32. Tuscaloosa: University of Alabama Press, 2010.

Brown, Mark B. *Science in Democracy: Expertise, Institutions, and Representation.* Cambridge: Massachusetts Institute of Technology Press, 2009.

Bryk, Anthony S., and Barbara Schneider. *Trust in Schools: A Core Resource for Improvement.* New York: Russell Sage, 2002.

Burkhalter, Stephanie, John Gastil, and Todd Kelshaw. "A Conceptual Definition and Theoretical Model of Public Deliberation in Small Face-to-Face Groups." *Communication Theory* 12, no. 4 (2002): 389–422.

Bush, George. *Public Papers of the Presidents of the United States: George Bush, 1989.* 2 vols. Washington, D.C.: Government Printing Office, 1990.

Bush, George W. *Public Papers of the Presidents of the United States: George W. Bush, 2001.* 2 vols. Washington, D.C.: Government Printing Office, 2003.

Butler, Judith, Jürgen Habermas, Charles Taylor, and Cornel West. *The Power of Religion in the Public Sphere.* Edited by Eduardo Mendieta and Jonathan VanAntwerpen. New York: Columbia University Press, 2011.

Calhoun, Craig. "Secularism, Citizenship, and the Public Sphere." In *Rethinking Secularism*, edited by Craig Calhoun, Mark Juergensmeyer, and Jonathan VanAntwerpen, 75–91. New York: Oxford University Press, 2011.

Campbell, Karlyn Kohrs. "Agency: Promiscuous and Protean." *Communication and Critical/Cultural Studies* 2, no. 1 (2005): 1–19.

Cappella, Joseph N., and Kathleen Hall Jamieson. *Spiral of Cynicism: The Press and the Public Good.* New York: Oxford University Press, 1997.

Carroll, William A. "The Constitution, the Supreme Court, and Religion." *American Political Science Review* 61, no. 3 (1967): 657–74.

Catterberg, Gabriela, and Alejandro Moreno. "The Individual Bases of Political Trust: Trends in New and Established Democracies." *International Journal of Public Opinion Research* 18, no. 1 (2005): 31–48.

Ceccarelli, Leah. "Let Us (Not) Theorize the Spaces of Contention." *Argumentation and Advocacy* 42, no. 1 (2005): 30–33.

———. "Manufactured Scientific Controversy: Science, Rhetoric, and Public Debate." *Rhetoric and Public Affairs* 14, no. 2 (2011): 195–228.

———. "Polysemy: Multiple Meanings in Rhetorical Criticism." *Quarterly Journal of Speech* 84, no. 4 (1998): 395–415.

Chemerinsky, Erwin. "The Segregation and Resegregation of American Public Education: The Court's Role." *North Carolina Law Review* 81, no. 4 (2002): 1597–1622.

Chetty, Raj, Nathaniel Hendren, Patrick Kline, and Emmanuel Saez. "Where Is the Land of Opportunity? The Geography of Intergenerational Mobility in the United States." National Bureau of Economic Research, Working Paper 19843. 2014. http://www.nber.org/papers/w19843.

Civil Rights Act of 1964, U.S. Statutes at Large 78 (1964): 241–68.

Cloud, Dana L., and Joshua Gunn. "Introduction: W(h)ither Ideology?" *Western Journal of Communication* 75, no. 4 (2011): 407–20.

Cohen, Joshua. "Deliberation and Democratic Legitimacy." In *Deliberative Democracy: Essays on Reason and Politics*, edited by James Bohman and William Rehg, 67–91. Cambridge: Massachusetts Institute of Technology Press, 1997.

Coleman, James S., et al. *Equality of Educational Opportunity.* Washington, D.C.: Government Printing Office, 1966.

Conquergood, Dwight. "Ethnography, Rhetoric, and Performance." *Quarterly Journal of Speech* 78, no. 1 (1992): 80–97.

Cornman, Stephen Q., Jumaane Young, and Kenneth C. Herrell. *Revenues and Expenditures for Public Elementary and Secondary Education: School Year 2009–10 (Fiscal Year 2010).* NCES 2013-305. Washington, D.C.: National Center for Education Statistics, 2012.

Crowley, Sharon. "Reflections on an Argument That Won't Go Away: Or, a Turn of the Ideological Screw." *Quarterly Journal of Speech* 78, no. 4 (1992): 450–65.

Cyphert, Dale. "Ideology, Knowledge, and Text." *Quarterly Journal of Speech* 87, no. 4 (2001): 378–95.

Daly, Alan J., and Kara S. Finnigan. "Exploring the Space Between: Social Networks, Trust, and Urban School District Leaders." *Journal of School Leadership* 22, no. 3 (2012): 493–530.

Davies, Gareth. *See Government Grow: Education Politics from Johnson to Reagan.* Lawrence: University Press of Kansas, 2007.

Davis, James A., and Tom W. Smith. *General Social Surveys, 1972–2008.* Chicago: National Opinion Research Center, 2009.

DeBray, Elizabeth H. *Politics, Ideology, and Education: Federal Policy during the Clinton and Bush Administrations.* New York: Teachers College Press, 2006.

Delagardelle, Mary L. "The Lighthouse Inquiry: Examining the Role of School Board Leadership in the Improvement of Student Achievement." In *The Future of School Board Governance: Relevancy and Revelation*, edited by Thomas L. Alsbury, 191–223. Lanham, Md.: Rowman and Littlefield, 2008.

DeMitchell, Todd A., and Richard Fossey. "Student Speech: School Boards, Gay/Straight Alliances, and the Equal Access Act." *BYU Education and Law Journal* 1 (2008): 89–124.

DeNardis, Lesley A. "From Equity to Adequacy: Evolving Legal Theories in School Finance Litigation: The Case of Connecticut." *International Journal of Education* 2,
no. 1 (2010): 1–17.

DeNavas-Walt, Carmen, Bernadette D. Proctor, and Jessica C. Smith. *Income, Poverty,
and Health Insurance Coverage in the United States: 2012.* U.S. Census Bureau
Current Population Reports, P60-245. Washington, D.C.: Government Printing
Office, 2013.

Dewey, John. "Creative Democracy—The Task before Us." In *John Dewey: The Later
Works, 1925–1953,* vol. 14, *1939–1941,* edited by Jo Ann Boydston, 224–30. Car-
bondale: Southern Illinois University Press, 1991.

———. *Democracy and Education: An Introduction to the Philosophy of Education.* 1916.
Repr., New York: Free Press, 1944.

———. *The Public and Its Problems.* 1927. Repr., Athens, Ohio: Swallow Press, 1954.

Dickinson, Hilary. "Beloit School Board Votes for 6.6% Boost in Tax Levy." *Beloit Daily
News,* October 30, 2009.

Dickman, Anneliese M., Sarah A. Kurhajetz, and Emily Van Dunk. "Choosing Integration: Chapter 220 in the Shadow of Open Enrollment." February 2003. http://
publicpolicyforum.org/research/choosing-integration-chapter-220-shadow
-open-enrollment.

Dougherty, Jack. *More Than One Struggle: The Evolution of Black School Reform in Milwaukee.* Chapel Hill: University of North Carolina Press, 2004.

Douglas, Heather E. *Science, Policy, and the Value-Free Ideal.* Pittsburgh: University of
Pittsburgh Press, 2009.

Duncombe, William, and John Yinger. "How Much More Does a Disadvantaged Student Cost?" *Economics of Education Review* 24, no. 5 (2005): 513–32.

Eagle Forum of Washington County. "West Bend School District Candidate Questionnaire." January 15, 2010. http://wbsbinfo.blogspot.com/2010_01_01_archive
.html.

Eagleton, Terry. *Ideology: An Introduction.* London: Verso, 1991.

Education Commission of the States. "K–12 Governance Structures Database, Wisconsin." 2013. http://ecs.force.com/mbdata/MBProfGov?SID=a0i70000006evYW
&rep=K12G&state=Wisconsin.

———. "Local Superintendents." 2013. http://ecs.force.com/mbdata/mbquestU?SID
=a0i70000006evYW&rep=K12G813&Q=Q0647.

Eisenhart, Christopher. "The Humanist Scholar as Public Expert." *Written Communication* 23, no. 2 (2006): 150–72.

Eliasoph, Nina. *Avoiding Politics: How Americans Produce Apathy in Everyday Life.* New
York: Cambridge University Press, 1998.

Elmbrook Enrollment Management Study Team. "Report on Team Recommendations and Findings." July 13, 2010. http://www.elmbrookschools.org/elmbrook
-school-district/board/meeting-agendas/2010-meeting-agendas/july-13-2010
-board-meeting.html.

Elmbrook School Board. "August 11 School Board Meeting." August 11, 2010. [Personal
transcript.]

———. "Finance and Operations Committee Meeting." October 19, 2009. [Personal
transcript.]

———. "July 13 School Board Meeting." July 13, 2010. [Personal transcript.]

———. "July 20 Special School Board Meeting." July 20, 2010. [Personal transcript.]

———. "October 12 School Board Meeting." October 12, 2010. [Personal transcript.]

———. "October 13 School Board Meeting." October 13, 2009. [Personal transcript.]

————. "October 19 Chapter 220 Planning Council Meeting." October 19, 2009. [Personal transcript.]

————. "October 26 Chapter 220 Planning Council Meeting." October 26, 2010. [Personal transcript.]

————. "October 26 School Board Meeting." October 26, 2010. [Personal transcript.]

————. "October 27 School Board Meeting." October 27, 2009. [Personal transcript.]

Elmbrook School District. "Annual Report, 2010–11." September 2011. http://www.elmbrookschools.org/elmbrook-school-district/annual-report.html.

————. "Annual Report, 2011–12." September 2012. http://www.elmbrookschools.org/elmbrook-school-district/annual-report.html.

————. "Chapter 220 and Open Enrollment Status Report." October 13, 2009.

Equal Access Act of 1984, U.S. Statutes at Large 98 (1984): 1302–4.

Estlund, David. "Beyond Fairness and Deliberation: The Epistemic Dimension of Democratic Authority." In *Deliberative Democracy: Essays on Reason and Politics*, edited by James Bohman and William Rehg, 173–204. Cambridge: Massachusetts Institute of Technology.

Everson v. Board of Education of the Township of Ewing, 330 U.S. 1 (1947).

Fabj, Valeria, and Matthew J. Sobnosky. "AIDS Activism and the Rejuvenation of the Public Sphere." *Argumentation and Advocacy* 31, no. 4 (1995): 163–84.

Farrell, Thomas B. *Norms of Rhetorical Culture*. New Haven: Yale University Press, 1993.

Felski, Rita. *Beyond Feminist Aesthetics: Feminist Literature and Social Change*. Cambridge, Mass.: Harvard University Press, 1989.

Festenstein, Matthew. *Negotiating Diversity: Culture, Deliberation, Trust*. Cambridge, U.K.: Polity Press, 2005.

Fischer, Frank. *Democracy and Expertise: Reorienting Policy Inquiry*. New York: Oxford University Press, 2009.

————. *Reframing Public Policy: Discursive Politics and Deliberative Practices*. Oxford: Oxford University Press, 2003.

Forsyth, Patrick B., Curt M. Adams, and Wayne K. Hoy. *Collective Trust: Why Schools Can't Improve Without It*. New York: Teachers College Press, 2011.

Fraser, Nancy. "Rethinking the Public Sphere: A Contribution to the Critique of Actually Existing Democracy." In *Habermas and the Public Sphere*, edited by Craig Calhoun, 109–42. Cambridge: Massachusetts Institute of Technology, 1992.

Friedland, Lewis A., Thomas Hove, and Hernando Rojas. "The Networked Public Sphere." *Javnost—The Public* 13, no. 4 (2006): 5–26.

Friedman, Milton. *Capitalism and Freedom*. Chicago: University of Chicago Press, 1962.

Fukuyama, Francis. *Trust: The Social Virtues and the Creation of Prosperity*. New York: Free Press, 1995.

Garver, Eugene. *Aristotle's "Rhetoric": An Art of Character*. Chicago: University of Chicago Press, 1994.

Gavan, Hillary. "4 of 5 Beloit Pupils on Lunch Subsidies." *Beloit Daily News*, March 20, 2012.

Giangreco, Michael F., and Steven J. Taylor. "'Scientifically Based Research' and Qualitative Inquiry." *Research and Practice for Persons with Severe Disabilities* 28, no. 3 (2003): 133–37.

Glauber, Bill. "State Voters Say 'I Do' to Marriage Amendment." *Milwaukee Journal Sentinel*, November 8, 2008.

Goodnight, G. Thomas. "Controversy." In *Argument in Controversy: Proceedings of the Seventh SCA/AFA Conference on Argumentation*, edited by Donn W. Parson, 1–13. Annandale, Va.: Speech Communication Association, 1991.

———. "The Personal, Technical, and Public Spheres of Argument: A Speculative Inquiry into the Art of Public Deliberation." *Journal of the American Forensic Association* 18, no. 4 (1982): 214–27.

Graham, Hugh Davis. *The Uncertain Triumph: Federal Education Policy in the Kennedy and Johnson Years.* Chapel Hill: University of North Carolina Press, 1984.

Graham, Patricia Albjerg. *Schooling America: How the Public Schools Meet the Nation's Changing Needs.* New York: Oxford University Press, 2005.

Greene, Ronald Walter. "Arguing with Money: Reasonableness and Change in *Citizens United v. Federal Election Commission.*" In *Reasoned Argument and Social Change,* edited by Robert C. Rowland, 537–44. Washington, D.C.: National Communication Association, 2011.

Gutmann, Amy, and Dennis Thompson. *Democracy and Disagreement: Why Moral Conflict Cannot Be Avoided in Politics and What Should Be Done about It.* Cambridge, Mass.: Harvard University Press, 1996.

———. *Why Deliberative Democracy?* Princeton: Princeton University Press, 2004.

Habermas, Jürgen. *Between Facts and Norms: Contributions to a Discourse Theory of Law and Democracy.* Translated by William Rehg. Cambridge: Massachusetts Institute of Technology, 1996.

———. *Between Naturalism and Religion: Philosophical Essays.* Translated by Ciaran Cronin. Malden, Mass.: Polity Press, 2008.

———. *Moral Consciousness and Communicative Action.* Translated by Christian Lenhardt and Sherry Weber Nicholsen. Cambridge: Massachusetts Institute of Technology Press, 1990.

———. *The Structural Transformation of the Public Sphere: An Inquiry into a Category of Bourgeois Society.* Translated by Thomas Burger. Cambridge: Massachusetts Institute of Technology Press, 1989.

———. *The Theory of Communicative Action.* Vol. 1, *Reason and the Rationalization of Society.* Vol. 2, *Lifeworld and System: A Critique of Functionalist Reason.* Translated by Thomas McCarthy. Boston: Beacon Press, 1984, 1987.

Habermas, Jürgen, Norbert Brieskorn, Michael Reder, Friedo Ricken, and Josef Schmidt. *An Awareness of What Is Missing: Faith and Reason in a Post-secular Age.* Translated by Ciaran Cronin. Malden, Mass.: Polity Press, 2010.

Hamari, Alan. "District Will Not Accept New Chapter 220 Students." *Brookfield Now,* October 26, 2010.

Hanna, Jason. "Library Fight Riles Up City, Leads to Book-Burning Demand." *CNN,* July 22, 2009. http://www.cnn.com/2009/US/07/22/wisconsin.book.row/.

Hardin, Russell. *Trust.* Cambridge, U.K.: Polity Press, 2006.

———. *Trust and Trustworthiness.* New York: Russell Sage, 2002.

Hariman, Robert. *Political Style: The Artistry of Power.* Chicago: University of Chicago Press, 1995.

Hartelius, E. Johanna. *The Rhetoric of Expertise.* Lanham, Md.: Lexington Books, 2011.

Hauser, Gerard A. "Attending the Vernacular: A Plea for an Ethnographical Rhetoric." In *The Rhetorical Emergence of Culture,* edited by Christian Meyer and Felix Girke, 157–72. New York: Berghahn Books, 2011.

———. *Vernacular Voices: The Rhetoric of Publics and Public Spheres.* Columbia: University of South Carolina Press, 1999.

Hauser, Gerard A., and Chantal Benoit-Barné. "Reflections on Rhetoric, Deliberative Democracy, Civil Society, and Trust." *Rhetoric and Public Affairs* 5, no. 2 (2002): 261–75.

Hayes, William. *No Child Left Behind: Past, Present, and Future.* Lanham, Md.: Rowman and Littlefield, 2008.

Heresco, Aaron. "Citizens Divided: Campaign Finance Reform, Deliberative Democracy, and *Citizens United.*" *Democratic Communiqué* 25, no. 2 (2012): 22–37.

Hess, Aaron. "Critical-Rhetorical Ethnography: Rethinking the Place and Process of Rhetoric." *Communication Studies* 62, no. 2 (2011): 127–52.

Hess, Frederick M. *School Boards at the Dawn of the 21st Century: Conditions and Challenges of District Governance.* Alexandria, Va.: National School Boards Association, 2002.

———. "When Education Research Matters." *Education Outlook* 1 (2008): 1–6.

Hessel, Kaellen. "West Bend School District Divided by Politics; Local, National Upheaval Affecting Proud District." *Milwaukee Journal Sentinel,* August 21, 2011.

Hetherington, Marc J. *Why Trust Matters: Declining Political Trust and the Demise of American Liberalism.* Princeton: Princeton University Press, 2004.

Hetzner, Amy. "Some Places' Integration Seats Vanish: Aid Formula Makes Big Players Prefer Open Enrollment to 220." *Milwaukee Journal Sentinel,* December 25, 2010.

Hicks, Darrin. "The Promise(s) of Deliberative Democracy." *Rhetoric and Public Affairs* 5, no. 2 (2002): 223–60.

Hochschild, Jennifer L. "What School Boards Can and Cannot (or Will Not) Accomplish." In *Besieged: School Boards and the Future of Education Politics,* edited by William G. Howell, 324–38. Washington, D.C.: Brookings Institution Press, 2005.

Honig, Meredith I., and Cynthia Coburn. "Evidence-Based Decision Making in School District Central Offices." *Educational Policy* 22, no. 4 (2008): 578–608.

Howard, Robert Glenn. "The Vernacular Mode: Locating the Non-institutional in the Practice of Citizenship." In *Public Modalities: Rhetoric, Culture, Media, and the Shape of Public Life,* edited by Daniel C. Brouwer and Robert Asen, 240–61. Tuscaloosa: University of Alabama Press, 2010.

Howe, Kenneth R. "The Question of Education Science: *Experiment*ism versus *Experi*mentalism." *Educational Theory* 55, no. 3 (2005): 307–21.

Howell, William G. "Introduction." In *Besieged: School Boards and the Future of Education Politics,* edited by William G. Howell, 1–23. Washington, D.C.: Brookings Institution Press, 2005.

Hoxby, Caroline H. "All School Finance Equalizations Are Not Created Equal." *Quarterly Journal of Economics* 116, no. 4 (2001): 1189–1231.

Iannaccone, Laurence, and Frank W. Lutz. *Politics, Power, and Policy: The Governing of Local School Districts.* Columbus, Ohio: C. E. Merrill, 1970.

"In a Decisive Victory, Obama Reshapes the Electoral Map." *New York Times,* November 6, 2008.

Inglehart, Ronald. "Postmodernism Erodes Respect for Authority, but Increases Support for Democracy." In *Critical Citizens: Global Support for Democratic Governance,* edited by Pippa Norris, 236–56. New York: Oxford University Press, 1999.

Ivie, Robert L. "Democratic Deliberation in a Rhetorical Republic." *Quarterly Journal of Speech* 84, no. 4 (1998): 491–505.

———. "Rhetorical Deliberation and Democratic Politics in the Here and Now." *Rhetoric and Public Affairs* 5, no. 2 (2002): 277–85.

Jackson, Kenneth T. *Crabgrass Frontier: The Suburbanization of the United States.* New York: Oxford University Press, 1985.

Jacobs, Lawrence R., Fay Lomax Cook, and Michael X. Delli Carpini. *Talking Together: Public Deliberation and Political Participation in America.* Chicago: University of Chicago Press, 2009.

Jacobsen, Rebecca, and Andrew Saultz. "Who Should Control Education?" *Public Opinion Quarterly* 76, no. 2 (2012): 379–90.

Jasinski, James. *Sourcebook on Rhetoric: Key Concepts in Contemporary Rhetorical Studies*. Thousand Oaks, Calif.: Sage, 2001.

———. "The Status of Theory and Method in Rhetorical Criticism." *Western Journal of Communication* 65, no. 3 (2001): 249–70.

Jeffrey, Julie Roy. *Education for Children of the Poor: A Study of the Origins and Implementation of the Elementary and Secondary Education Act of 1965*. Columbus: Ohio State University Press, 1978.

Jennings, John F. *Why National Standards and Tests? Politics and the Quest for Better Schools*. Thousand Oaks, Calif.: Sage, 1998.

"Jobless Rate Up Again, 17.7%." *Beloit Daily News*, April 23, 2009.

Johnson, Lyndon Baines. *Public Papers of the Presidents of the United States: Lyndon B. Johnson, 1965*. 2 vols. Washington, D.C.: Government Printing Office, 1966.

———. *The Vantage Point: Perspectives of the Presidency, 1963–1969*. New York: Holt, Rinehart, and Winston, 1971.

Kaestle, Carl F. *Pillars of the Republic: Common Schools and American Society, 1780–1860*. New York: Hill and Wang, 1983.

Kava, Russ. "Open Enrollment Program." Wisconsin Legislative Fiscal Bureau. Informational Paper 27. January 2013.

———. "School Integration (Chapter 220) Aid." Wisconsin Legislative Fiscal Bureau. Informational Paper 27. January 2011.

Kava, Russ, and Layla Merrifield. "State Aid to School Districts." Wisconsin Legislative Fiscal Bureau. Informational Paper 26. January 2011.

Keith, William M. *Democracy as Discussion: Civic Education and the American Forum Movement*. Lanham, Md.: Lexington Books, 2007.

Keränen, Lisa. "Mapping Misconduct: Demarcating Legitimate Science from 'Fraud' in the B-06 Lumpectomy Controversy." *Argumentation and Advocacy* 42, no. 2 (2005): 94–113.

King, Martin Luther, Jr. "Letter from Birmingham Jail." In *Blessed Are the Peacemakers: Martin Luther King Jr., Eight White Religious Leaders, and the "Letter from Birmingham Jail,"* edited by S. Jonathan Bass, 237–56. Baton Rouge: Louisiana State University Press, 2001.

———. "The Quest for Peace and Justice." In *Peace*, edited by Frederick W. Haberman, 333–46. New York: Elsevier, 1972.

Kitcher, Phillip. *Science in a Democratic Society*. Amherst, N.Y.: Prometheus Books, 2011.

Kock, Christian, and Lisa S. Villadsen. "Introduction: Citizenship as a Rhetorical Practice." In *Rhetorical Citizenship and Public Deliberation*, edited by Christian Kock and Lisa S. Villadsen, 1–10. University Park: Pennsylvania State University Press, 2012.

Koski, William S., and Rob Reich. "When 'Adequate' Isn't: The Retreat from Equity in Educational Law and Policy and Why It Matters." *Emory Law Journal* 56, no. 3 (2006): 545–617.

Kozol, Jonathan. *Savage Inequalities: Children in America's Schools*. New York: Crown, 1991.

Kramer, Roderick M. "Trust and Distrust in Organizations: Emerging Perspectives, Enduring Questions." *Annual Review of Psychology* 50 (1999): 569–98.

Krippendorf, Klaus. "Reliability." In *The International Encyclopedia of Communication*, edited by Wolfgang Donsbach, 4174–79. Malden, Mass.: Blackwell, 2008.

———. "Validity." In *The International Encyclopedia of Communication*, edited by Wolfgang Donsbach, 5245–51. Malden, Mass.: Blackwell, 2008.

Kristula-Green, Noah. "How Badly Have Republicans Alienated Women?" *Daily Beast*, April 20, 2012. http://www.thedailybeast.com/articles/2012/04/20/women -and-the-gop.html.

Kritek, William J. "Voluntary Desegregation in Wisconsin." *Integrated Education* 15, no. 6 (1977): 83–87.

Krugman, Paul. *End This Depression Now!* New York: W. W. Norton, 2012.

Kubisiak, Kristen J. "Charter School Facing Obstacles." *Daily News*, November 20, 2010.

———. "Charter School Proposal Rejected; School Board Spurns Crossroads Academy on 4–3 Vote." *Daily News*, November 23, 2010.

———. "Day of Silence Not Lacking in Controversy." *Daily News*, April 16, 2011.

———. "Ethics Complaints against School Board Members Dismissed." *Daily News*, January 18, 2011.

———. "Incumbents Lead the Way." *Daily News*, February 17, 2010.

———. "School Board: 'Ins' Are Out; Conservative Challengers Knock Off Incumbents." *Daily News*, April 7, 2010.

Kuehl, Rebecca A. "The Rhetorical Presidency and 'Accountability' in Education Reform: Comparing the Presidential Rhetoric of Ronald Reagan and George W. Bush." *Southern Communication Journal* 77, no. 4 (2012): 329–48.

Lafont, Cristina. "Religion and the Public Sphere: What Are the Deliberative Obligations of Democratic Citizenship?" *Philosophy and Social Criticism* 35, nos. 1–2 (2009): 127–50.

———. "Religion in the Public Sphere: Remarks on Habermas's Conception of Public Deliberation in Postsecular Societies." *Constellations* 14, no. 2 (2007): 239–59.

Land, Deborah. "Local School Boards under Review: Their Role and Effectiveness in Relation to Students' Academic Achievement." *Review of Educational Research* 72, no. 2 (2002): 229–78.

Lenard, Patti Tamara. "Rebuilding Trust in an Era of Widening Wealth Inequality." *Journal of Social Philosophy* 41, no. 1 (2010): 73–91.

Lewicki, Roy J., Daniel J. McAllister, and Robert J. Bies. "Trust and Distrust: New Relationships and Realities." *Academy of Management Review* 23, no. 3 (1998): 438–58.

Lippmann, Walter. *The Phantom Public*. 1927. Repr., New Brunswick, N.J.: Transaction, 1993.

Luhmann, Niklas. *Trust and Power*. New York: John Wiley & Sons, 1979.

Lynch, John. "Information at the Intersection of the Public and Technical Spheres: A Reply to Majdik." *Rhetoric and Public Affairs* 14, no. 2 (2011): 369–78.

Lyne, John, and Henry F. Howe. "The Rhetoric of Expertise: E. O. Wilson and Sociobiology." *Quarterly Journal of Speech* 76, no. 2 (1990): 134–51.

Lyon, Arabella. *Deliberative Acts: Democracy, Rhetoric, and Rights*. University Park: Pennsylvania State University Press, 2013.

Macedo, Stephen. "Property-Owning Plutocracy: Inequality and American Localism." In *Justice and the Metropolis*, edited by Clarissa Rile Hayward and Todd Swanstrom, 33–58. Minneapolis: University of Minnesota Press, 2011.

———. "School Reform and Equal Opportunity in America's Geography of Inequality." *Perspectives on Politics* 1, no. 4 (2003): 743–55.

Mackie, Gerry. "Patterns of Trust in Western Europe and Their Genesis." In *Trust in Society*, edited by Karen S. Cook, 245–82. New York: Russell Sage, 2001.

Maeroff, Gene I. *School Boards in America: A Flawed Exercise in Democracy*. New York: Palgrave Macmillan, 2010.

Maher, Craig, Mark Skidmore, and Bambi Statz. "State Policy Consequences for Wisconsin's School Districts: Spending Disparities, Finance Formulas, and Revenue Restrictions." *Marquette Law Review* 90, no. 3 (2007): 621–65.

Majdik, Zoltan P. "Judging Direct-to-Consumer Genetics: Negotiating Expertise and Agency in Public Biotechnological Practice." *Rhetoric and Public Affairs* 12, no. 4 (2009): 571–606.

Majdik, Zoltan P., and William M. Keith. "Expertise as Argument: Authority, Democracy, and Problem-Solving." *Argumentation* 25, no. 3 (2011): 371–84.

Markovits, Elizabeth. *The Politics of Sincerity: Plato, Frank Speech, and Democratic Judgment*. University Park: Pennsylvania State University Press, 2008.

———. "The Trouble with Being Earnest: Deliberative Democracy and the Sincerity Norm." *Journal of Political Philosophy* 14, no. 3 (2006): 249–69.

Marquardt, Randy. "Announcement." *Common Sense* (blog), January 11, 2010. http://randy-marquardt.blogpost.com/.

———. *Common Sense Citizens*. Accessed August 7, 2012. http://cscwc.com/testimonials.

———. Letter to the editor. *Daily News*, October 31, 2009.

———. Letter to the editor. *Daily News*, February 2, 2010.

———. "Results Are In!" *Common Sense* (blog), April 6, 2010. http://randy-marquardt.blogspot.com/.

Mayer, Roger C., James H. Davis, and F. David Schoorman. "An Integrative Model of Organizational Trust." *Academy of Management Review* 20, no. 3 (1995): 709–34.

Maziarka, Ginny. Letter to the editor. *Daily News*, May 7, 2011.

McArdle, Nancy, Theresa Osypuk, and Dolores Acevedo-García. "Segregation and Exposure to High-Poverty Schools in Large Metropolitan Areas: 2008–09." September 2010. http://diversitydata.org/Publications/school_segregation_report.pdf.

McCarthy, Martha M. "Religious Influences in Public Schools: The Winding Path toward Accommodation." *Saint Louis University Public Law Review* 23, no. 2 (2004): 572–74.

McDermott, Kathryn A. *Controlling Public Education: Localism versus Equity*. Lawrence: University Press of Kansas, 1999.

McGuinn, Patrick J. *No Child Left Behind and the Transformation of Education Policy, 1965–2005*. Lawrence: University Press of Kansas, 2006.

McIntush, Holly G. "Defining Education: The Rhetorical Enactment of Ideology in *A Nation at Risk*." *Rhetoric and Public Affairs* 3, no. 3 (2000): 419–43.

———. "Political Truancy: George Bush's Claim to the Mantle of 'Education President.'" In *The Rhetorical Presidency of George H. W. Bush*, edited by Martin J. Medhurst, 102–18. College Station: Texas A&M University Press, 2006.

Medhurst, Martin J. "Mitt Romney, 'Faith in America,' and the Dance of Religion and Politics in American Culture." *Rhetoric and Public Affairs* 12, no. 2 (2009): 195–222.

Meyer, Michaela D. E. "Women Speak(ing): Forty Years of Feminist Contributions to Rhetoric and an Agenda for Feminist Rhetorical Studies." *Communication Quarterly* 55, no. 1 (2007): 1–17.

Middleton, Michael K., Samantha Senda-Cook, and Danielle Endres. "Articulating Rhetorical Field Methods: Challenges and Tensions." *Western Journal of Communication* 75, no. 4 (2011): 386–406.

Miller, Carolyn R. "The Presumptions of Expertise: The Role of *Ethos* in Risk Analysis." *Configurations* 11, no. 2 (2003): 163–202.

Miner, Barbara J. *Lessons from the Heartland: A Turbulent Half-Century of Public Education in an Iconic American City.* New York: Free Press, 2013.

Mishler, William, and Richard Rose. "Five Years after the Fall: Trajectories of Support for Democracy in Post-Communist Europe." In *Critical Citizens: Global Support for Democratic Government*, edited by Pippa Norris, 78–99. New York: Oxford University Press, 1999.

Misztal, Barbara A. *Trust in Modern Societies.* Cambridge, U.K.: Polity Press, 1996.

Moses, Michele S., and Michael J. Nanna. "The Testing Culture and the Persistence of High Stakes Testing Reforms." *Education and Culture* 23, no. 1 (2007): 55–72.

Mouffe, Chantal. *Agonistics: Thinking the World Politically.* London: Verso, 2013.

———. *The Democratic Paradox.* London: Verso, 2000.

Mountford, Meredith. "Historical and Current Tensions among Board-Superintendent Teams: Symptoms or Cause?" In *The Future of School Board Governance: Relevancy and Revelation*, edited by Thomas L. Alsbury, 81–114. Lanham, Md.: Rowman and Littlefield, 2008.

Muckelbauer, Dan. "School Board OKs 10.9 Levy Increase." *Daily News*, October 27, 2009.

———. "School Board Starts Cutting." *Daily News*, October 6, 2009.

———. "School Levy Increase Rejected." *Daily News*, September 29, 2009.

Murphy, John M. "The Language of the Liberal Consensus: John F. Kennedy, Technical Reason, and the 'New Economics' at Yale University." *Quarterly Journal of Speech* 90, no. 2 (2004): 133–62.

———. "Mikhail Bakhtin and the Rhetorical Tradition." *Quarterly Journal of Speech* 87, no. 3 (2001): 259–77.

Mutz, Diane C. *Hearing the Other Side: Deliberative versus Participative Democracy.* New York: Cambridge University Press, 2006.

National Center for Education Statistics. *Digest of Education Statistics: 2012.* Accessed August 21, 2012. http://nces.ed.gov/programs/digest/d12/tables/dt12_202.asp.

National Commission on Excellence in Education. *A Nation at Risk: The Imperative for Educational Reform.* Washington, D.C.: Government Printing Office, 1983.

Newton, Kenneth. "Trust, Social Capital, Civil Society, and Democracy." *International Political Science Review* 22, no. 2 (2001): 201–14.

Nixon, Richard. *Public Papers of the Presidents of the United States: Richard Nixon, 1972.* Washington, D.C.: Government Printing Office, 1974.

No Child Left Behind Act of 2001, U.S. Statues at Large 115 (2001): 1425–2094.

Norris, Pippa. *Democratic Deficits: Critical Citizens Revisited.* New York: Cambridge University Press, 2011.

Nussbaum, Martha. "Education and Democratic Citizenship: Capabilities and Quality Education." *Journal of Human Development* 7, no. 3 (2006): 385–95.

Obama, Barack. *Public Papers of the Presidents of the United States: Barack Obama, 2009.* 2 vols. Washington, D.C.: Government Printing Office, 2010.

Offe, Claus. "How Can We Trust our Fellow Citizens?" In *Democracy and Trust*, edited by Mark E. Warren, 42–87. Cambridge, U.K.: Cambridge University Press, 1999.

Orman, Sarah. "Being Gay in Lubbock: The Equal Access Act in Caudillo." *Hastings Women's Law Journal* 17, no. 2 (2006): 227–46.

Pace, Ian, and Nicholas Schoob. "West Bend High School Gay-Straight Alliance School-Sponsored Club Application." March 25, 2011.

Palczewski, Catherine Helen. "Argument in an Off Key: Playing with the Produc-
    tive Limits of Argument." In *Arguing Communication and Culture*, edited by
    G. Thomas Goodnight, 1–23. Washington, D.C.: National Communication As-
    sociation, 2002.

Pascoe, C. J. *Dude, You're a Fag: Masculinity and Sexuality in High School*. Berkeley:
    University of California Press, 2011.

Patterson, Orlando. "Liberty against the Democratic State: On the Historical and Con-
    temporary Sources of American Distrust." In *Democracy and Trust*, edited by
    Mark E. Warren, 151–207. New York: Cambridge University Press, 1999.

Payne, Elizabethe, and Melissa Smith. "LGBTQ Kids, School Safety, and Missing the
    Big Picture: How the Dominant Bullying Discourse Prevents School Profes-
    sionals from Thinking about Systemic Marginalization or . . . Why We Need to
    Rethink LGBTQ Bullying." *QED: A Journal in GLBTQ Worldmaking* (Fall 2013):
    1–36.

Penta, Leo J. "Hannah Arendt: On Power." *Journal of Speculative Philosophy* 10, no. 3
    (1996): 210–29.

Perry, Barbara A. "Justice Hugo Black and the 'Wall of Separation between Church and
    State.'" *Journal of Church and State* 31, no. 1 (1989): 55–72.

Peterson, Mark. "Common Sense Dictates Who to Elect to School Board." *Daily News*,
    January 30, 2010.

———. "Peeking Behind the Right-Wing Political Curtain." *Daily News*, March 13,
    2010.

———. "'Right Thing' vs. 'Legal Thing.'" *Daily News*, June 17, 2011.

Pezzullo, Phaedra. "Resisting 'National Breast Cancer Awareness Month': The Rheto-
    ric of Counterpublics and Their Cultural Performances." *Quarterly Journal of
    Speech* 89, no. 4 (2003): 345–65.

Pirson, Michael, and Deepak Malhotra. "Foundations of Organizational Trust: What
    Matters to Different Stakeholders?" *Organization Science* 22, no. 4 (2011):
    1087–1104.

Pitkin, Hanna Fenichel. *The Concept of Representation*. Berkeley: University of Califor-
    nia Press, 1967.

Pratt, Carolyn. "Protecting the Marketplace of Ideas in the Classroom: Why the Equal
    Access Act and the First Amendment Require the Recognition of Gay/Straight
    Alliances in America's Public Schools." *First Amendment Law Review* 5, no. 2
    (2007): 370–99.

Public Policy Forum. "Interdistrict Chapter 220: Changing Goals and Perspectives."
    January 2000. http://publicpolicyforum.org/research/interdistrict-chapter-220
    -changing-goals-perspectives.

Pupil Nondiscrimination Act, Wisconsin Statutes and Annotations, 2009–10, §118.13.

Putnam, Robert D. *Bowling Alone: The Collapse and Revival of American Community*.
    New York: Simon and Schuster, 2000.

———. "Tuning In, Tuning Out: The Strange Disappearance of Social Capital in
    America." *PS: Political Science and Politics* 28, no. 4 (1995): 664–83.

Rank, Dave. "Pencils Sharp for School Budget." *Daily News*, September 30, 2009.

Ranson, Stewart. "Markets or Democracy for Education." *British Journal of Educational
    Studies* 41, no. 4 (1993): 333–52.

Ravitch, Diane. *The Death and Life of the Great American School System: How Testing and
    Choice Are Undermining Education*. New York: Basic Books, 2010.

———. *The Troubled Crusade: American Education, 1945–1980*. New York: Basic Books,
    1983.

———. "Why Public Schools Need Democratic Governance." *Phi Delta Kappan*, March 2010.

Rawls, John. "The Idea of Public Reason Revisited." *University of Chicago Law Review* 64, no. 3 (1997): 765–807.

———. *Political Liberalism.* Rev. ed. New York: Columbia University Press, 1996.

Rebell, Michael A. "Fiscal Equity Litigation and the Democratic Imperative." *Journal of Education Finance* 24, no. 1 (1998): 23–50.

Reed, Douglas S. "Not in My Schoolyard: Localism and Public Opposition to Funding Schools Equally." *Social Science Quarterly* 82, no. 1 (2001): 34–50.

Reese, William J. *America's Public Schools: From the Common School to "No Child Left Behind."* Baltimore: Johns Hopkins University Press, 2005.

Reich, Robert B. "How to End the Great Recession." *New York Times*, September 2, 2010.

Reschovsky, Andrew, and Jennifer Imazeki. "Achieving Educational Adequacy through School Finance Reform." *Journal of Education Finance* 26, no. 4 (2001): 373–96.

———. "Let No Child Be Left Behind: Determining the Cost of Improving Student Performance." *Public Finance Review* 31, no. 3 (2003): 263–90.

Reynolds, Laurie. "Skybox Schools: Public Education as Private Luxury." *Washington University Law Quarterly* 82, no. 3 (2004): 755–819.

Rhodebeck, Ashley. "Kerry Shows Off New Facility." *Beloit Daily News*, June 24, 2009.

Riddle, Wayne C., and Rebecca R. Skinner. *The Elementary and Secondary Education Act, as Amended by the No Child Left Behind Act: A Primer.* Report RL33960. Washington, D.C.: Congressional Research Service, January 8, 2008.

Riley, Richard W. "Reflections on Goals 2000." *Teachers College Record* 96, no. 3 (1995): 380–88.

Robinson, Owen B. "It's for the Children." *Daily News*, March 30, 2010.

———. "Lessons from Our Budget Discussion." *Daily News*, November 3, 2009.

Romano, Rick. "Gibson Recalls Tenure Fondly, Looks Ahead." *Brookfield Now*, June 6, 2012.

Rorty, Richard. "Religion in the Public Square: A Reconsideration." *Journal of Religious Ethics* 31, no. 1 (2003): 141–49.

Rothstein, Richard. *Class and Schools: Using Social, Economic, and Educational Reform to Close the Black-White Achievement Gap.* Washington, D.C.: Economic Policy Institute, 2004.

Rowland, Robert C. "The Relationship between the Public and the Technical Spheres of Argument: A Case Study of the Challenger Seven Disaster." *Central States Speech Journal* 37, no. 3 (1986): 136–46.

Ryan, James E. *Five Miles Away, a World Apart: One City, Two Schools, and the Story of Educational Opportunity in Modern America.* New York: Oxford University Press, 2010.

———. "The Perverse Incentives of the *No Child Left Behind Act.*" *New York University Law Review* 79, no. 3 (2004): 932–89.

Sandel, Michael J. *Democracy's Discontent: America in Search of a Public Philosophy.* Cambridge, Mass.: Harvard University Press, 1996.

Schiappa, Edward. "Defining Marriage in California: An Analysis of Public and Technical Argument." *Argumentation and Advocacy* 48, no. 4 (2012): 213–27.

Schneiberg, Scott. Letter to the editor. *Daily News*, March 17, 2010.

Schoorman, F. David, Roger C. Mayer, and James H. Davis. "An Integrative Model of Organizational Trust: Past, Present, and Future." *Academy of Management Review* 32, no. 2 (2007): 344–54.

Schudson, Michael. "The 'Public Sphere' and Its Problems: Bringing the State (Back) In." *Notre Dame Journal of Law, Ethics, and Public Policy* 8, no. 2 (1994): 529–46.

Sedler, Robert A. "The Profound Impact of *Milliken v. Bradley*." *Wayne Law Review* 33, no. 5 (1986): 1693–1722.

Sheppard, Blair H., and Dana M. Sherman. "The Grammars of Trust: A Model and General Implications." *Academy of Management Review* 23, no. 3 (1998): 422–37.

Slavin, Robert E. "Evidence-Based Education Policies: Transforming Educational Practice and Research." *Educational Researcher* 31, no. 7 (2002): 15–21.

Smith, Anne. "Scientifically Based Research and Evidence-Based Education: A Federal Policy Context." *Research and Practice for Persons with Severe Disabilities* 28, no. 3 (2003): 126–32.

Smith-Sanders, Alana K., and Lynn M. Harter. "Democracy, Dialogue, and Education: An Exploration of Conflict Resolution at Jefferson Junior High." *Southern Communication Journal* 72, no. 2 (2007): 109–26.

Staton, Ann Q., and Jennifer A. Peeples. "Education Reform Discourse: President George Bush on 'America 2000.'" *Communication Education* 49, no. 4 (2000): 303–19.

Steinberger, Elizabeth Donohoe. "Superintendent–School Board Relations That Work: Despite Changing Casts, These Four School Communities Stayed on Track." *School Administrator* 51, no. 7 (1994): 8–14.

Steiner, Mark Allan. "Reconceptualizing Christian Public Engagement: 'Faithful Witness' and the American Evangelical Tradition." *Journal of Communication and Religion* 32, no. 2 (2009): 289–318.

Stolee, Michael. "The Milwaukee Desegregation Case." In *Seeds of Crisis: Public Schooling in Milwaukee since 1920*, edited by John L. Rury and Frank A. Cassell, 229–68. Madison: University of Wisconsin Press, 1993.

Stone, Deborah. *Policy Paradox: The Art of Political Decision Making.* Rev. ed. New York: W. W. Norton, 1997.

Sutton, Jeffrey S. "*San Antonio Independent School District v. Rodriguez* and Its Aftermath." *Virginia Law Review* 94, no. 8 (2008): 1963–86.

Taylor, Charles Alan. "On the Public Closure of Technical Controversy." In *Argument in Controversy: Proceedings of the Seventh SCA/AFA Conference on Argumentation*, edited by Donn W. Parson, 263–69. Annandale, Va.: Speech Communication Association, 1991.

Tell, Dave. "Augustinian Political Theory and Religious Discourse in Public Life." *Journal of Communication and Religion* 30, no. 2 (2007): 213–35.

Terkel, Amanda. "Glenn Grothman, Wisconsin Pol Who Sponsored Equal Pay Repeal, Turns Down Women's Issues Debate." *Huffington Post*, April 20, 2012. http://www.huffingtonpost.com/2012/04/20/glenn-grothman-wisconsin-equal-pay-repeal-debate_n_1440602.html.

Toch, Thomas. *In the Name of Excellence: The Struggle to Reform the Nation's Schools, Why It's Failing, and What Should Be Done.* New York: Oxford University Press, 1991.

Tracy, Karen. *Challenges of Ordinary Democracy: A Case Study in Deliberation and Dissent.* University Park: Pennsylvania State University Press, 2010.

Troup, Calvin L. "Civic Engagement from Religious Grounds." *Journal of Communication and Religion* 32, no. 2 (2009): 240–67.

Tseng, Vivian. "The Uses of Research in Policy and Practice." *Social Policy Report* 26, no. 2 (2012): 1–16.

Tyack, David. *Seeking Common Ground: Public Schools in a Diverse Society.* Cambridge, Mass.: Harvard University Press, 2003.

U.S. Census Bureau. "Local Governments and Public School Systems by Type and State." *Census of Governments: 2007.* Accessed August 22, 2013. http://www .census.gov/govs/cog/GovOrgTab03ss.html.

———. *2007–2011 American Community Survey.* Accessed October 26, 2012. http://fact finder.census.gov/faces/tableservices/jsf/pages/productview.xhtml?src=bkmk.

———. "Washington County, Wisconsin." Accessed August 3, 2012. http://quickfacts .census.gov/qfd/states/55/55131.html.

———. "Wisconsin Population of Counties by Decennial Census: 1900 to 1990." Accessed August 3, 2012. http://www.census.gov/population/cencounts/wi1900 90.txt.

U.S. Senate Subcommittee on Education. *Elementary and Secondary Education Act of 1965.* 98th Cong., 1st sess., 1965.

Uslaner, Eric M. *The Moral Foundations of Trust.* New York: Cambridge University Press, 2002.

———. "Producing and Consuming Trust." *Political Science Quarterly* 115, no. 4 (2000–2001): 569–90.

———. "Social Capital, Television, and the 'Mean World': Trust, Optimism, and Civic Participation." *Political Psychology* 19, no. 3 (1998): 441–67.

Vorwald, Courtney. "When Parental and Minors' Rights Conflict: Minors' Constitutional Rights and Gay-Straight Alliances." *Journal of Gender, Race, and Justice* 13, no. 2 (2010): 465–90.

Wallinger, Michael J. "Regulatory Rhetoric: Argument in the Nexus of Public and Technical Spheres." In *Spheres of Argument: Proceedings of the Sixth SCA/AFA Conference on Argumentation,* edited by Bruce E. Gronbeck, 71–80. Annandale, Va.: Speech Communication Association, 1989.

Walsh, Camille. "Erasing Race, Dismissing Class: *San Antonio Independent School District v. Rodriguez.*" *Berkeley La Raza Law Journal* 21 (2011): 133–71.

Walzer, Michael. *Interpretation and Social Criticism.* Cambridge, Mass.: Harvard University Press, 1987.

Warner, Michael. *Publics and Counterpublics.* New York: Zone Books, 2002.

Warren, Mark E. "Deliberative Democracy and Authority." *American Political Science Review* 90, no. 1 (1996): 46–60.

———. "Introduction." In *Democracy and Trust,* edited by Mark E. Warren, 1–21. Cambridge, U.K.: Cambridge University Press, 1999.

Washington County Clerk. "Election Summary Report, General Election, November 4, 2008." *Washington County,* November 20, 2008. http://www.co.washington .wi.us/departments.iml?Detail=263.

Weaver, Justin. "School District OKs Levy Hike." *Beloit Daily News,* October 30–31, 2010.

Weigand, Dave. "Have You Been Disappointed in Local Government?" *Dave Weigand for School Board* (blog), January 21, 2010. http://weigandforschoolboard.blog spot.com/.

———. "Navigating Charter School Choice for West Bend District." *Daily News,* October 22, 2010.

West Bend School Board. "Annual Meeting of the West Bend School District." September 28, 2009. [Personal transcript.]

———. "Committee of the Whole Meeting." May 9, 2011. [Personal transcript.]

———. "June Board Meeting." June 13, 2011. [Personal transcript.]

———. "May Board Meeting." May 9, 2011. [Personal transcript.]

———. "November Board Meeting." November 22, 2010. [Personal transcript.]

———. "October Board Meeting." October 26, 2009. [Personal transcript.]

West Bend School District. "Board Policy 370, Exhibit B." March 25, 2011. http://www
.boarddocs.com/wi/wbsdwi/Board.nsf/files/8GKVK278758D/$file/GSA%20
Application%20Information.pdf.

———. "Board Policy 370, Exhibit C: Criteria for School Sponsored Co-curricular and
Clubs, Criteria for Non-school Sponsored Clubs." March 25, 2011. http://www
.boarddocs.com/wi/wbsdwi/Board.nsf/files/8GKVK278758D/$file/GSA%20
Application%20Information.pdf.

———. "Board Policy 370: Extracurricular Activities and Programs." October 8, 2007.
http://www.boarddocs.com/wi/wbsdwi/Board.nsf/files/8GKVK278758D/$file
/GSA%20Application%20Information.pdf.

Willard, Charles Arthur. "Authority." *Informal Logic* 12, no. 1 (1990): 11–22.

———. *Liberalism and the Problem of Knowledge: A New Rhetoric for Modern Democracy.*
Chicago: University of Chicago Press, 1996.

———. "Valuing Dissensus." In *Argumentation: Across the Lines of Discipline,* edited by
Frans H. van Eemeren, Rob Grootendorst, J. Anthony Blair, and Charles Arthur
Willard, 145–57. Dordrecht, Holland: Foris, 1987.

Williams, Bart. Letter to the editor. *Daily News,* January 28, 2010.

———. Letter to the editor. *Daily News,* March 31, 2011.

Wisconsin Department of Public Instruction. "Enrollment and Participation Reports:
October 2010." Accessed October 26, 2012. http://fns.dpi.wi.gov/fns_progstat.

———. "School District Tax Apportionment Equalized Values: October 2010." Accessed November 7, 2012. https://www2.dpi.state.wi.us/safr_ro/tax_apportion
ment_all_districts.asp?year=2011#E.

———. "2010–2011 Comparative Revenue per Member." Accessed October 26, 2012.
http://sfs.dpi.wi.gov/sfs_cmprv.

Wisconsin Department of Workforce Development. "Local Area Unemployment Statistics, 2010–11." *Wisconsin's Worknet.* Accessed October 26, 2012. http://worknet
.wisconsin.gov/worknet/downloads.aspx?menuselection=da&pgm=LAUS.

Wisconsin Information Network for Successful Schools. *WINSS Successful School
Guide: Data Analysis.* Accessed May 15, 2013. http://data.dpi.state.wi.us/data/.

"Wisconsin's Median Income Plummets, Census Figures Show." *Milwaukee Journal-
Sentinel,* September 21, 2011.

Wiseman, Alexander W. "The Uses of Evidence for Educational Policymaking: Global
Contexts and International Trends." *Review of Research in Education* 34 (2010):
1–24.

Witte, John F., and Christopher A. Thorn. "Who Chooses? Voucher and Interdistrict
Choice Programs in Milwaukee." *American Journal of Education* 104, no. 1
(1996): 186–217.

Wolf, Clint. "Beloit Schools Miss Goals." *Beloit Daily News,* June 9, 2009.

Wundrow, Hillary. "New Corporate Campus: Kerry Plans $45 Million Project at I-90/
I-43 Junction." *Beloit Daily News,* April 20, 2007.

Wuthnow, Robert. "The Role of Trust in Civic Renewal." In *Civil Society, Democracy,
and Civic Renewal,* edited by Robert K. Fullinwider, 209–30. New York: Rowman
and Littlefield, 1999.

Wyckoff, Paul Gary. *Policy and Evidence in a Partisan Age: The Great Disconnect.* Washington, D.C.: Urban Institute Press, 2009.

Young, Iris Marion. *Inclusion and Democracy.* New York: Oxford University Press,
2000.

Zarefsky, David. *President Johnson's War on Poverty: Rhetoric and History.* Tuscaloosa:
University of Alabama Press, 1986.

————. "Strategic Maneuvering in Political Argumentation." *Argumentation* 22, no. 3 (2008): 317–30.

Zarling, Kathy. Kathy Zarling to West Bend School Board, memorandum. May 9, 2011.

Zeidel, Rebecca. "Forecasting Disruption, Forfeiting Speech: Restrictions on Student Speech in Extracurricular Activities." *Boston College Law Review* 53, no. 1 (2012): 303–43.

Zmerli, Sonja, and Ken Newton. "Social Trust and Attitudes toward Democracy." *Public Opinion Quarterly* 72, no. 4 (2008): 706–24.

INDEX

RHETORICAND**DEMOCRATIC**DELIBERATION

Other books in the series:

Typeset by
BOOKCOMP, INC.

Printed and bound by
SHERIDAN BOOKS

Composed in
SCALA

Printed on
NATURES NATURAL